REPORT ON THE
M·7
OPERATION

*38TH
INFANTRY
DIVISION*

"THE AVENGERS OF BATAAN"

19 JANUARY 1945
to
30 JUNE 1945

Published by Books Express Publishing
Copyright © Books Express, 2011
ISBN 978-1-83931-016-4

Books Express publications are available from all good retail and online booksellers. For
publishing proposals and direct ordering please contact us at: info@books-express.com

INTRODUCTION

This report describes the part played by the 38th Infantry Division in the M-7 operation on LUZON from 29 January - 30 June 1945.

All phases of the operation are covered. The hectic planning phase on LEYTE, the landing on the ZAMBALES Coast, the bitter opening battle in the ZIG ZAG PASS, the liberation of BATAAN and ZAMBALES PROVINCE, the capture of the MANILA BAY Forts, and the operations at FT STOTSENBURG and East of MANILA, are covered. All assigned missions were accomplished and over 20,000 Japanese were killed.

That stage of operations known as "mopping up" is often such only from the viewpoint of higher headquarters. From the viewpoint of this division and its regimental combat team, these actions on LUZON always became full scale attacks against well fortified and desperately defended positions. Of such were the operations of the 149th Infantry Regiment West of FT STOTSENBURG and the 152d Infantry Regiment on WOODPECKER RIDGE East of MARIKINA.

A narrative such as this must, of necessity, list only chronological events with supporting journals and files. These are of value to students of military history and to contemporary commanders for lessons learned from both mistakes and successes. Nothing appears concerning the great human factor, except to state that all ranks were imbued with the will to move in on the Jap and kill him.

Humble tribute is paid to the valor of the infantry soldier and abounding admiration and wonder for his fortitude, his patience and his indomitable spirit are keenly felt by all commanders of this division.

As a result of the operations in BATAAN in which the entire province was liberated, the 38th Infantry Division proudly adds to its division insignia the phrase -

THE AVENGERS OF BATAAN

WILLIAM C. CHASE
Major General, U.S. Army
Commanding

THE CHAIN OF COMMAND

GHQ
★
USAFFE

INITIALLY **EIGHT ARMY**-Operation
CAME UNDER CONTROL OF
SIXTH ARMY
ON LANDING AT **SAN NARCISO** ·····

XI CORPS
★
38TH INFANTRY DIVISION

HEADQUARTERS 38TH INFANTRY DIVISION
APO 38

ASSIGNMENT	NAME	ASN
Commanding General	Maj Gen HENRY L. C. JONES Departed Hq Sixth Army 6 Feb 45	03168
Aide-de-Camp	Capt MILTON S. COOPER ADC to Div Comdr; departed Hq Sixth Army 6 Feb 45	0407479
Commanding General	Maj Gen WILLIAM C. CHASE Asgd & jd fr 1st Cav Div & assumed command 7 Feb 45 Aptd Maj Gen 20 Mar 45	04739
Aide-de-Camp	Capt HENRY M. FREIDENGER Asgd & jd fr Hq 1st Cav Div Luzon PI 11 Feb 45; departed TDY Comd & Gen Staff Sch, Ft Leavenworth, Kansas 4 May 45	0450197
Aide-de-Camp	1st Lt BURNS T. TILTON Asgd & jd fr 1st Cav Div Luzon PI & Asgd ADC to Div Comdr 4 Mar 45	01031276
Asst Div Comdr	Brig Gen ROY W. EASLEY Assumed command 6 Feb 45; Reld Div Comdr & Asgd Asst Div Comdr 7 Feb 45; departed to Misc Group Hq USAFFE 2 Mar 45	0172501
Aide-de-Camp	1st Lt JAMES C. TAYLOR ADC to Asst Div Comdr; departed to Misc Group Hq USAFFE 3 Mar 45	01306660
Asst Div Comdr	Brig Gen ROBERT H. SOULE Asgd & jd fr 11th A/B Div & Asgd Asst Div Comdr 17 Mar 45; Aptd Brig Gen 12 Apr 45	011888
Aide-de-Camp	1st Lt NELSON N. LAMPERT Asgd & jd fr Co E 151st Inf for dy as ADC to Asst Div Comdr 20 Apr 45; detailed to ADC 27 Apr 45	01304081
Div Arty Comdr	Brig Gen WILLIAM SPENCE Asgd & jd fr 93d Inf Div & assumed command 8 Nov 44	04447

ASSIGNMENT	NAME	ASN
Aide-de-Camp	1st Lt DENSLO B. GREEN Asgd & jd fr 93d Inf Div & Asgd ADC to Div Arty Comdr 8 Nov 44	0534264
Aide-de-Camp	1st Lt ROBERT A. TEWKSBURY Asgd 38th Div as ADC to Div Arty Comdr 8 June 44	0523414
Chief of Staff	Colonel A. J. HASTINGS	011721
G-1	Lt Col EARL V. DAVIS Evac to 36th Evac Hosp Luzon, PI 27 Feb 45	0391536
G-1	Lt Col GARRETT W. OLDS Detailed to GSC, Reld as AG Asgd G-1, 2 Mar 45	0179718
Asst	Maj JOHN L. VIOTTI Detailed to GSC 23 Mar 45 Promoted to Maj 16 Apr 45	01288145
Actg Asst (PCAU)	Maj ROY M. WHITE Civil Affairs Officer; Trfd to MP Command USAFFE 1 June 45	0320003
Actg Asst (PCAU)	1st Lt ANTHONY CANCELOSI Civil Affairs Officer	01303460
Asst	CWO DAVID S. MASON Promoted to CWO 22 Apr 45	W2109408
G-2	Lt Col OLLIE J. WILSON Evac to 60th Gen Hosp Luzon PI 10 May 45	0359154
G-2	Maj RICHARD F. JEFFERS	0327474
Asst	Maj THOMAS F. McNEAL Atchd and jd fr 152d Inf for dy as Sup-Evac Officer (Asst G-4) 18 Jan 45	0240050
Asst	Capt ROBERT D. OWENS (KIA Olongapo, Luzon, PI 5 Feb 45)	0350808

ASSIGNMENT	NAME	ASN
Actg Asst	Capt EUGENE RADER Atchd & jd fr 138th FA Bn for dy as Intelligence Staff O (Asst G-2) 17 May 45	0409987
Actg Asst	Capt WAYNE C. DUCKETT Asgd Actg Asst G-2 15 May 45	01283739
Asst (CIC)	1st Lt MURRAY SCHWARTZ Atchd fr USAFFE 20 Dec 44 for dy as Mil Int O (CIC)	01323976
Asst (PI Team)	1st Lt MORTON M. SCHNEIDER Aerial Photo Interpreter	01039997
Asst (OB Team)	1st Lt JAMES B. BROUSSARD Order of Battle Analyst; promoted to 1st Lt 2 Feb 45	01061636
Asst (ATIS)	1st Lt ROY F. LITTLE Interpreter (Mil Int O); Promoted to 1st Lt 25 Feb 45; Departed to 43d Inf Div 12 Apr 45	0558448
Asst (ATIS)	2d Lt LEONARD M. MENDELSON (Mil Int O); departed to 24th Inf Div 19 Jan 45	0558472
Asst (ATIS)	1st Lt YOSHIKAZU HIGASHI Interpreter (Mil Int O); promoted to 1st Lt 11 Apr 45	02037059
Asst (ATIS)	2d Lt WARREN R. JOHNSON Asgd & jd fr Hq 43d Inf Div for dy as Mil Int O, 15 Apr 45	0558440
G-3	Colonel ALEXANDER G. KIRBY Promoted to Col 14 Apr 45	0212867
Asst	Lt Col MENLO M. PURLEE Promoted to Lt Col 2 May 45	0372205
Asst (I & E O)	Capt ARNETT McKENNAN Asgd to dy as I & E Officer 20 Feb 45	01175797
Liaison O	Capt DARWIN C. EBINGER	0452448
Liaison O	Capt WILLIAM M. TERRY	01304144

ASSIGNMENT	NAME	ASN
GLO	Capt FRED B. TUGGLE Atchd & jd fr Hq Sixth Army 23 Apr 45 for dy as Air Liaison Officer; Asgd Hq 38th Div 12 May 45	0398804
Liaison O	1st Lt UTHO T. BARNES Jd for TDY fr 149th Inf 24 May 45	01293524
Liaison O	1st Lt JOHN S O'CONNOR Jd for TDY fr 152d Inf 24 May 45	01306460
G-4	Lt Col FRED. C. DYER Reld Asgmt and Asgd Hq XIV Corps 8 June 45	0220739
G-4	Maj PHILLIP M. LORTON Trfd fr 38th Div Arty 8 June & assumed duties as AC of S, G-4	0411018
Asst	Maj EDWARD J. LICHTENSTEIN	01573365
Asst	WOJG JAMES B. MARSH Motor Transport Officer Evac to 36th Evac Hosp 27 Mar 45	W2109408
Adjutant General	Lt Col JOHN FISSELL Assumed duties as AG 2 Mar 45 Promoted to Lt Col 22 Mar 45	0408089
Asst	Maj CARL C. DUNHAM Promoted to Maj 22 Mar 45	0411002
Asst	WOJG HOWARD E. LIGHT Asst Adj Gen (Misc)	W2135036
Personnel	Capt HENRY W. TURNEY Asgd & jd fr 151st Inf for dy as Asst Adj Gen (Personnel Officer) 8 May 45. Detailed to AGD 30 May 45	0336547
Asst	CWO CECIL J. HILL	W2109402
Asst	WOJG WESLEY C. BERRY Aptd WOJG 23 Apr 45 & Asgd dy as Asst Adj Gen (Personnel) (formerly M/Sgt this Hq)	W2135295

ASSIGNMENT	NAME	ASN
Classification	1st Lt JAMES J. SEYBOLD (Class & Asgmt O); promoted to 1st Lt 1 Feb 45	O1686323
Postal O	Capt MARTIN PRIPSTEIN	O1000649
Inspector General	Lt Col VIRGIL P. POWNALL Evac to 80th Gen Hosp Luzon PI 28 May 45	O147842
Asst	Capt WILBUR E. CHELLGREN Evac to 36th Evac Hosp 1 Mar 45	O1285546
Asst	WOJG NORMAN ELDRIDGE	W2109410
Judge Advocate	Lt Col MAURICE D. BURTON Evac to 30th Gen Hosp Luzon PI 11 May 45	O277232
Judge Advocate	Lt Col ALLEN R. COZIER	O202208
Asst	1st Lt FRANCIS E. CASH Promoted to 1st Lt 6 Feb 45	O2052020
Asst	WOJG RAYMOND E. KUSCHKE Aptd WOJG 23 Apr 45 & Asgd dy as Asst JAG (Adm Asst Legal) (formerly S/Sgt this Hq)	W2135296
Finance O	Lt Col JOE F. MINER	O281796
Asst	1st Lt HRANT AKMAKJIAN Promoted to 1st Lt 17 Apr 45	O1281794
Asst	CWO FREDERIK B. JOHNSON Promoted to CWO 5 Apr 45	W2109409
Chemical O	Lt Col HAROLD L. ANDERSON Departed to Rotation Det Base "K" Leyte PI 16 Apr 45	O301640
Chemical O	Lt Col MARTIN T. OLSEN Asgd & jd fr Hq 43rd Inf Div for dy as Div Chem O 13 Apr 45	O389016
Asst	Capt FRANK E. BOBO, Jr Promoted to Capt 16 Apr 45	O372186

ASSIGNMENT	NAME	ASN
Chaplain	Lt Col JAMES J. McMAHON	026443
Asst	Maj FREDERICK J. WESTENDORF	0336113
Actg Asst	Capt RICHARD F. DENBO	0419930
Div Surgeon	Lt Col FRANK B. RAMSEY	0278183
Asst	Capt ROBERT S. WHITING	01541960
Dental Surgeon	Maj JAMES F. FAVORITE	0333945
Neuropsychiatrist	Maj JULES V. COLEMAN	0486259
Div Med Insp	Maj ALVIN R. LAMB Evac to 36th Evac Hosp Castillejos Luzon PI 2 Feb 45	0119902
Div Med Insp	Maj HARVEY C. BLANTON Asgd & jd fr 113th Med Bn for dy as Div Med Insp 20 Mar 45	0369695
Asst	Capt HERBERT A. ANDERSON Asgd fr 259th Repl Co Leyte PI 14 Apr 45; jd 3 May 45 & Asgd Asst Div Med Insp	0473219
Special Service and PRO	Maj PEYTON HOGE	0408914
Actg Asst	Capt MILTON J. BUBLITZ Evac to 30th Gen Hosp 4 June 45	0331454
Actg Asst	Capt WILLIAM W. VAN PELT Correspondent (Atchd fr GHQ SWPA); departed to GHQ SWPA 1 Mar 45	01286928
Actg Asst	1st Lt MAURICE P. MURPHY Atchd & jd fr 151st Inf 18 Apr 45 for dy as Special Service O (Asst)	01306452

PRIOR HISTORY

The 38th Infantry Division was reorganized after the First World War. The first elements were organized in 1920, and the Division as such Federally recognized 16 March 1923.

From then until January 1941, the whole Division (less 150th Infantry) trained together as a Division each summer training period.

On 17 January 1941 the 38th Infantry Division, then a square division composed of National Guard units from Indiana, Kentucky and West Virginia, was inducted into Federal Service at Camp Snelby, near Hattiesburg, Mississippi. In April and May 1941, the first Selectees were received, bringing the Division up to Peace Time T/O.

At Camp Snelby the Division underwent basic training and field maneuvers which ultimately led to active participation in the THIRD ARMY MANEUVERS in Louisiana in August-September 1941.

The Division furnished numerous personnel for newly activated Divisions, and large numbers of our best personnel for Officer Candidate Schools of all branches between October 1941 and the maneuvers in Louisiana in September-October-November 1942. These men were replaced from replacement training centers. Upon entering actual combat, only about 25% of original National Guard personnel remained.

Following the 1942 Louisiana Maneuvers and Amphibious Training at Camp Gordon Johnston, Florida, intensive unit training and tests occurred at Camp Livingston, Louisiana. Fall of 1943 found the Division staging for overseas movement. Arriving in the Hawaiian Islands, beach defense of the Island of Oahu, further amphibious training, and jungle training occupied the next six months. The Division then moved to ORO BAY in NEW GUINEA where practical jungle training and unit training were carried on in preparation for final combat staging. In December 1944 the Division moved to LEYTE, participating in combat patrolling in the mopping up phase of that operation. The Division staged for the M-7 Operation at LEYTE.

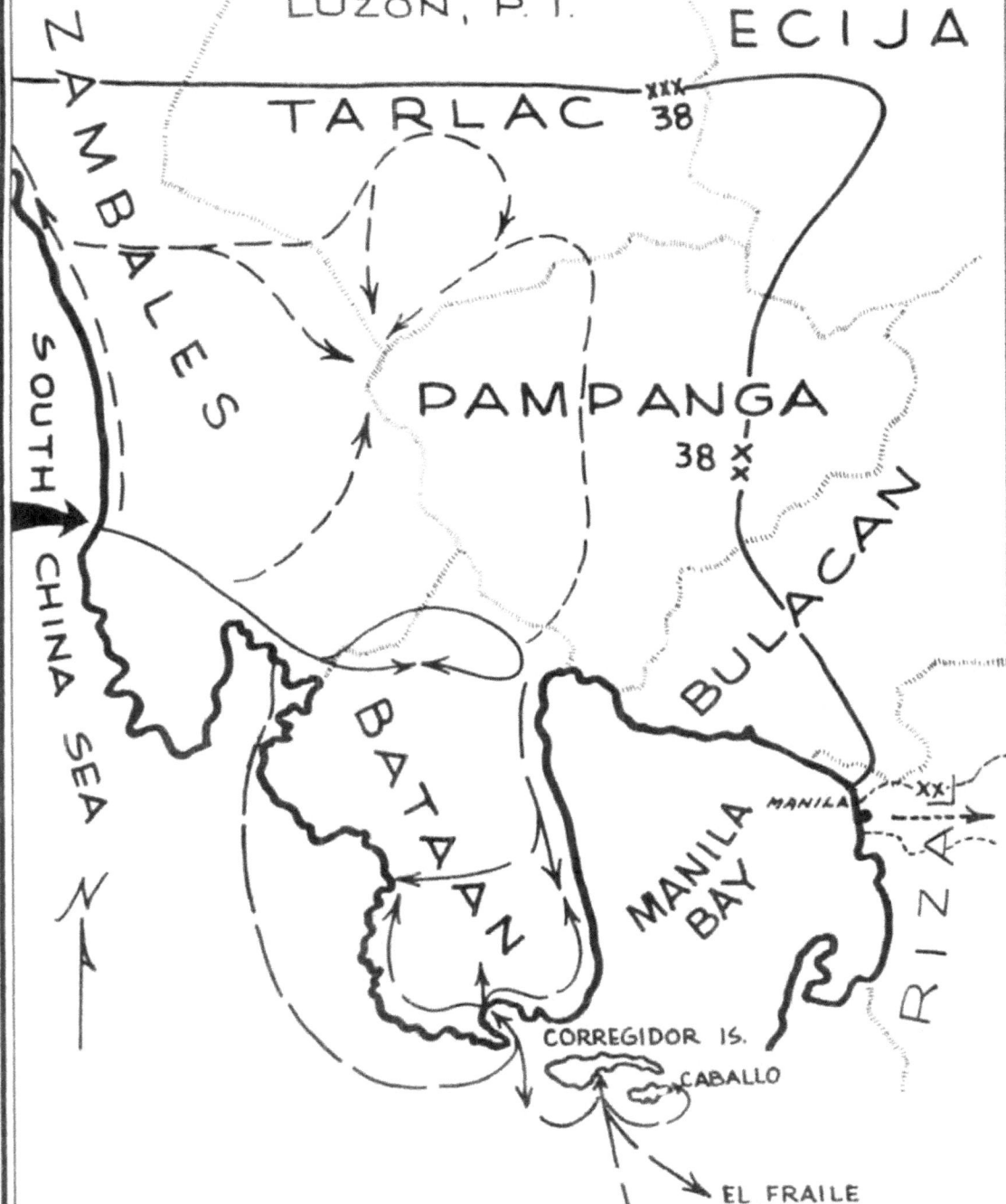

THE AVENGERS' BATTLEGROUND
LUZON, P.I.

ECIJA

TARLAC
XXX
38

ZAMBALES

SOUTH CHINA SEA

PAMPANGA
38 XX

BULACAN

BATAAN

MANILA BAY

MANILA
XX

RIZAL

CORREGIDOR IS.

CABALLO

EL FRAILE

CARABAO

· LEGEND ·
— INITIAL LANDING - ZIG-ZAG
– – BATAAN - ADJACENT ISLANDS
– – STOTSENBURG AREA
· · · · OPERATION EAST OF MANILA

MISSION

On 19 January 1945 the 38th Infantry Division Reinf, was directed by FO #3, Hq XI Corps 19 January 1945, to participate in the M-7 Operation.

The mission of the operation was first to effect landings in Southern ZAMBALES Province, secure the airfield in the vicinity SAN MARCELINO and the naval base and its facilities on SUBIC BAY, to seize and occupy the general line DINALUPIHAN - HERMOSA, sealing off BATAAN from Northern LUZON and thus denying the enemy freedom of movement between the PAMPANGA Plains and BATAAN Peninsula. A subsequent mission to assure our complete control of BATAAN Peninsula was assigned on 30 January and consisted of an amphibious assault on the MARIVELES area coordinated with an amphibious and airborne attack on the Island of CORREGIDOR, a rapid movement South from HERMOSA, and the seizure of the BAGAC-PILAR Road. When the M-7 Operation was concluded, the 38th Infantry Division had destroyed all the Japanese forces in ZAMBALES and PAMPANGA Provinces, liberated BATAAN, and furnished a battalion and other units to the force that captured CORREGIDOR. During the "Mopping Up" phase, the 38th Infantry Division relieved the 43d Infantry Division in operation against the enemy forces between FT STOTSENBURG and MT PINATUBO. Following the completion of the FT STOTSENBURG operation the 38th Infantry Division relieved the 6th Infantry Division in the operation against the Japanese in the area East of MANILA. These were full scale actions. In accomplishing these missions the Division had various units attached from time to time.

TROOP LIST

38th Inf Div
Hq 38th Inf Div
Hq Co, MP Plat 38th Inf Div
149th Inf Regt
151st Inf Regt (- Co E)
152d Inf Regt
Hq & Hq Btry 38th Inf Div Arty
138th FA Bn (105mm How)
139th FA Bn (105mm How)
163d FA Bn (105mm How)
11th FA Bn (155mm How)
113th Engr C Bn
113th Med Bn
38th Sig Co
738th Ord Co
64th Port Surg Hosp
592d JASCO (- Det)
603d Tk Co (- 1 Plat)
18th SAP (- Det)

The 150th FA Bn (155mm How), the 38th Rcn Tr, Co E 151st Inf, 38th Div Band and detachments of other units were enroute from ORO BAY, NEW GUINEA. They arrived at SUBIC BAY on 11 February 1945.

38th Div rear echelon arrived from LEYTE at SUBIC BAY 31 March 1945.

TERRAIN

The M-7 Operation was laid in the mountains of BATAAN, ZAMBALES and PAMPANGA Provinces (see sketch). Initially it was an attack that closely followed the course of the Japanese attack against the elements of the American Army which withdrew to BATAAN in December 1941.

The high ZAMBALES mountain range extends from the Southern tip of BATAAN to LINGAYEN Gulf. Except for small coastal plains, the terrain is mountainous with several peaks over five thousand feet in height. Heavy forest and steep walled valleys make movement over this range difficult for troops. The coastal area between SAN NARCISO and SAN ANTONIO is more extensive than usual with a depth of about ten miles.

Vegetation is generally heavy forest on the higher slopes. Bamboo thickets and dense underbrush on the lower slopes make movement and vision as difficult as in the jungle terrain found in NEW GUINEA, except on trails or roads. Vegetation on the coastal plain consists mainly of cultivated crops, with rice paddies predominating. At the time of the M-7 Operation the weather was dry and practically all rice paddies were hard and negotiable.

Main roads are Routes 7 and 110. Route 7 is an all-weather road which in the zone of our operations crosses the ZAMBALES Range from OLONGAPO to DINALUPIHAN in a tortuous track called the ZIG-ZAG Pass Road. Route 110 is an all-weather road from MARIVELES on the South to DINALUPIHAN, very rough South of ORION and reasonably good North therefrom.

From a study of the map of the area it is readily apparent that he who controls BATAAN controls MANILA Bay. There are many sites for air strips along the coastal plains while SUBIC Bay offers protected anchorages for ships and sea planes. Highway 7, the ZIG-ZAG Pass road, offers the only land movement for vehicles through the ZAMBALES range South of the LINGAYEN area. The extremely rugged terrain of BATAAN makes an ideal situation for a last stand defense.

PLANNING AND MOVEMENT PHASE

The planning phase of the M-7 Operation began with the M-3 Operation on 25 December 1944 when the Division G-2, G-3, and G-4 were called to Headquarters Eighth Army to receive instructions. Immediately following this, Eighth Army issued Field Order #8 setting up the units involved, the shipping available, the estimated capacity in vehicles, personnel, tonnage and the dates of resupply convoys. The smaller units involved were scattered from BRISBANE to LEYTE, and of those on LEYTE, many were dispersed from CARRIGARA to AMBUYOG with no telegraph or telephone communications. Teams of officers were sent out to locate and inform them of their projected participation and to acquire the necessary logistics. It was soon found that published TO & Es were useless as reference documents, first because some special groups had none, and second because many units were authorized special equipment in excess of T/E.

In assigning the shipping where several units moved on the same vessel, it was necessary to direct how many and what type of vehicles would be taken. With the exception of the Engineer Group who were assigned a group of shipping estimated to carry their special equipment, this was done. In arriving at the allotment, essential service units received especial attention and the least reduction in vehicles.

This vehicle allotment made to combat units is not recommended for future operations. In the M-3 Operation the area to be occupied initially was very small and motor transportation from D-day to D/10 was not a major item. This received consideration in arriving at the number of vehicles to be taken, the final allotment being based on the bringing forward of additional vehicles on D/5 and D/10. The D/5 and D/10 ships were taken away later, resulting in the M-7 Operation being carried out with what proved to be too few vehicles for the extended area covered.

On 19 January, when the planning had reached the stage of assembling the TQMs, S-3s, and representatives of the 592d EB & S Regt to discuss detailed loading and unloading, the M-3 Operation was cancelled and the M-7 began. Due to lack of definite knowledge of the operation several days were lost in the planning phase. When definite information became available loading plans continued, being varied from time to time as variations occurred in number and types of ships to be furnished, and as the usual last minute accomodations for observers and specialists were made.

Since the time was short and the XI Corps staff was unacquainted with the details of what had been done, it was wisely decided that the 38th Infantry Division continue with the loading and embarkation, including many units now assigned as Corps troops. Loading and embarkation of the 34th RCT was placed under the direction of XI Corps and is not covered in this report.

Variations between the printed characteristics of the ships and the actual characteristics, plus the decisions of the ships' captains, called for changes in the plans after the arrival of the Navy TQMs, and in some cases after the supplies were moving from the beaches to the transports. This was particularly true of ammunition.

Difficulty in loading and embarkation was occasioned by the great distances, in some cases up to 45 miles, between units and the loading points and the poor communications between them. The use of the telephone varied inversely with the daily rainfall and the distance involved, frequently failing altogether. Much assistance was given by the Transportation Section, XI Corps.

At sailing time, all units and all vehicles originally allotted, plus a few additional where the space permitted, were aboard.

The trip to LUZON was without incident, the weather being clement, and with no enemy action. The debarkation area was reached in the early morning of 29 January. During the trip a message was received that the Japanese had withdrawn from the SAN ANTONIO, SAN NARCISO, SAN MARCELINO area, and it was decided to withhold the preliminary naval bombardment.

COMBAT PHASE

The M-7 Operation covered a very extensive area including the major portions of the ZAMBALES, BATAAN, and PAMPANGA Provinces of LUZON, PHILIPPINE ISLANDS. (See sketch).

In order to simplify and place into an understandable sequence the combat phase of the M-7 Operation will be divided into four parts:

```
INITIAL LANDING - ZIG-ZAG    (29 Jan to 14 Feb 1945)
BATAAN - ADJACENT ISLANDS    (11 Feb to 17 Apr 1945)
STOTSENBURG AREA             ( 7 Mar to 30 Apr 1945)
EAST OF MANILA               (30 Apr to 30 June 1945)
```

Each of these may further be divided into what appears to be separate actions, although the continuity will be retained insofar as clearness will permit.

The INITIAL LANDING - ZIG-ZAG action may be considered one continuous operation. American forces successfully landed, secured air strip facilities vicinity of SAN MARCELINO, and meeting no opposition, rapidly advanced into the SUBIC BAY - OLONGAPO area securing the port facilities thereof. There in the ZIG-ZAG Pass area, extending from SANTA RITA East to DINALUPIHAN, the Japanese forces made an unsuccessful attempt to prevent the accomplishment of the original mission. In the meantime, and as ZIG-ZAG developed, the GRANDE ISLAND at the entrance to SUBIC Bay was secured by an amphibious landing.

Closely following and even before the ZIG-ZAG action terminated, the BATAAN - ADJACENT ISLANDS Operation began. Concurrently, the occupation of the PILAR - BAGAC Road, the East coast road (Highway 110) and the successful amphibious landing at MARIVELES were made. Assistance to the 503d Parachute Infantry in its capture of CORREGIDOR was also given. Amphibious assaults of CABALLO Island, EL FRAILE Island (Fort Drum), and CARABAO Island, all in the entrance to MANILA BAY, followed the collapse of Japanese resistance on CORREGIDOR.

The third or STOTSENBURG Area portion of the M-7 Operation centers around the mountainous area between FT STOTSENBURG and MT PINATUBO, the highest mountain in the CABUSILAN Mountain Range. In this operation our forces, other than those engaged at STOTSENBURG, also pushed North from SAN FELIPE to PALAUIG BAY and East from BOTOLAN along the CAPAS Trail into the O'DONNELL - MORIONES area. This cut off the enemy's escape routes North into the LINGAYEN sector.

The fourth part of the M-7 Operation was the destruction

of the enemy forces EAST OF MANILA. This operation drove the Japanese East of the MARIQUINA River – BOSO BOSO River line, and destroyed or dispersed all effective units in that area.

Classification of these operations may fall between the combat phase and the mopping up phase as they were not the initial operations in those areas. Participation by our forces began upon relief of the Divisions then in contact, but unlike other engagements in the mopping up phase, they developed into major operations against stiff organized enemy resistance.

The "Mopping Up" Phase began at different times for different units of the Division, and some regiments became engaged in an active operation afterward. Hence this must be discussed in piecemeal, rather than as a separate Phase.

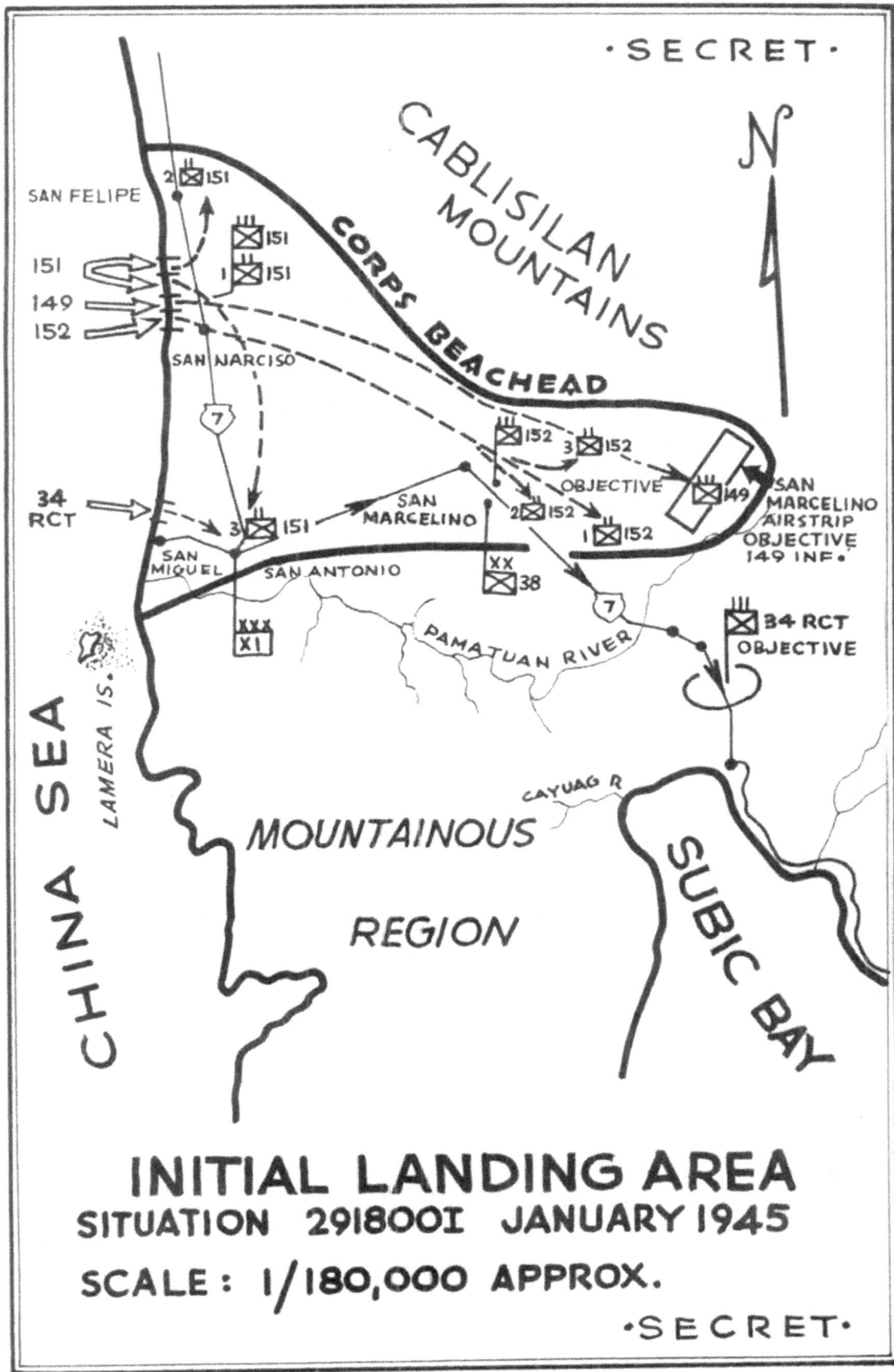

CABLISILAN MOUNTAINS

CORPS BEACHEAD

N

SAN FELIPE

2 ⊠ 151

⊠ 151

1 ⊠ 151

151 →

149 →

152 →

SAN NARCISO

7

⊠ 152

3 ⊠ 152

OBJECTIVE

⊠ 149

SAN MARCELINO AIRSTRIP OBJECTIVE 149 INF.

34 RCT →

3 ⊠ 151

SAN MARCELINO

2 ⊠ 152

1 ⊠ 152

SAN MIGUEL

SAN ANTONIO

XX ⊠ 38

7

⊠ 34 RCT OBJECTIVE

XXX X1

PAMATUAN RIVER

CHINA SEA

LAMERA IS.

CAYUAG R

MOUNTAINOUS

REGION

SUBIC BAY

INITIAL LANDING AREA
SITUATION 291800I JANUARY 1945
SCALE: 1/180,000 APPROX.

INITIAL LANDING ZIG-ZAG

At 290830 January the first waves hit Red and Yellow Beach. Prior reconnaissance by Navy and Division staff officers in a patrol boat at 0630 had shown that the beaches were crowded with cheering FILIPINOS, the American flag proudly flying in their midst. Their enthusiastic greeting actually delayed the initial progress, but their willing help was of great assistance in getting vehicles and supplies ashore.

Due to the narrowness of the beach the 38th Division landed regiments abreast, battalions in column, with the 152d Infantry on the right, the 149th Infantry in the center, and the 151st Infantry on the left. The 151st Infantry in addition landed one battalion on Yellow Beach to protect left flank.

The regiments immediately moved rapidly inland, meeting no opposition. The 149th Infantry seized the SAN MARCELINO Airstrip by 1600. The 152d Infantry secured their sector of the Corps beachhead by 1400. The 1st Battalion 151st Infantry reached SAN FELIPE and set up a defensive line North of that town by 1330. During the same period the 3d Battalion 151st Infantry (-) moved South to SAN ANTONIO to secure Blue Beach and cover the right flank of the Corps beachhead. This was completed at 1800 without confusion or interruption to traffic. The 151st Infantry was then placed in Corps reserve.

The following day, 30 January, the 149th Infantry and 152d Infantry moved to the pass South of CASTILLEJOS. This same day the 2d Battalion 151st Infantry made a shore-to-shore operation, landing on GRANDE Island in SUBIC Bay without opposition.

The mission initially assigned the 34th RCT by XI Corps was to advance rapidly via SAN MARCELINO, CASTILLEJOS, and SUBIC and seize OLONGAPO. This was accomplished against minor resistance. On 31 January the 152d Infantry was ordered to relieve the 34th RCT astride Highway 7 North of Olongapo, and the 34th RCT ordered back to the OLONGAPO-SUBIC area.

On 31 January the mission assigned the 38th Division was to clear Highway 7, the OLONGAPO-DINALUPIHAN road, and establish contact with elements of XIV Corps in the vicinity of DINALUPIHAN. To accomplish this, the Division was directed to advance one regiment astride Highway 7 and one regiment East by a parallel trail North of Highway 7 to DINALUPIHAN. The latter regiment was to turn West and strike the ZIG-ZAG area from the rear via Highway 7. The 152d Infantry was designated to advance East on Highway 7, relieving the 34th RCT, and the 149th Infantry (less 1st Battalion in Division Reserve) to take the North trail, the Western end of which was SANTA RITA.

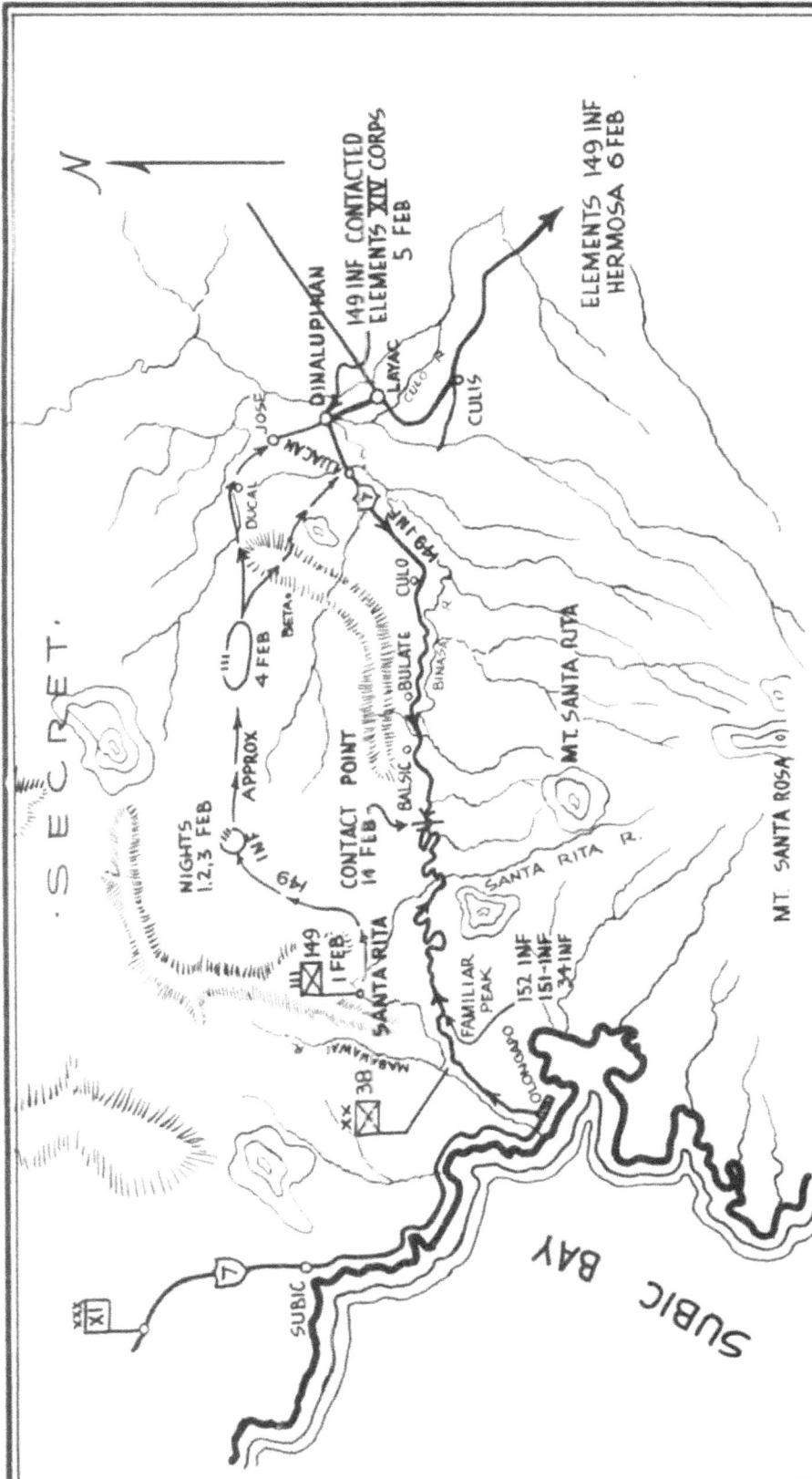

OLONGAPO – DINALUPIHAN
ZIG-ZAG PASS   SCALE 1:180,000 APPROX

Map labels: SECRET. N. Subic Bay, SUBIC, OLONGAPO, SANTA RITA, MABAYUAN, FAMILIAR PEAK, MT SANTA RITA, MT SANTA ROSA, SANTA RITA R., BALSIC, BULATE, CULO, BINASA R., CULIS, LAYAC, CULO R., JOSE, LIAC-AN, DINALUPIHAN, DUCAL, PAETAN.

NIGHTS 1,2,3 FEB   APPROX   4 FEB
CONTACT POINT 14 FEB
149 INF 1 FEB
38
149 INF
149 INF CONTACTED ELEMENTS XIV CORPS 5 FEB
ELEMENTS 149 INF HERMOSA 6 FEB
152 INF 151 INF 34 INF
XI
7

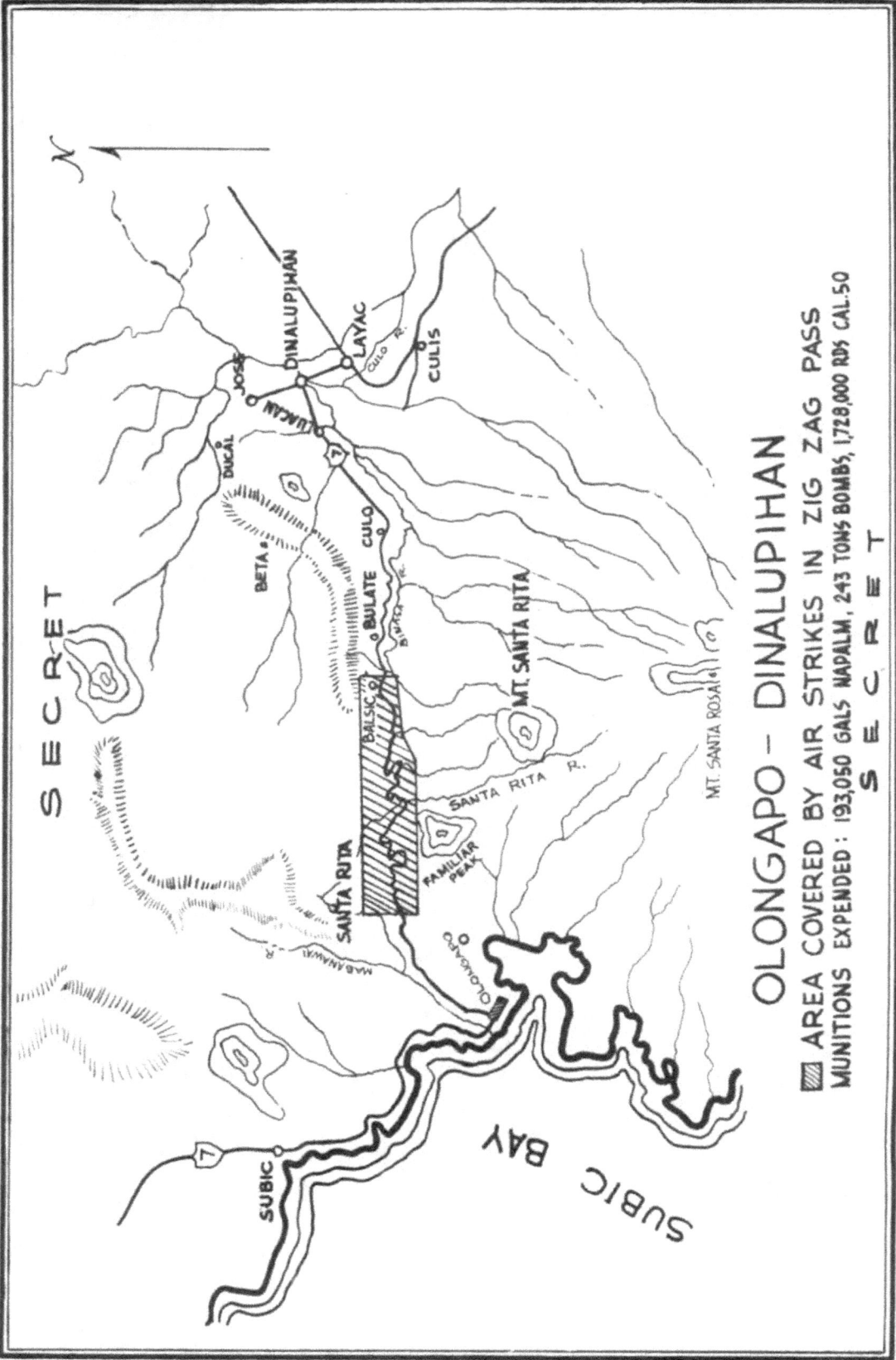

SECRET

OLONGAPO – DINALUPIHAN

▨ AREA COVERED BY AIR STRIKES IN ZIG ZAG PASS
MUNITIONS EXPENDED: 193,050 GALS NAPALM, 243 TONS BOMBS, 1,728,000 RDS CAL.50

S E C R E T

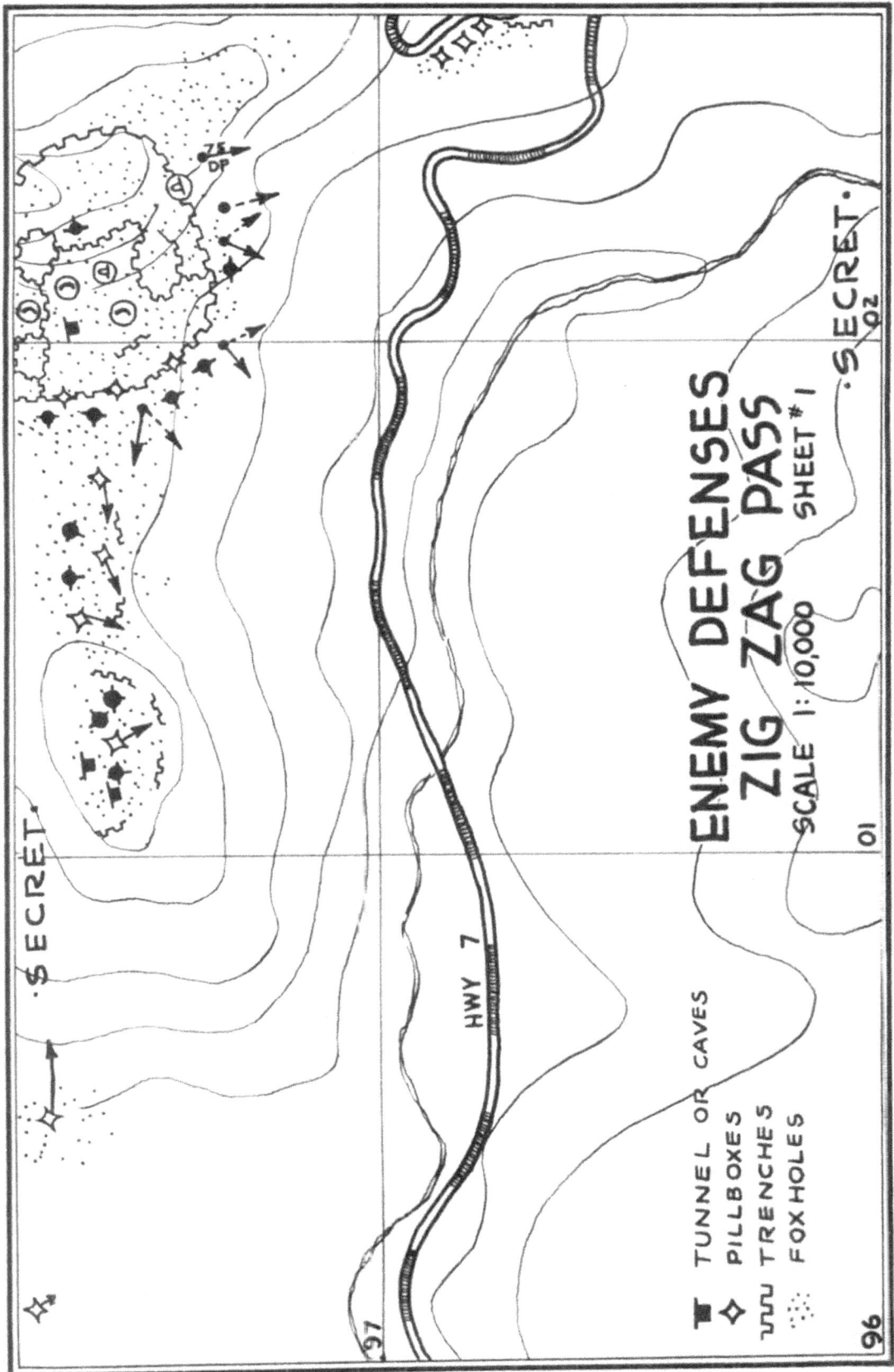

ENEMY DEFENSES
ZIG ZAG PASS
SHEET #1
SCALE 1:10,000

·SECRET·

·SECRET·

HWY 7

▮ TUNNEL OR CAVES
◇ PILLBOXES
ᴗᴗᴗ TRENCHES
⁙ FOX HOLES

96   01   02

97

ZZ
DP

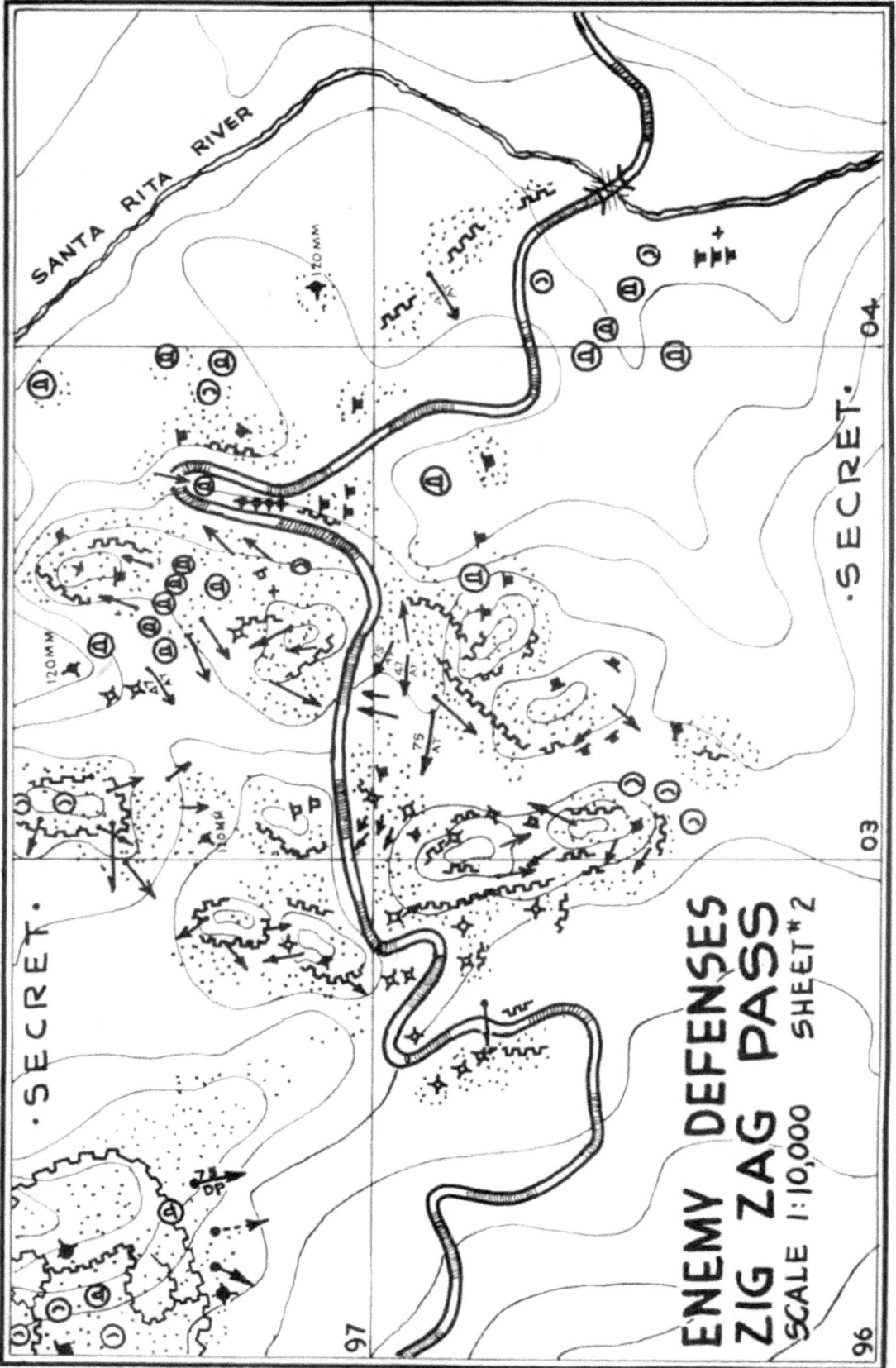

ENEMY DEFENSES
ZIG ZAG PASS
SCALE 1:10,000   SHEET #2

SANTA RITA RIVER

SECRET.

120 MM

120 MM

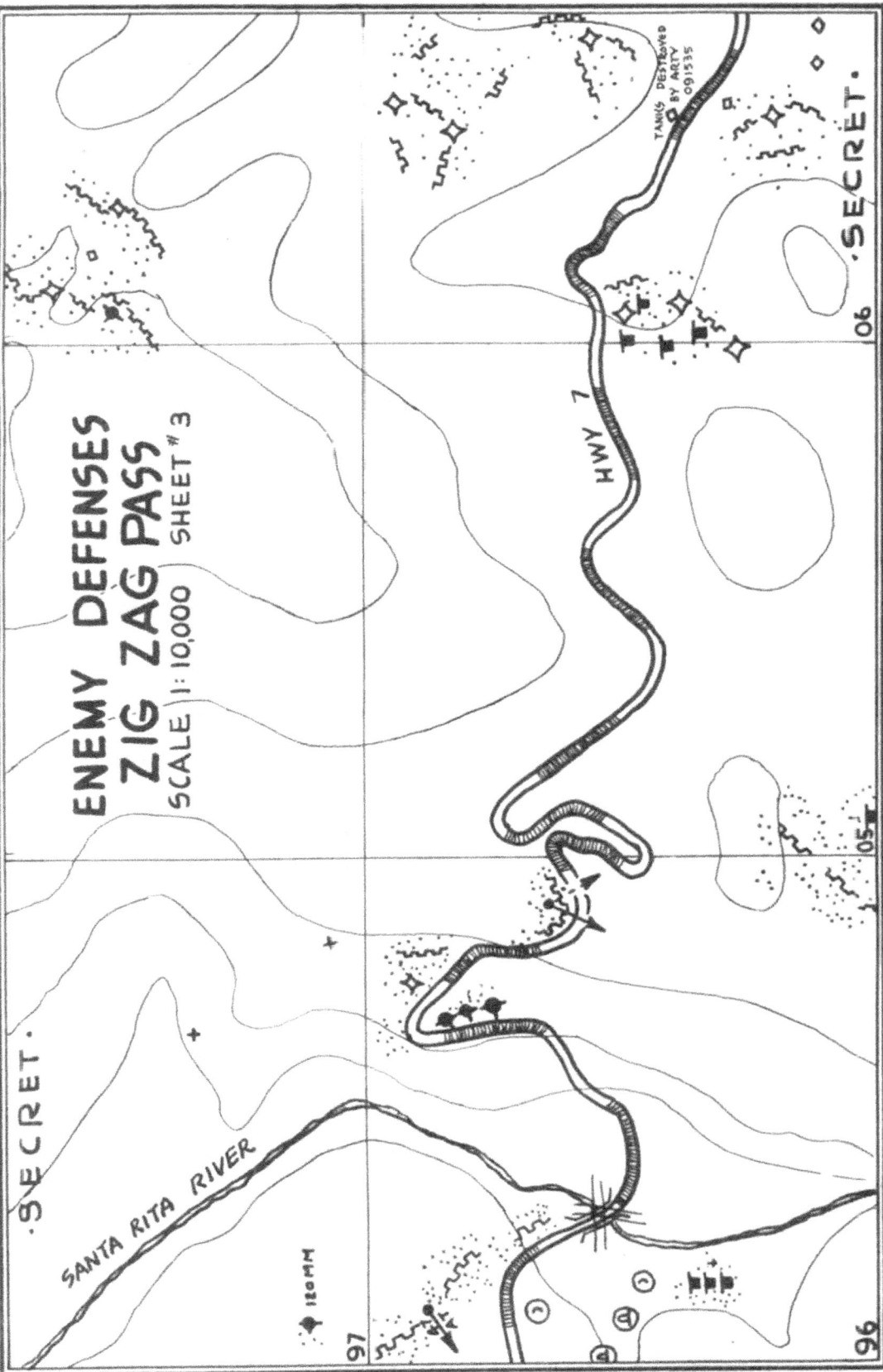

ENEMY DEFENSES
ZIG ZAG PASS
SCALE 1: 10,000   SHEET #3

·SECRET·

SANTA RITA RIVER

HWY 7

TANKS DESTROYED
BY ARTY
091535

·SECRET·

150MM

97

96

06

05

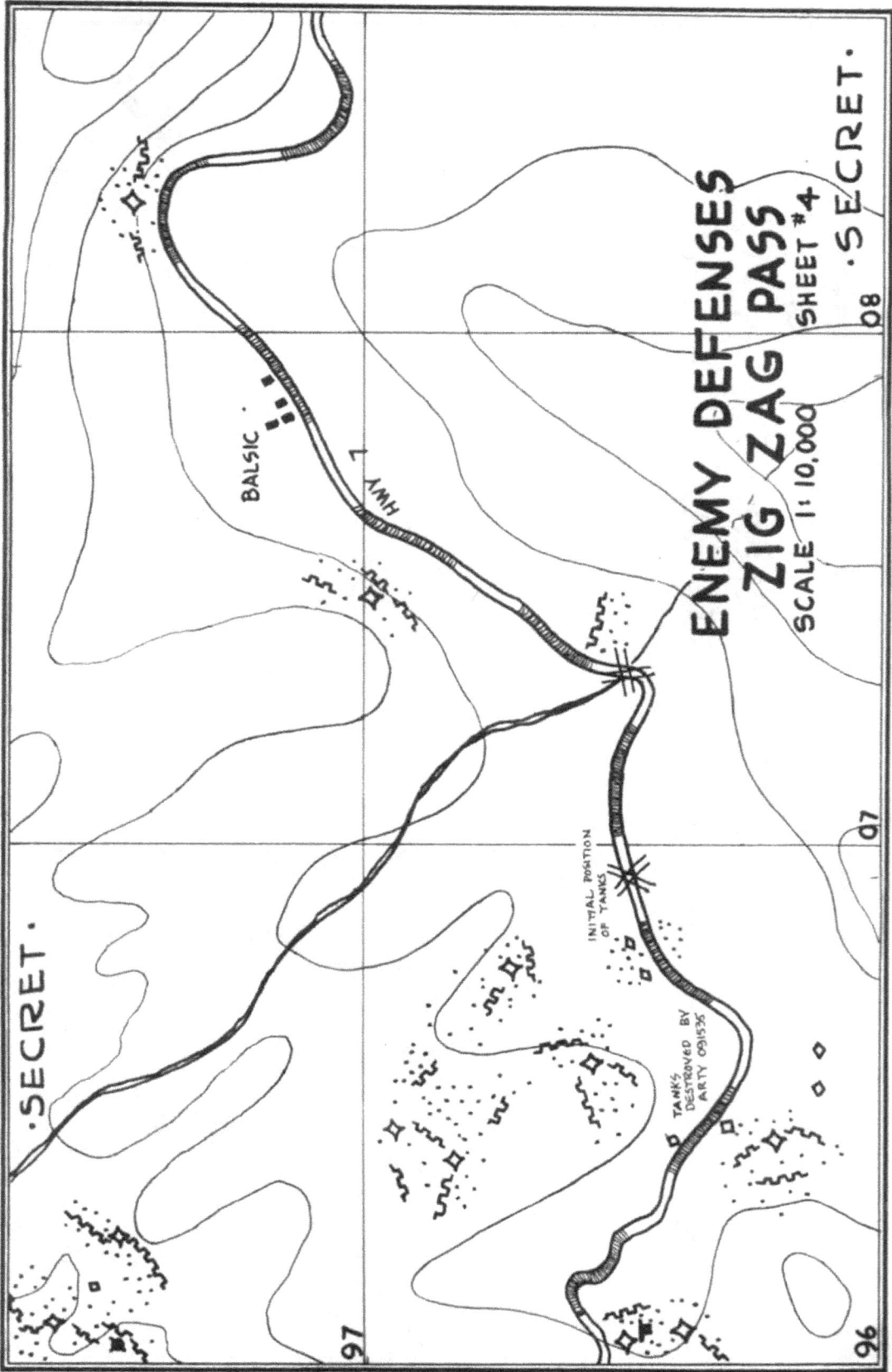

ENEMY DEFENSES
ZIG ZAG PASS
SCALE 1: 10,000   SHEET #4

·SECRET·

·SECRET·

BALSIC

HWY 1

INITIAL POSITION
OF TANKS

TANKS
DESTROYED BY
ARTY 091535

08

07

97

96

In the SAN NARCISO-SAN FELIPE area the 151st Infantry continued extensive patrolling as Corps reserve.

Relief of the 34th RCT, less 63d FA Bn attached to the 38th Division Artillery, was started by the 152d Infantry while the 149th Infantry, less 1st Battalion in Division reserve, closed in vicinity SANTA RITA. By 311800 January the 149th Infantry was prepared to move East via an uncharted trail North of Highway 7.

On 1 February the 152d Infantry completed relief of the 34th RCT, some elements of the 34th Infantry not moving until the following day. During this relief elements of both regiments became involved in actions against enemy strong points. Heavy fire from prepared enemy positions was by-passed by the leading 1st Battalion as the 152d Infantry proceeded East on Highway 7 toward ZIG-ZAG Pass on 1 February. These positions were subsequently reduced by the 2d Battalion that followed. By 1200 the regiment had advanced three and one half miles inland, neutralizing all enemy positions up to that point. Each yard gained was marked by increased resistance.

Meanwhile the 2d Battalion 149th Infantry with Co C 113th Medical Battalion, 1 Platoon Co A 113th Engineer Battalion, and 64th Portable Surgical Hospital, started East to DINALUPIHAN over a trail reported North of Highway 7, known as the SANTA RITA Trail. This trail, beginning at SANTA RITA on the West and emerging at BETA on the East, was a Negrito trail used by the Guerrillas during the period of enemy occupation. The route, reported as paralleling Highway 7 at about 1500 to 2000 yards, proved to be in error. It developed that this trail was actually 8000 to 10,000 yards North of the Highway. It crossed a series of extremely difficult and heavily wooded ridges and ravines, much of it overgrown. Difficulties were added to the march in that all equipment was hand carried, including a complete Portable Surgical Hospital, and water on the higher ridges was very scarce. To supply these columns it was necessary to provide daily air drop service along the route of march. This mountain march over trails known only to the native guides covered a period of five days.

A discussion of the terrain and the enemy's plan of defense of the ZIG-ZAG Pass will make clear the account that follows.

From OLONGAPO, Highway 7 was constructed on flat land about 2 miles, abruptly entering a narrow mountain valley. In the next 5 miles the road reaches an elevation of approximately 800 feet by a series of loops and hairpin curves around and between hills which completely dominate the Highway. It was around the sides and on the tops of these hills that the Japan-

ese entrenchments were placed, the defenses on each hill interlocking with the fires from adjacent hills. This defense was
well planned in depth as is indicated on the accompanying
sketch.

A curious fact is that little or no attempt was made to
defend or place harassing fire on the flat ground leading from
OLONGAPO, although the first entrenched hills afforded an excellent opportunity. They had, however, previously destroyed
their reconstructed port installations and some civilian res-
idences.

Continuing for the next 8 miles the first hills encountered upon leaving OLONGAPO were intricately entrenched. Sited
in the rear of the strongest defenses were excellently emplaced
and camouflaged 10cm and 75mm artillery and 120mm mortars, with
ranges to key points predetermined and evidently registered on,
prior to our attack. Maps captured later indicated these
places, in which our forces experienced heavy mortar and artillery fire. These mortars and artillery pieces were scattered
across the zone, and although this gave excellent defensive
dispersion, it also made the massing of fires impossible. 47mm
AT guns were interspersed between the artillery pieces, effectively covering the few available routes of tank approach.

The second element characterizing the defense was the
lack of width of the defended zone. To the North there was a
large hill mass, the Northern slope being the South bank of
the SANTA RITA River. This bank was a vertical cliff varying
from 40 to 100 feet in height and rising from a rough, narrow
stream bed. The Japanese had overlooked the possibility of
troops moving between the cliff and their Northern positions.
Our units were able to flank these enemy positions consist-
ently from the North, although even a flanking attack was a
frontal one because of the all-around defense employed on
each hill. To the South the ground fell off into a saddle
between the road and FAMILIAR PEAK, which was covered with
heavy jungle and considered impassable. The enemy mission
was to block the use of Highway 7 which could be effectively
accomplished from their positions astride the road.

The third, and most difficult element of the whole defense was the system of well dug-in positions. Each hill top
was crowned with a series of foxholes, each about 5 to 6 feet
deep and with tunnels of 4 to 8 feet extending from the bottom of the foxhole. Many of these foxholes were then partially covered with logs and earth, leaving one hole facing to
the front and another to the rear. Each foxhole was connected to the next by a shallow communicating trench. Carefully
planned and sited MG positions, pillboxes, and dugouts were
interspersed throughout the area. A direct hit by artillery

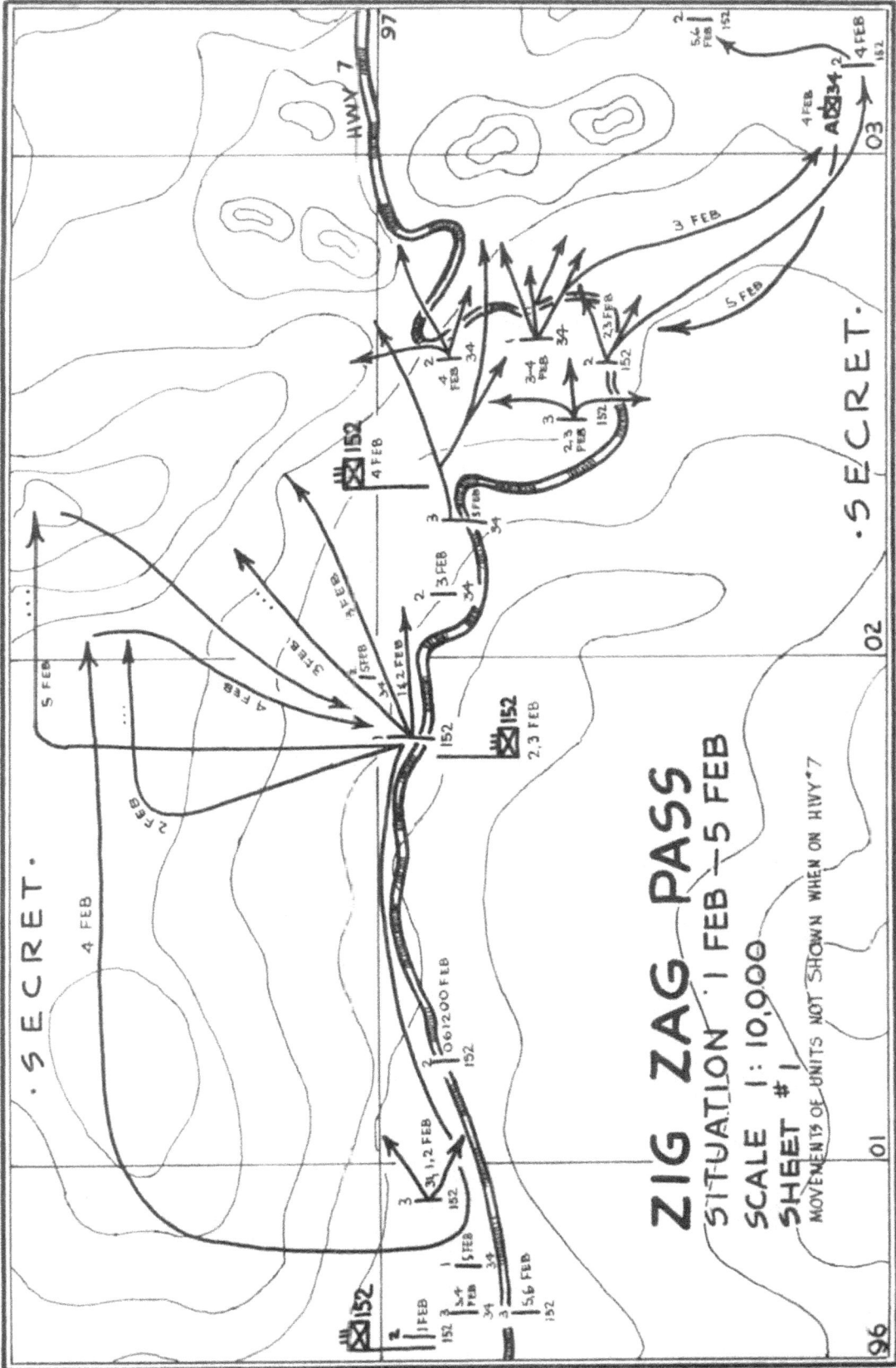

ZIG ZAG PASS

SITUATION 1 FEB - 5 FEB

SCALE 1:10,000

SHEET #1

MOVEMENTS OF UNITS NOT SHOWN WHEN ON HWY #7

·SECRET·

·SECRET·

or mortars, or attack by the individual riflemen were the only means of silencing the fire of each foxhole or emplacement. In the area were spider-holes, command post caves, and caves containing ample food and ammunition. Thus each hill top was a fortress which had to be reduced in turn. Behind these hill tops were stores of rations and supplies. Effective concealment for all these installations was given by the maze of trees, underbrush, and bamboo thickets with which the whole area of the pass is liberally covered.

During the morning of 2 February the 152d Infantry mopped up scattered groups that were bypassed the previous day. When the entire area up to the leading elements of the 1st Battalion was cleared the Regiment advanced abreast the Highway, 2d Battalion on the right, 3d Battalion on the left, 1st Battalion in reserve. Having advanced to a point on the Highway (02.6-96.9) offensive action was hindered by the extremely steep slopes rising on the North of the Highway giving the enemy great strength in the defense of the pass. His prepared positions on commanding ground delivered extremely accurate mortar and machine gun fire that withstood our attack till late in the period when the Regiment dug in for the night. All Battalions suffered severe mortar and artillery fire during the night and were subjected to continued attempts at infiltration.

On 2 February the 2d and 3d Battalions 149th Infantry closed in bivouac approximately 8000 yards North of Highway 7. The exact location is still a controversial question. As the result of two messages, one undelivered due to failure of radios, and one garbled in transmission, instructions were issued for the return of the Regiment to SANTA RITA. The 2d Battalion, Company A 113th Medical Battalion and 1 Platoon Company A 113th Engineer Battalion returned to SANTA RITA arriving at 1930, 2 February. That night instructions were given to proceed again to DINALUPIHAN, and releasing the 1st Battalion 149th Infantry from Division Reserve.

During the night of 2-3 February orders were received directing the 34th RCT under XI Corps control to relieve the 152d Infantry in place, pass through the 152d Infantry and continue the attack, clearing the road to DINALUPIHAN. The 152d Infantry was to follow the 34th RCT, when bypassed, mopping up any enemy resistance left behind, and maintaining the lines of communication.

On 3 February the 34th Infantry began to pass through the 152d Infantry, but when the leading battalion advanced beyond the line of the 152d Infantry, it encountered such heavy resistance that it could not advance. This caused both units to be jammed in the area along Highway 7, causing heavy casualties from enemy mortar and artillery fire. The 152d

Terrain North of Highway 7 up which 152d attacked
on 2-3 February 1945. Destroyed Pill-box in center.

Visibility Zero

Infantry sent patrols to the North of the Highway, to determine the enemy's right (North) flank.

The 1st and 2d Battalions and Regimental Headquarters 149th Infantry with Company A 113th Medical Battalion, one Platoon Company A 113th Engineer (C) Battalion left SANTA RITA, reaching the bivouac of the 3d Battalion that evening.

The 152d Infantry on 4 February mopped up close-in enemy positions and sent the 1st Battalion West down the Highway, then North, and East against the enemy's right flank. During the move East several Japanese positions were encountered by the 1st Battalion and taken. Late in the afternoon, a large enemy position was encountered and engaged. At about 1630 intense enemy fire caused the loss of all the officers, except one, in two rifle companies, and one half the NCOs in the three rifle companies. The Battalion moved down to the road to reorganize.

The 34th Infantry attempted to advance down the Highway with units on both sides of the road but was stopped by the hostile resistance. The tanks supporting the 34th Infantry tried to break through down the road, but when the Infantry were left behind, the Japanese attacked them with lunge mines, so the tanks withdrew. A Company was sent to the right (South) flank to locate the flank of the enemy's position, but became lost in the FAMILIAR PEAK area, and was reported cut off and surrounded. At 2050 4 February the 34th Infantry was attached to the 38th Infantry Division.

The 149th Infantry continued its march East in two columns, toward DINALUPIHAN. The 3d Battalion halted for the night 1500 yards Northwest of BETA. The balance of the Regiment halted behind the 3d Battalion on the trail.

On 5 February the 34th Infantry was assigned the mission of advancing on the South side of the Highway, with the 152d Infantry on the North. Elements of the 34th Infantry were in advance of the 152d Infantry, and in attempting to maneuver around their opposition, moved North of the road. This caused such confusion that instructions were issued that no artillery concentrations would be fired West of the SANTA RITA River without permission of the Regimental Commanding Officer of the sector concerned. This inevitably caused a delay in the placing of close-in artillery fires. The 34th Infantry, unable to advance, and suffering heavy casualties, requested to be withdrawn, and the 151st Infantry was ordered to relieve them on 6 February.

This same day, 5 February, the 149th Infantry completed its march to DINALUPIHAN, established contact with elements of XIV Corps and set up a road block at LAYAC. The 2d Battalion

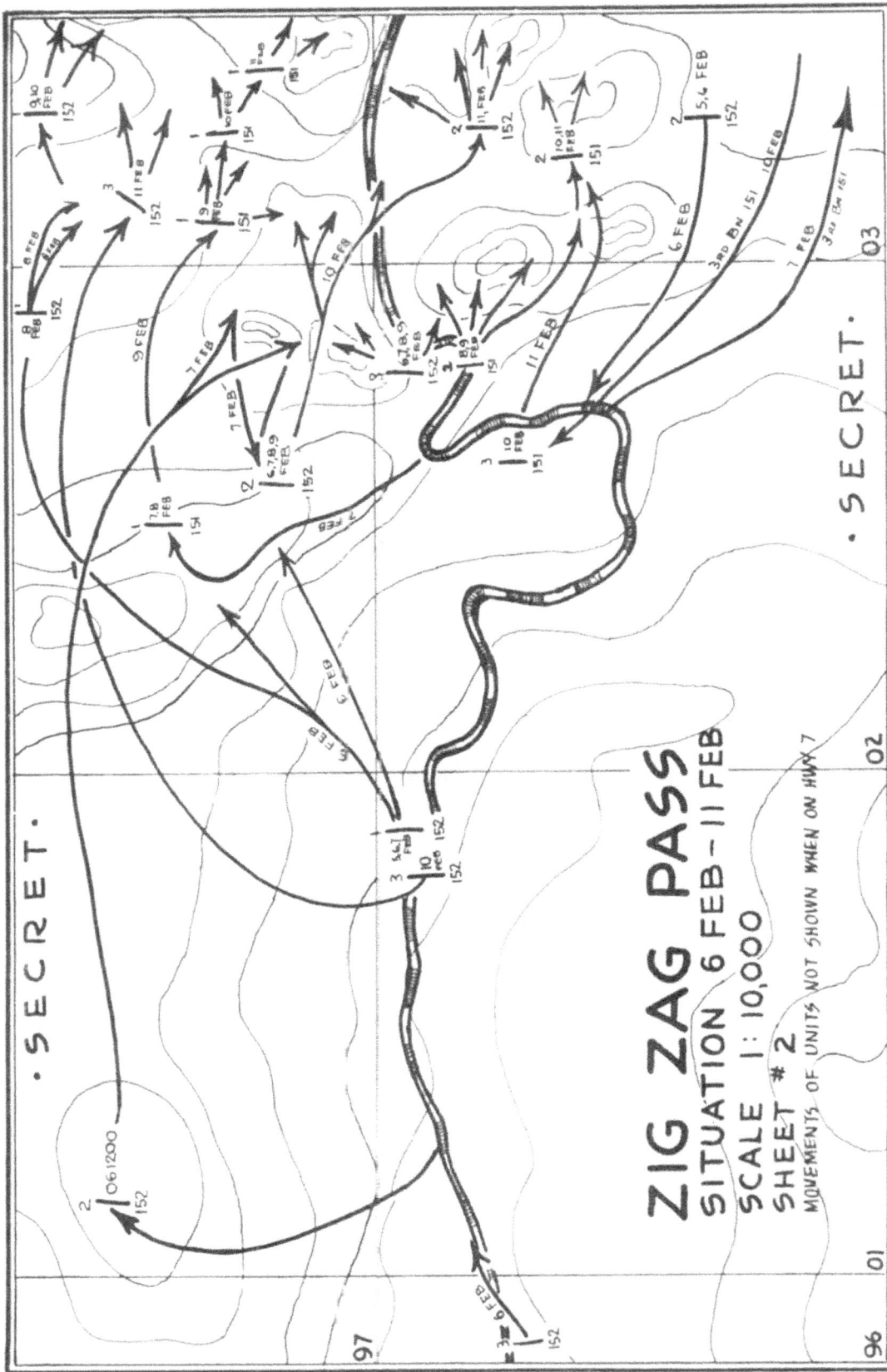

ZIG ZAG PASS

SITUATION 6 FEB – 11 FEB

SCALE 1:10,000

SHEET #2

MOVEMENTS OF UNITS NOT SHOWN WHEN ON HWY 7

152d Infantry moved South of the Highway and occupied commanding ground 800 yards North of FAMILIAR PEAK. Contact was made with A Company 34th Infantry, guides were furnished them and A Company returned to the Highway at the Horseshoe Bend. The 1st Battalion 152d Infantry continued its drive East along the ridge North of Highway 7 reducing enemy emplacements. Late in the period strong enemy underground works were encountered and the Battalion went into a perimeter for the night.

On 6 February the 34th Infantry was detached from the 38th Infantry Division and moved to the rear, the 151st Infantry taking over their sector. Air strikes and heavy artillery preparations were placed on the Japanese ZIG-ZAG defenses in preparation for a coordinated attack to the East by the 151st Infantry and the 152d Infantry. The 2d Battalion 152d Infantry was moved back into Division Reserve North and West of the Horseshoe Bend with the mission of protecting the left rear of the 152d Infantry. The 149th Infantry prepared for their advance to the West against ZIG-ZAG, and relieved elements of the XIV Corps in the DINALUPIHAN area. To the North of Highway 7 the 152d Infantry continued to advance slowly against a number of prepared positions and under heavy machine gun and mortar fire. The advance in all sectors was assisted by the accurate supporting fire of the Division Artillery, and coordinated air strikes. As of this date the Division had advanced from OLONGAPO inland a distance of approximately 9000 yards.

On 6 February Maj Gen H. L. C. Jones was relieved from command of the 38th Infantry Division.

On 7 February Maj Gen William C. Chase (then Brig Gen) took command of the 38th Infantry Division.

On 7 February 1945 the 149th Infantry advanced West against sniper fire until 1500 when they encountered an organized enemy position 800 yards East of BALSIC. Company A bypassed it. By 1800 the battalion had overcome all opposition. A second position was encountered 400 yards East of BALSIC and the 1st Battalion halted for the night.

The 2d Battalion 152d Infantry was committed from Division Reserve and continued the advance to the East on the North of the Highway, assaulted and secured enemy strong point (03.0-97.2) after a brisk fight. The mission of the 1st Battalion was to follow the 2d Battalion and secure 2d Battalion's left flank. The 3d Battalion continued methodically to assault and mop up the enemy positions in their front against strong opposition on their North.

The 3d Battalion 151st Infantry was ordered to proceed to

FAMILIAR PEAK. On arrival they sent patrols to the SANTA RITA River bridge and to the East along the South side of Highway 7 in an effort to contact the 149th Infantry. No contact was made with the enemy or 149th Infantry and the battalion went into perimeter 400 yards South of SANTA RITA River bridge.

On 8 February Company G 149th Infantry attached to the 1st Battalion 149th Infantry attacked and destroyed the enemy position encountered at the close of the previous period. The 1st Battalion less Company B reverted to Regimental reserve. The 2d Battalion attacked through the 1st Battalion and advanced 400 yards West of BALSIC where they encountered enemy machine gun and mortar fire. Artillery was placed on this Japanese position following which the Battalion overran it. After a further advance of 300 yards another strong position was encountered, reduced and occupied. In the early evening two Japanese tanks attacked the perimeter from across the creek. Rifle grenades and bazookas proved ineffective, so artillery fire was called for and the tanks withdrew. At 1830 the 3d Battalion 151st Infantry advancing East on the South side of the road was attached to 149th Infantry.

The 151st Infantry (less 3d Battalion) was ordered to pass through and relieve the 152d Infantry. Relief of the 152d Infantry was slowed up by enemy mortar concentrations, which were silenced by artillery and the relief continued. At 1300 the 1st Battalion 151st Infantry and 2d Battalion 151st Infantry (less Company E which had not arrived on LUZON from ORO BAY) were in position, and supported by tanks, moving forward, the 2d Battalion against a strong point at (03.2-96.8). After limited gains the Battalions at 1800 went into perimeters for the night, the 1st Battalion at (03.1-97.2), the 2d Battalion at (02.8-96.9), and the 3d Battalion at (04.8-95.8).

After relief by the 151st Infantry the 1st Battalion 152d Infantry advanced East in a zone North of the 1st Battalion 151st Infantry. It reduced numerous enemy strong points in the advance from the vicinity of (02.8-97.5) to the vicinity of (03.3-97.6). The 2d Battalion 152d Infantry reorganized in the position it was holding in Division Reserve. The 3d Battalion was engaged in mopping up operations.

On 9 February, while the 1st Battalion 149th Infantry was in Regimental Reserve protecting the rear and flanks of the Regiment, the 2d Battalion 149th Infantry attacked through heavy undergrowth against enemy automatic fire. Three tanks, protected by machine guns and snipers were encountered during the day. Rockets and grenades could not immobilize the tanks, however the machine guns on one were put out of action by two direct bazooka hits. At 1532 an artillery plane located 2

Japanese tank destroyed by 149th Infantry
in their drive West through ZIG-ZAG Pass

An aerial view of ZIG-ZAG Pass at it's Eastern exit near BALSIC.
In the lower right hand corner an enemy tank blazes from a
direct hit by our artillery. In the center of the picture the
artillery scores another direct hit on an ammunition dump just
off the road.

ZIG ZAG PASS

SITUATION II FEB – 14 FEB

SCALE 1 : 10,000

SHEET # 3

MOVEMENTS OF UNITS NOT SHOWN WHEN ON HWY 7

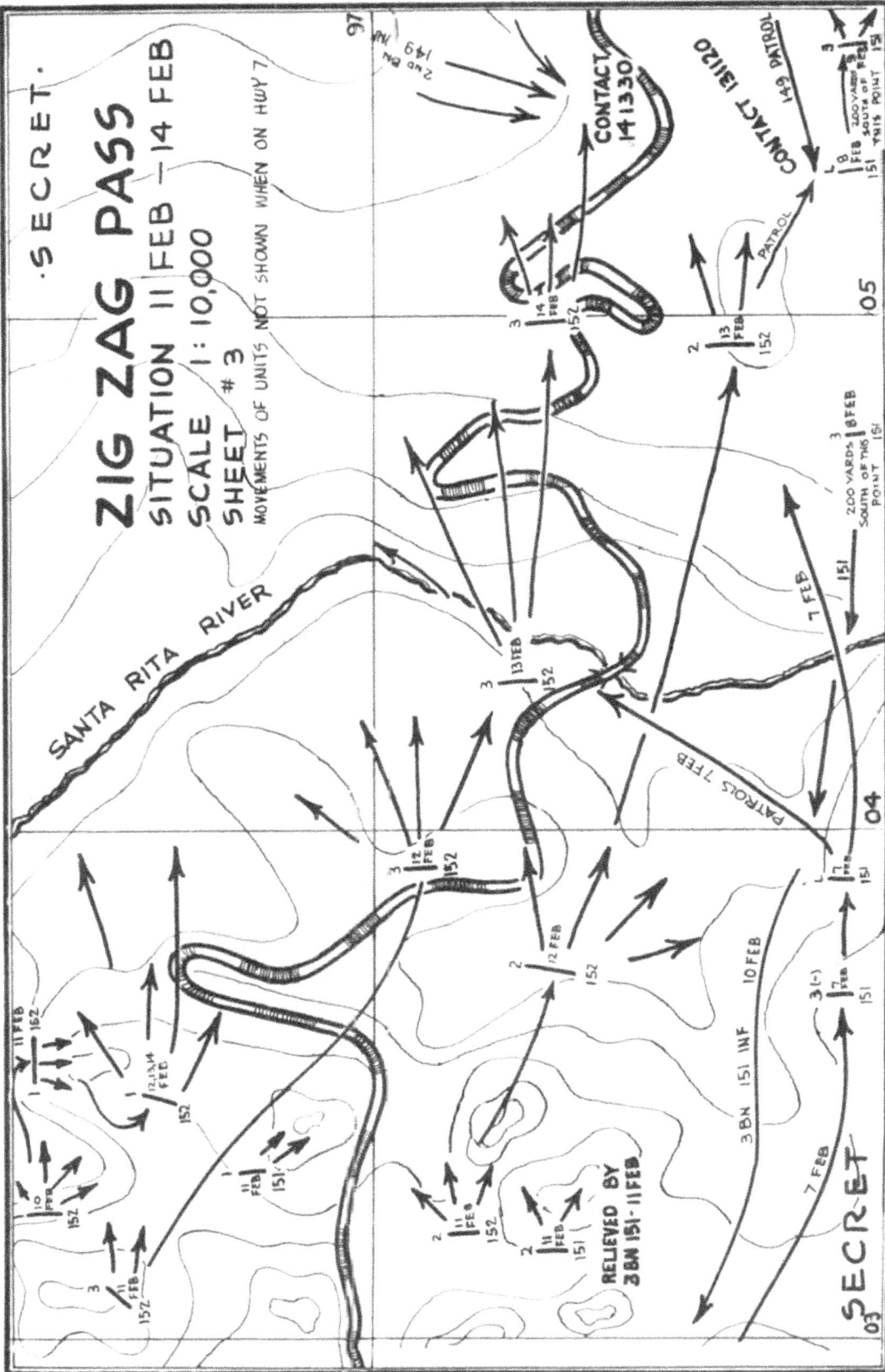

SANTA RITA RIVER

2nd BN 149 INF

CONTACT 141330

CONTACT 131120

149 PATROL

PATROL

8 FEB
200 YARDS
SOUTH OF THIS
POINT 151

3 14 FEB 152

2 13 FEB 152

3 8 FEB
200 YARDS
SOUTH OF THIS
POINT 151

7 FEB

PATROLS 7 FEB

7 FEB

3 13 FEB 152

3 12 FEB 152

2 12 FEB 152

7 FEB 151

3 BN 151 INF 10 FEB

3(-) 7 FEB 151

3 11 FEB 152

12,13,14 FEB 152

11 FEB

11 FEB 151

10 FEB 152

3 11 FEB 152

2 11 FEB 152

2 11 FEB 151

RELIEVED BY
2 BN 151 – 11 FEB

7 FEB

03

04

05

97

tanks and artillery fire was placed on them resulting in one direct hit at 9000 yards. The 3d Battalion continued extensive patrolling with nil contact in the vicinity of ORANI. Control of 3d Battalion 151st Infantry reverted back to 151st Infantry, as effective control could not be exercised by the 149th Infantry due to tank activity in between.

The 151st Infantry, on 9 February, was ordered to continue the attack. The 2d Battalion made slow progress but developed a net work of machine gun emplacements. Tanks were brought up to assist in the reduction of these positions. One tank exhausted its ammunition supply and one tank was knocked out. The 2d Battalion 151st Infantry was short Company E and two platoons of Company G. To assist them, Companies F and G of the 152d Infantry were attached to the 2d Battalion 151st Infantry. During the middle of the day, the 2d Battalion 151st Infantry encountered heavy resistance. Hard fighting at close ranges ensued, lasting till dark, when the 2d Battalion 151st Infantry moved into a perimeter on an adjacent hill occupied the previous night. The 2d Battalion 152d Infantry as Division Reserve was committed between the 1st and 2d Battalions of the 151st Infantry, (Company F 152d Infantry reverting to Battalion control) through this gap they continued the attack against stubborn resistance reaching and holding their objective. The 152d Infantry (less 2d Battalion) during the period had reduced and mopped up strong points at (03.1-96.5) and (03.5-97.5), against strong resistance.

On 9 February the 3d Battalion 151st Infantry attempted to contact the 149th Infantry South of Highway 7. The action of the 149th Infantry with the Japanese tanks, and the artillery concentrations in between the two units prevented contact.

On 10 February the 149th Infantry 1st Battalion, launched an attack from the vicinity of point (06.9-96.1) on the South of the Highway, Company C in the lead. They advanced 800 yards where contact was made with the tanks again. The 2d Battalion, in a deployed formation on the North side of the road, advanced slowly, here also a tank was encountered and fired on without effect. The tank withdrew to a concealed position. At 1700 the Battalion moved into the perimeter of the previous night. The 151st Infantry organized Companies F and G together with Company G, 152d Infantry, into an assault detachment to reduce an elaborate system of tunnels holding up the advance. After two assaults it was reduced and 25 Japanese killed. The entire day was spent reducing like installations, all mutually supporting and well manned. The 152d Infantry continued the attack to the East against stubborn resistance, the 2d Battalion 152d Infantry (less Company G) reaching and holding ground

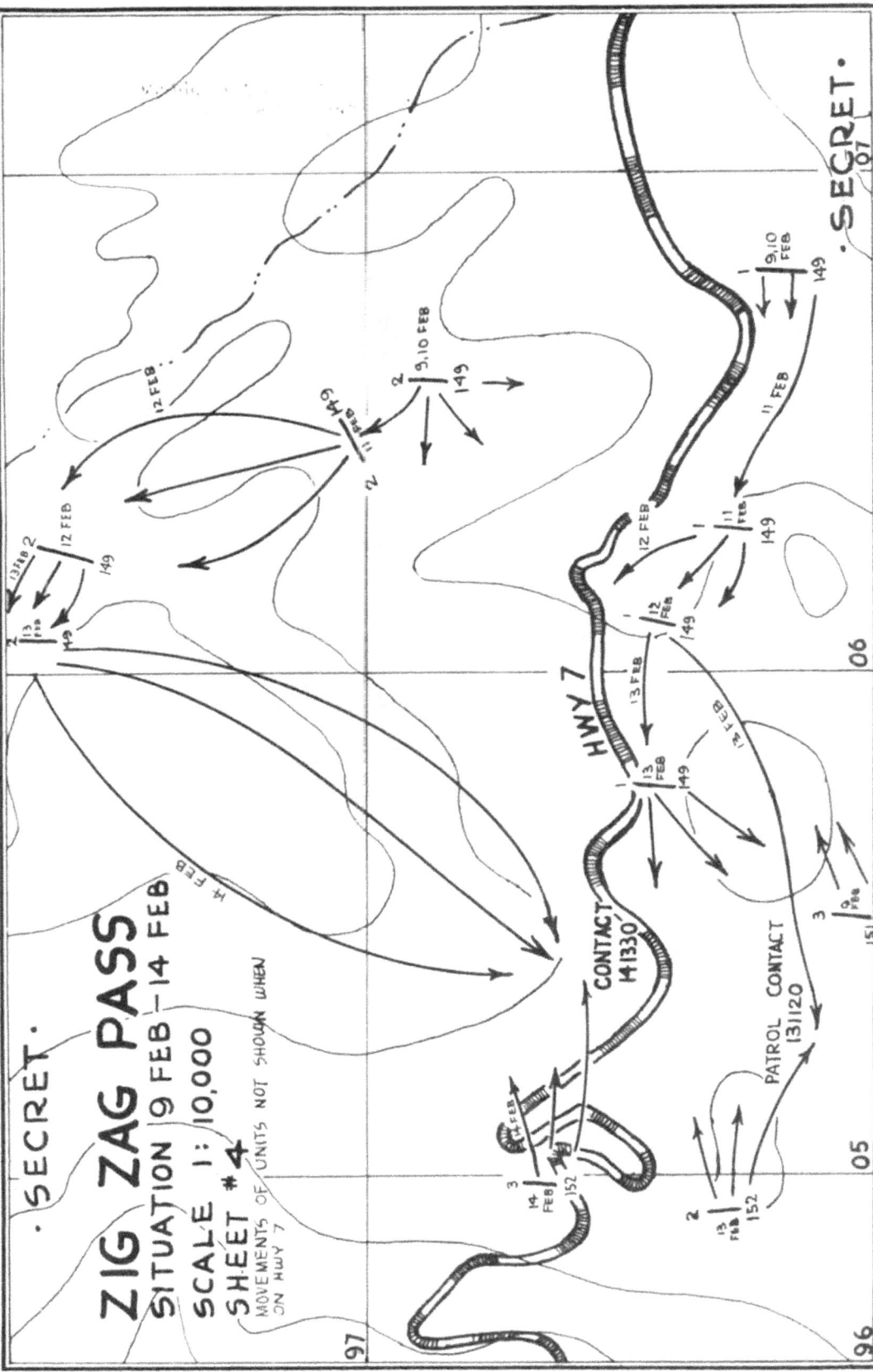

· SECRET ·

ZIG ZAG PASS
SITUATION 9 FEB – 14 FEB
SCALE 1: 10,000
SHEET # 4
MOVEMENTS OF UNITS NOT SHOWN WHEN ON HWY 7

HWY 7

CONTACT 141330

PATROL CONTACT 131120

· SECRET ·

One of the World's largest field mortars (120mm) captured
intact by infantrymen of the 152d Infantry during the
battle of ZIG-ZAG Pass. Three others were destroyed.

Hill (03.0-96.8) just South of Highway 7 that
withstood attack for six days until taken by
2d Bn 151st Infantry and 2d Bn 152d Infantry.

Terrain confronting 149th Infantry West of
Balsic where engagements with Japanese tanks
occurred.

in the vicinity of (03.3-96.7). The 3d Battalion 152d Infantry, relieved by 2d Battalion 151st Infantry, moved to (01.8-96.8) and remained there, replacing 2d Battalion 152d Infantry as Division reserve. The 1st Battalion 152d Infantry operated on the left (North) flank and reduced heavily armed, well entrenched positions on Hill (03.7-97.7).

During the preceeding action, elements of the 152d Infantry had been committed to assist the 151st Infantry. Elements of the 151st Infantry, engaged North of the Highway, had to be assisted by the 152d Infantry. They could not be disengaged. To simplify control, all units North of Highway 7 were placed under command of Lt Col McIntosh, 152d Infantry, and all units South of Highway 7 under command of Col Ralf Paddock, 151st Infantry.

On 10 February the 3d Battalion 151st Infantry was ordered to return to the Regiment and moved to the vicinity of the Horse Shoe Bend.

On 11 February the 3d Battalion 151st Infantry relieved the 2d Battalion 151st Infantry and Companies F and G 152d Infantry were detached from the 2d Battalion 151st Infantry and reverted to 2d Battalion 152d Infantry. 2d Battalion 151st Infantry was put in Regimental reserve; they continued mopping up operations in the vicinity of (03.3-96.7). The forces moving East through the ZIG-ZAG Pass were in order from North to South as follows: 1st Battalion 152d Infantry on the left flank, 3d Battalion 152d Infantry to the rear of and on the left flank of 1st Battalion 151st Infantry who had its right flank on Highway 7. The 2d Battalion 152d Infantry on the South of the Highway with its left flank on the Highway. 3d Battalion 151st Infantry on the right flank. The 2d Battalion 151st Infantry in Regimental reserve mopped up around its position.

The 2d Battalion 152d Infantry advanced to the enemy position at (03.3-96.7), which was reduced after a sharp fight and occupied for the night. The 3d Battalion 152d Infantry met moderate resistance and advanced to (03.6-97.4). The 151st Infantry was receiving heavy fire from (03.5-97.2) which checked the entire advance. To prepare for another mission the 151st Infantry was relieved by 152d Infantry and ordered to an assembly area near OLONGAPO. The entire regiment had closed in their rear area at 1800. 1st Battalion 149th Infantry attacked on the South side Highway 7 following an air strike. In their drive Westward aggressive action disclosed strongly entrenched positions (06.3-96.2) which were reduced and occupied after hard fighting. The 2d Battalion 149th Infantry after an advance of 300 yards, encountered an enemy tank. 81mm mortar fire placed

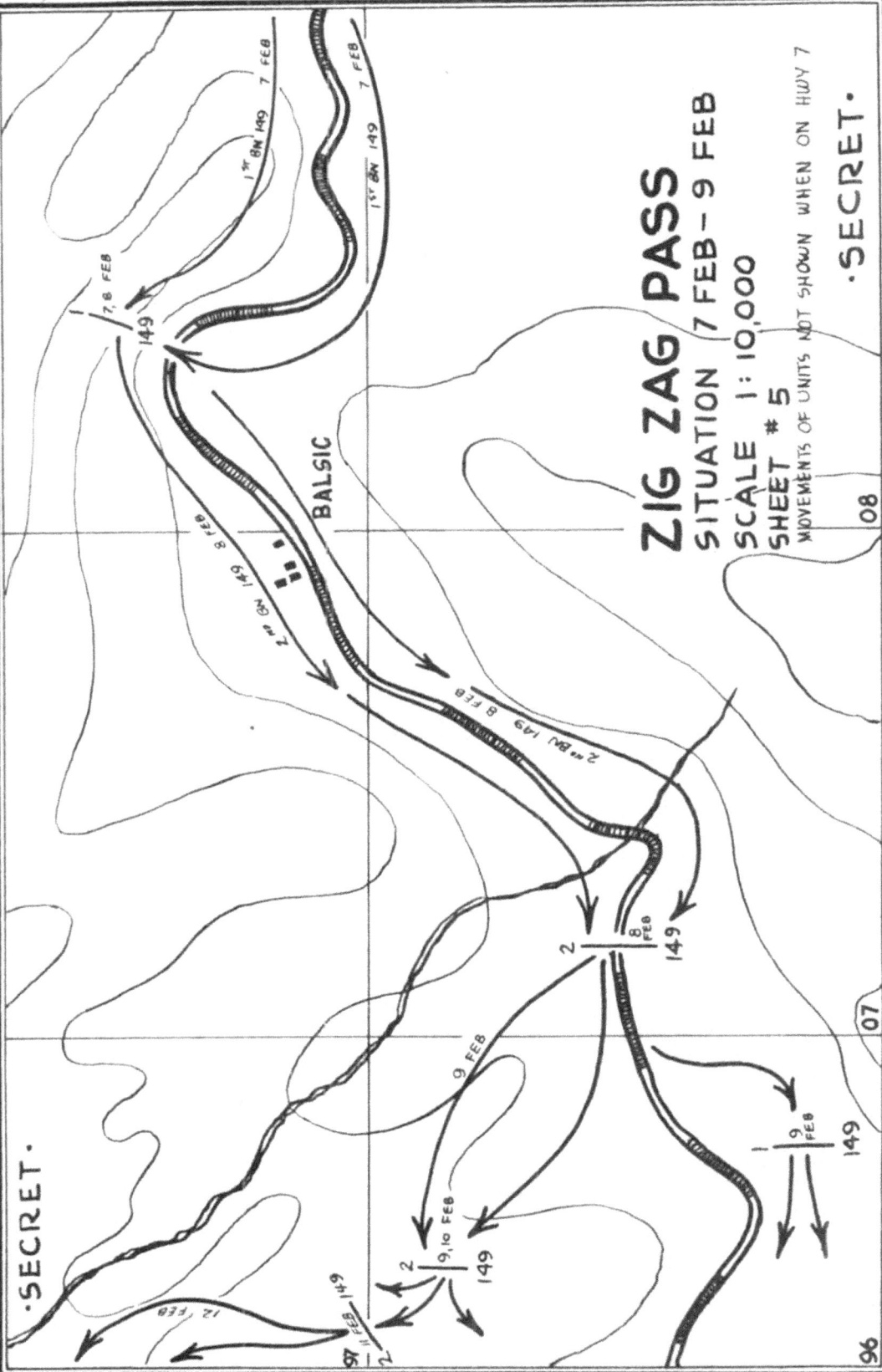

ZIG ZAG PASS
SITUATION 7 FEB - 9 FEB
SCALE 1 : 10,000
SHEET # 5
MOVEMENTS OF UNITS NOT SHOWN WHEN ON HWY 7

·SECRET·

·SECRET·

BALSIC

on the tank forced it to withdraw. The Battalion at the end
of the day dug in (06.4-96.9).

On 12 February the 149th Infantry was continuing their attack to the West. The 1st Battalion on the South side of the
road encountered Japanese positions that withstood artillery
and mortar fire. Attacking with BAR's, grenades, and rifles
the positions were taken and its 60 Japanese defenders killed
at a cost of 1 casualty to the Battalion. During the day the
Battalion advanced several hundred yards. The 2d Battalion
attacked to the North from positions on the right of Highway
7. Near the close of the day a strongly fortified position was
located 400 yards North of the Highway in dense undergrowth.
The approaches to this position were well covered by enemy machine gun fire. To combat this situation the Battalion withdrew and called for artillery fire on the position during the
night.

The 152d Infantry assaulted the position that had checked
the advance the previous day. Strong points (03.5-96.9) which
included mortar and artillery positions were assaulted and destroyed after fierce fighting by the 1st Battalion. The 2d
and 3d Battalions advanced against strong opposition, and
seized and held their objective North and South of point (03.8-
96.65). Vast quantities of enemy ammunition and supplies were
captured during the day.

On 13 February a patrol from Company A 149th Infantry contacted a patrol from the 152d Infantry at point (02.5-96.15).
The day was spent reducing minor strong points and the 1st Battalion 149th Infantry remained in the perimeter of the preceding night. The 2d Battalion 149th Infantry attacked the
strong point on the North side of the highway that had checked
their advance at the close of preceding day. Following an artillery preparation it was reduced and occupied against heavy
fire. The attack continued to the Northwest, and an advance of
200 yards was made. The 149th Infantry was now within 800
yards of the 152d Infantry.

The advance of the 152d Infantry continued against sniper
and machine gun resistance. The 3d Battalion gained and held
its objective North of the highway at the (05) grid line. The
2d Battalion reduced and occupied enemy positions on high
ground (05.5-96.25).

On 14 February the 149th Infantry 1st Battalion advanced
on the South side of highway 7 where minor enemy positions were
encountered and eliminated. Contact was made with the 152d Infantry at (05.2-96.6) and Highway 7 was open to traffic at
1330. The 2d Battalion 149th Infantry attacked from the East

and Northeast. Grenades and close combat fighting overcame all resistance encountered. By 1600 all organized resistance had been eliminated and junction was made with 1st Battalion 152d Infantry attacking from the West.

On 15 February the 149th and 152d Infantry started mopping up the scattered enemy resistance remaining in the ZIG-ZAG Pass. On 16 February the 149th Infantry was ordered to move East to DINALUPIHAN to participate in operations on the East coast of BATAAN. The 152d Infantry was given the mission of securing Highway 7 from OLONGAPO to DINALUPIHAN and to continue mopping up operations in the ZIG-ZAG Pass.

At the close of the ZIG-ZAG fight the Division had killed 1846 Japanese and taken 18 prisoners.

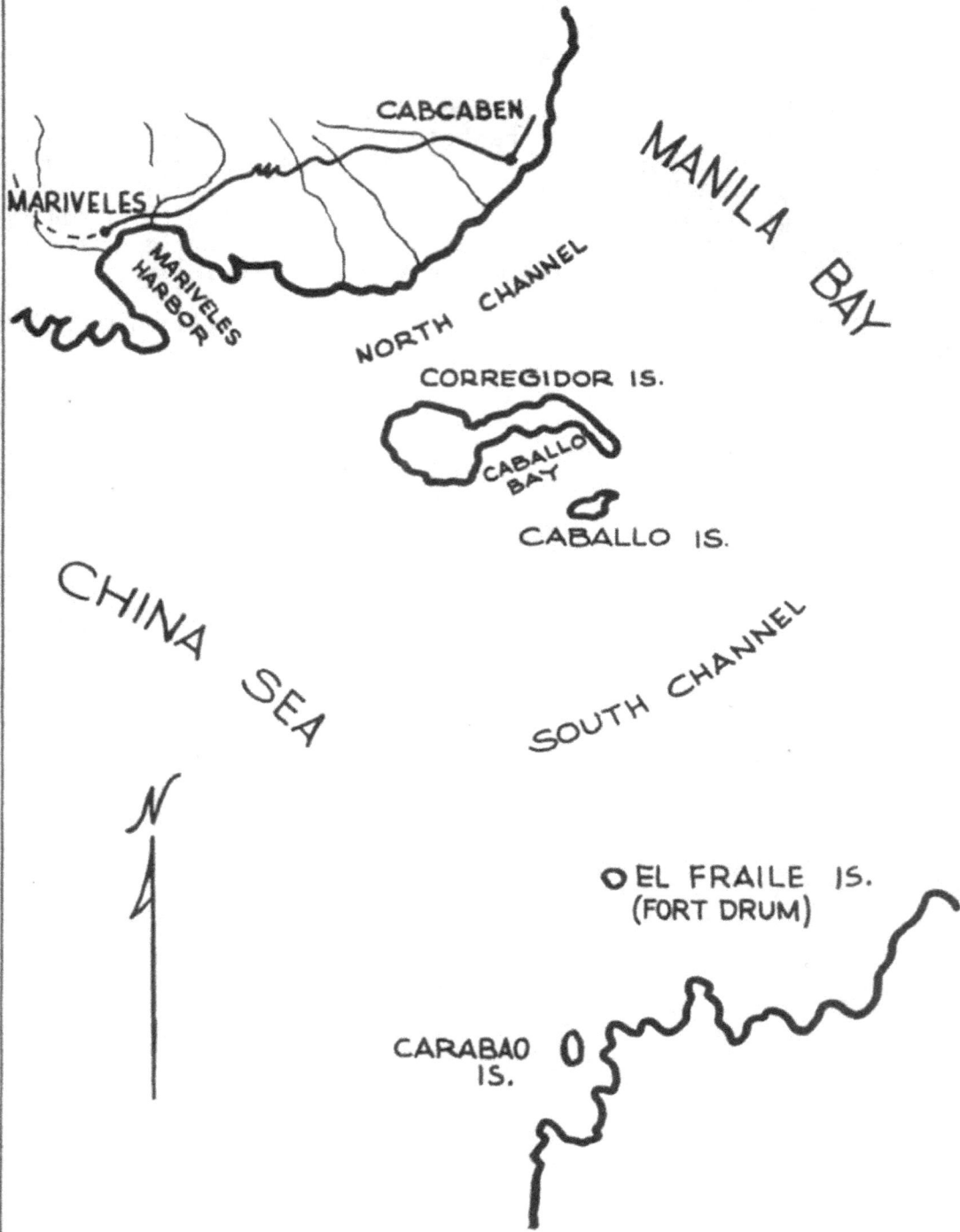

CORREGIDOR · CABALLO · EL FRAILE · CARABAO
SCALE 1:180,000 APPROX

BATAAN - ADJACENT ISLANDS

Field Order 6, headquarters XI Corps, dated 17 February 1945 gave the 38th Infantry Division Reinf the additional mission of securing the PILAR - BAGAC Road and the destruction of all enemy forces on the BATAAN Peninsula. Enemy forces were estimated to number 4000 - 8000 on BATAAN with 3000 of these on the PILAR - BAGAC Road. This later proved to be much too high.

XI Corps directed that two separate forces carry out this mission. The SOUTH FORCE composed of the 151st Infantry Reinf was to land at MARIVELES, secure a beachhead and the air strip immediately to the North, and advance North on Highway 110 to make a junction with the EAST FORCE advancing South. The EAST FORCE was to consist of the 149th Infantry. Due to their engagement in the ZIG-ZAG, the 1st Infantry RCT from XIV Corps was substituted. The mission of this force was to move South along Highway 110 from DINALUPIHAN, to establish contact with the SOUTH FORCE, and to secure Highway 111, the PILAR - BAGAC Road.

Constructed through the mountainous foothills formed by MT NATIB on the North and MT MARIVELES on the South, the PILAR-BAGAC Road consists of curves and hairpin turns similar to those in the ZIG-ZAG PASS. Densely wooded high cliffs and deep gorges afforded excellent defensive installations. But, to the disadvantage of the Japanese forces, they had constructed interlocking and deeply entrenched defensive positions intended to repel attacking forces advancing from BAGAC on the West coast. It was evident that the enemy had hastily occupied and improved positions from which our own American forces had so sucessfully repelled the Japanese occupation of BATAAN in 1942.

Ample support was available from the 5th Air Force. Day after day Highway 111 from PILAR to BAGAC and the coast North and South of BAGAC was subjected to 500 and 1000 pound demolition bombs, fragmentation bombs, NaPalm bombs, and strafing. As the ground forces pushed from the East coast numerous heavy air strikes were placed in advance of the leading elements. Continuous air observation by the Air Force and by our own Artillery liaison planes located enemy activities and installations North and South of the road as they hastily attempted to shift their defenses to repel an easterly attack. These offered excellent air targets and were consequently pounded day after day.

Much credit is due to 5th Air Force in this portion of

the M-7 Operation. As complete clearance of the PILAR - BAGAC Road developed, it was quite evident that air strikes had completely demoralized the enemy and prohibited an effective defense. This enabled the ground forces to rapidly advance with only scattered opposition.

On 14 February a detachment of the 38th Division Headquarters flown by Artillery liaison planes from OLONGAPO and commanded by Brig Gen William Spence, was joined at ORANI by the 1st Infantry Regiment reinforced by the 1st Field Artillery Battalion, Company C 754th Tank Battalion, Company C 640th Tank Destroyer Battalion, and Company A 6th Engineer (C) Battalion.

From 14 to 17 February the southward advance to PILAR by the EAST FORCE was unopposed, except for a brisk action at ORION.

On night of 14-15 February a large group of Japanese attacked the CP of the 2d Battalion 1st Infantry at ORION. After a sharp fight lasting several hours, during which elements of nearby rifle companies were called in, the Japanese were driven off leaving behind approximately 85 dead.

The movement was not as rapid as was desired, however, because of the many demolished bridges and poor bypasses encountered. Guerrillas had burned a number of bridges as Japanese force had withdrawn into BATAAN. Those that they had not burned were only capable of the lightest traffic or had been destroyed by the retreating enemy. Upon evidence that friendly forces were moving South the Guerrillas had constructed some bypasses, but the limited amount of material and the often poorly selected area with steep and shifty banks caused them to require constant improvement by the Engineers to allow limited traffic. Even this was subject to limitations as the changing tide only permitted use of a number of the bypasses between 0600 and 1700 hours. The work of Company A 6th Engineer (C) Battalion was excellent in overcoming these difficulties.

On 17 February, Brig Gen William C. Chase, Commanding General 38th Division, assumed direct command of the forces on the East coast of BATAAN. The 149th Infantry, 38th Cavalry Reconnaissance Troop, 138th Field Artillery Battalion (105mm Howitzer), 163d Field Artillery Battalion (105mm Howitzer), 150th Field Artillery Battalion (155mm Howitzer), 983d Field Artillery Battalion (240mm Gun), and 113th Engineer (C) Battalion had moved through the ZIG-ZAG PASS and were concentrating near BALANGA. With only light opposition the 2d Battalion 1st Infantry had advanced to ORION with leading ele-

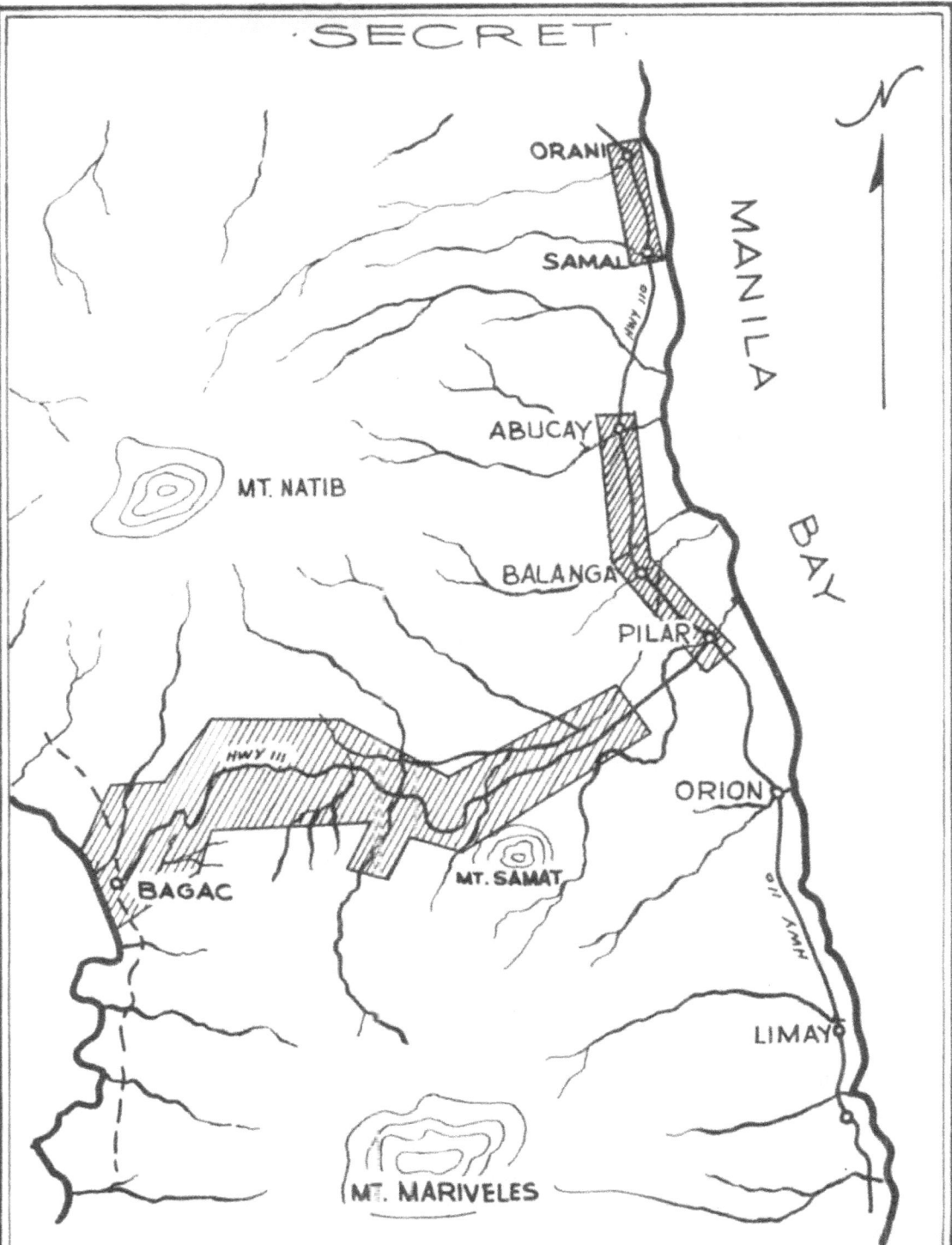

ORANI

SAMAL

MANILA

ABUCAY

MT. NATIB

BALANGA

PILAR

BAY

ORION

BAGAC

MT. SAMAT

HWY 111

LIMAY

MT. MARIVELES

PILAR — BAGAC ROAD

AREA COVERED BY AIR STRIKES 14 FEBRUARY 1945

MUNITION EXPENDED: 63,640 GALS NAPALM, 261 TONS BOMBS, 705,600 RDS CAL. 50

SCALE 1:180,000 APPROX

ments at LIMAY, thus securing the South flank. Leading elements of the 1st and 3d Battalions 1st Infantry astride Highway 111 had pushed West into the foothills of MT SAMAT while elements of the 149th Infantry, moving to join the action, patrolled West along the trails eminating from Highway 110 between ORANI and BALANGA. The 38th Cavalry Reconnaissance Troop, given the mission of establishing contact with the 151st Infantry, effected contact on 18 February at LIMAY. By now, Highway 110, the East coast of BATAAN, and one third of Highway 111, were secure.

The majority of enemy contacts thus far had developed mainly from small parties of Japanese, mostly Navy and Service personnel, landing along the coast in an effort to escape from MANILA and the East shores of MANILA BAY. Guerrilla outposts scattered every 1000 yards or so along the coast reported these landings which were quickly investigated by our own forces. As the 38th Division and its reinforcing elements occupied areas all along Highway 110 from ORANI to LIMAY, several interesting minor engagements resulted. Service units and our Combat Engineers were frequently called upon to investigate these landings, and destroy these Japanese parties. Artillery liaison planes reconnoitered the coast line daily to direct fire on barges and small boats trying to land.

The 738th Ordnance Light Maintenance Company featured in one of these contacts. Voluntarily, a detachment of mechanics and shop personnel under the Company Commander engaged an enemy party which had landed near the mouth of BALANGA River in an effort to join the defending forces on PILAR - BAGAC Road. The enemy was soon killed or dispersed with members of the Ordnance Company receiving only light casualties. From thenceforth the 738th Ordnance Company was known as the 738th "Combat" Ordnance Company to the men in the Division.

Returning to the PILAR - BAGAC action, a coordinated attack by the 1st Infantry and the 149th Infantry was initiated on 19 February. The 3d and 2d Battalions of the 149th Infantry, in that order, began an effort to flank the enemy by moving West from BALANGA into the area of the barrio BANI. The remainder of the Regiment moved West with the 1st Battalion advancing North of Highway 111 approximately 1000 yards and parallel to the Highway.

In the meantime, the 1st and 3d Battalions of the 1st Infantry continued advancing to the West, sending patrols 1000 yards along trails leading North and South from the highway. Numerous minor contacts were made, but not of enough importance to hinder the advance. The 2d Battalion 1st Infantry at ORION dispatched patrols West from points along Highway 110 in

N

MANILA
BAY

ORANI

SAMAL

HWY 110

20 FEB

ABUCAY

2 ⊠ 152

XX
⊠ 38

MT NATIB

BALANGA

⊞ 149

ENEMY SMALL BOAT LANDINGS

I&R ⊠ 149
TO MORON
23 FEB

ABO ABO R.

BANI

2
19 FEB
⊞ 149

PILAR

3 19 FEB
149

HWY 111

TIAWIR R.

20 FEB

20 FEB

3
20 FEB

149

2

149

3
18 FEB

2 ⊞ 1

149

19 FEB

149

19 FEB

ORION

3
20 FEB

20 FEB

149

19 FEB

⊞ 38

3
20 FEB

149

I+R ⊠ 1
20 FEB
BAGAC

⊡ 38

19 FEB

CHINA SEA

⊡ 38
RCN

MT SAMAT

I+R ⊠ 151

PANTINGAN R.

20 FEB

19 FEB

LIMAY

CONTACT 18 FEB

20 FEB

MT MARIVELES

PATROLS ⊠ 151

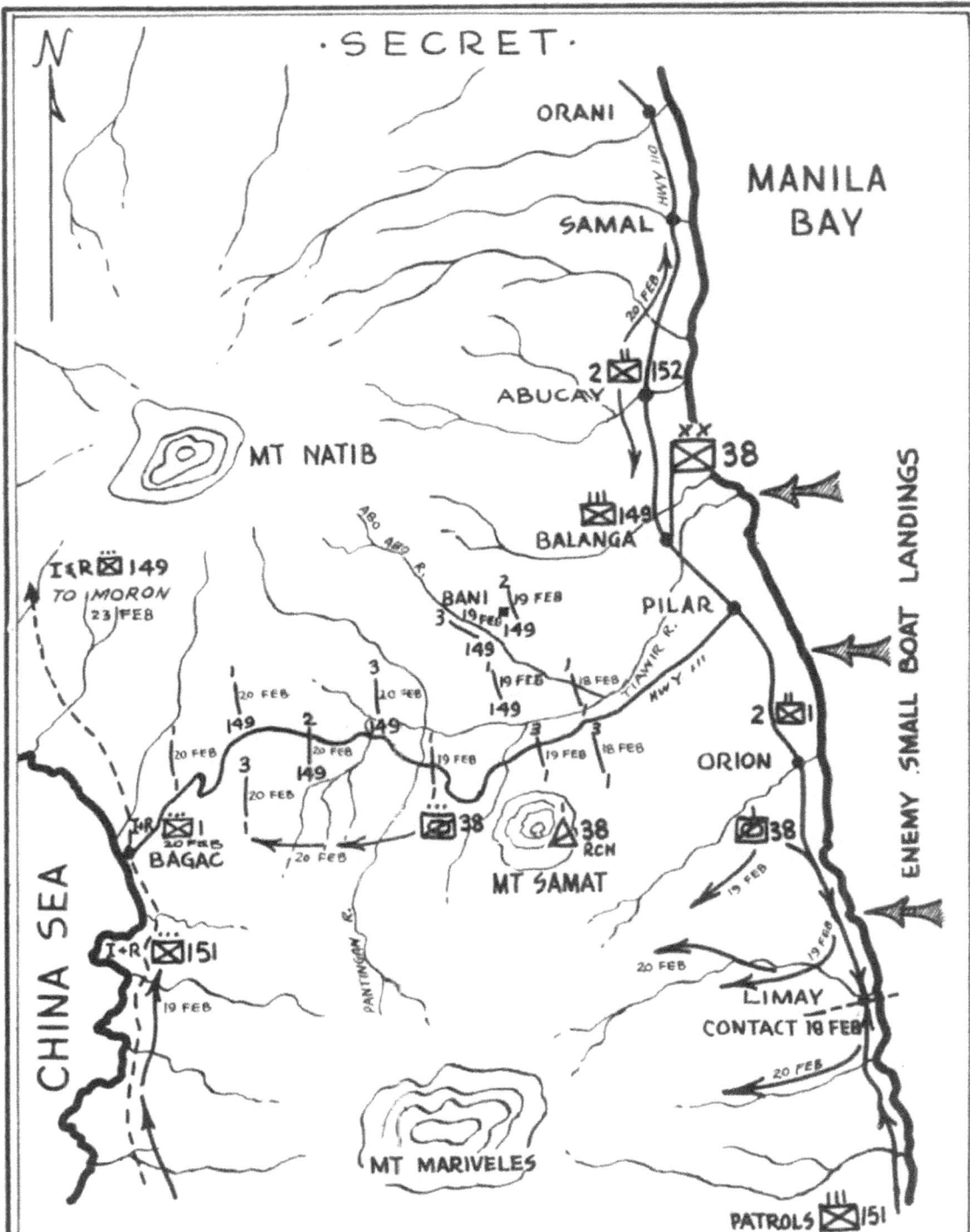

PILAR — BAGAC ROAD
18 – 20 FEBRUARY
SCALE: 1:180,000 APPROX

A reinforced dugout encountered by the
149th Infantry in the PILAR-BAGAC area.

their sector.

This same day, 19 February, the major enemy resistance during the entire PILAR - BAGAC campaign was encountered by the 3d Battalion 149th Infantry in the vicinity of BANI. Along the right bank of the ABO ABO River 1000 yards West of BANI an entrenched enemy force employing mortars, machine guns, and riflemen attempted to slow their advance. Maneuvering their forces, supported by artillery, organic mortars, and machine guns, the 3d Battalion developed this position as resistance grew stronger late in the day. At this point the 2d Battalion, having been delayed most of the day by action in front of the 3d Battalion, assisted by sending elements around left (South) flank. As the day was drawing to a close both Battalions went into perimeters for the night. Continuing the attack on 20 February, it was found that the enemy had withdrawn during the night, leaving numerous dead and quantities of supplies and equipment.

The action of 20 February was highlighted by the rapid advance of the 1st Infantry and the 149th Infantry along Highway 111. With the 1st and 3d Battalions, 1st Infantry leading and meeting only slight resistance, the town of BAGAC was entered and radio contact was established between the I & R Platoon 151st Infantry and the I & R Platoon 1st Infantry.

The I & R Platoon 151st Infantry had, on 19 February gained the overlooking hills on a coastal trail 2000 yards South of BAGAC, watched an air strike, and returned to MARIVELES. Returning on the 20th, they entered BAGAC on 21 February.

On 21 February physical contact was established between the 1st Infantry and the 151st Infantry, and the I & R Platoon 149th Infantry moved to MORON. This effectually cleared the West coast of BATAAN.

On the East coast the 2d Battalion, 152d Infantry had moved through the ZIG-ZAG PASS to ABUCAY and had taken over road and bridge guard responsibilities from ORANI to BALANGA. The 38th Cavalry Reconnaissance Troop and the 2d Battalion 1st Infantry had secured Highway 110 to the unfordable LAMAO River just South of the town of LAMAO.

Not all of the Reconnaissance Troop and 2d Battalion 1st Infantry had been committed to the South however. Reconnaissance and combat patrols had moved West into the foothills of MT SAMAT and MT MARIVELES, meeting only slight resistance from enemy stragglers. Reconnaissance Troop observation posts were established on MT SAMAT while their patrols worked the

- 34 -

PANTINGAN River and the trails leading West into BAGAC.

Thus, after only seven days, the 38th Infantry Division (Reinf) with the assistance of the 1st Infantry, 1st Field Artillery Battalion, Company C 640th Tank Destroyer Battalion, Company C 754th Tank Battalion, and Company A 6th Engineer (C) Battalion had secured control of the BATAAN Peninsula. Concurrently with the PILAR - BAGAC action, the 151st Infantry had successfully landed at MARIVELES and had secured the remainder of Highway 110 and the trail from MARIVELES to BAGAC. This action is covered in the following section.

The 1st Infantry, 1st Field Artillery Battalion, Company A 6th Engineer (C) Battalion and Company A 6th Medical Battalion were detached from the 38th Division on 21 February, passing to the control of XIV Corps. Only the mopping up phase remained in the destruction of all Japanese Forces on the BATAAN Peninsula.

LANDING ON MARIVELES AND CORREGIDOR

FO # 5 Corrected Copy, Headquarters XI Corps 10 February 1945 gave the 38th Division the mission of landing at MARI-VELES at H-Hour on D-Day; seizing and securing a beach head and rapidly establishing control over the southern tip of BATAAN; to amphibiously land elements of the Rock Force (less 503d Parachute Regimental Combat Team) at MARIVELES; reload these units for shore to shore movement and land them on SAN JOSE BEACH, CORREGIDOR ISLAND, at 1030I on D/1. Upon landing, these troops were to be attached to 503d Parachute Regimental Combat Team.

It was estimated that the enemy strength in the MARIVELES-BATAAN area would not exceed 5000, but this was based on guerrilla reports, and proved to be grossly exaggerated.

The mission was assigned the 151st Regimental Combat Team, Col Ralf C. Paddock Commanding. On 11 February the 151st Infantry was relieved by the 152d Infantry in the action on the ZIG-ZAG Pass, returning the same day to a staging area North of OLONGAPO. In addition to the 151st Regimental Combat Team, the Division was assigned the mission of transporting the 3d Battalion 34th Infantry with attachments to MARIVELES, and staging them from there on D/1 to land on CORREGIDOR.

Plans were rapidly made, and on 12 February FO # 13, Headquarters 38th Infantry Division was issued. On 13 February ammunition and supplies were gathered on the beaches at SUBIC and OLONGAPO.

The 151st Regimental Combat Team (the South Force) was composed of the following:

> 151st Infantry
> 139th Field Artillery Battalion
> 24th Reconnaissance Troop
> Battery C, 950th AAA AW Battalion
> Company B, 113th Engineer (C) Battalion
> Company B, 113th Medical Battalion
> Detachment 38th Signal Company
> Detachment 738th Ordnance Company
> Detachment 38th Div Hq and Hq Co
> Detachment 38th Div MP Platoon
> 1st Platoon, 603d Tank Company (-)
> Detachment 592d EB & SR
> Detachment 592d JASCO
> 6th SAP (- Detachment)
> Detachment 636th Ordnance Am Co

The 3d Battalion 34th Infantry had these attachments:

Battery A, 950th AAA AW Battalion
18th Portable Surgical Hospital (Reinf)
174th Ordnance Service Detachment (Bomb
    Disposal Squad)
Detachment 592d EB & SR
Detachment 98th Signal Battalion
Detachment 1st Plat 603d Tank Company
Detachment 592d JASCO
Detachment 6th SAP
3d Plat, Antitank Company, 34th Infantry
3d Plat, Cannon Company, 34th Infantry

For the assault shipping there were available 3 APDs, 5 LCIs, 1 LST, 10 LSMs, and 25 LCMs.

On 14 February the troops moved to the beaches, were embarked by 1500, and the convoy sailed at 1800.

H-Hour was initially set for 0900, 15 February, but due to a change in the bombing and bombardment schedule on CORREGIDOR, was set back to 1000.

Prior to H-Hour a heavy Air and Naval bombardment was carried out on CORREGIDOR and on the beach at MARIVELES to neutralize any Japanese weapons thereon. As the men entered the landing craft, one Japanese gun opened fire from the ROCK, firing 4 rounds and causing a few casualties before being smothered by Naval gunfire.

The assault waves landed at 1000 without opposition, 1st Battalion 151st Infantry on the left, 3d Battalion 151st Infantry on the right, and promptly secured the beachhead. The 2d Battalion 151st Infantry (Reserve) landed and relieved the 3d Battalion on the 1st phase line. The 3d Battalion then advanced rapidly East on Highway 110 toward CABCABEN.

The LSM carrying the 24th Reconnaissance Troop (- 1 Plat) struck a mine, causing the loss of all their equipment and heavy casualties. The other Platoon landed, and promptly began patrolling to the North.

By 1740, 15 February, the 3d Battalion had cleared the road as far as PARANG (26-49) destroying several pillboxes and machine guns enroute, and bivouacked for the night.

At the same time the 1st and 2d Battalions had secured the Regimental beachhead and patrols were working down the coast on both sides of the bay. The 3d Battalion 34th Infantry landed and bivouacked for the night.

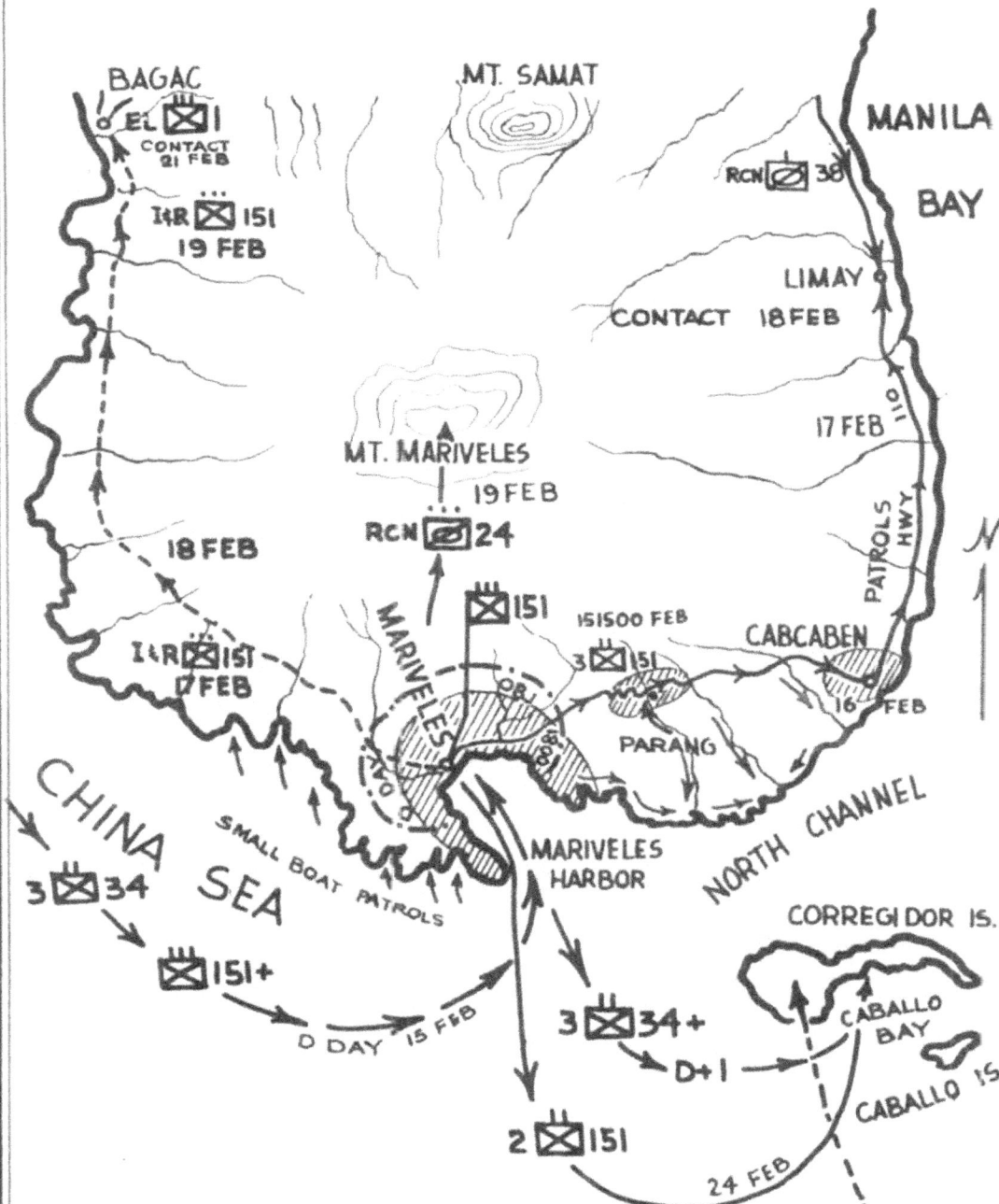

BAGAC

EL 1
CONTACT
21 FEB

I&R 151
19 FEB

MT. SAMAT

MANILA

BAY

RCN 38

LIMAY
CONTACT 18 FEB

17 FEB

MT. MARIVELES
19 FEB

RCN 24

151
151500 FEB

3 151

PARANG

CABCABEN

16 FEB

PATROLS HWY

CHINA SEA

SMALL BOAT PATROLS

3 34

151+

D DAY 15 FEB

MARIVELES
HARBOR

NORTH CHANNEL

CORREGIDOR IS.

CABALLO
BAY

3 34+
D+1

2 151

24 FEB

CABALLO IS

503
D+1

MARIVELES-CORREGIDOR
SCALE 1:180,000
AREA COVERED BY AIR STRIKES
MUNITIONS EXPENDED: 271 TON BOMBS, 597,600 RDS. CAL. 50

Squat, bulky LSMs poured out a steady stream of men, vehicles and supplies at MARIVELES. Despite deep water, congestion on the beach was at a minimum as alligators and bulldozers quickly stalled trucks and sent them rumbling inland.

A patrol of the 151st Infantry moves through
the shambles of MARIVELES, reduced to the ground
by the fierce naval and air bombardment that
preceded the 151st Infantry's amphibious assault.

An interesting event on 15 February was the report by Air Support planes. A motor column advancing rapidly down Highway 110 from the North was sighted, and permission was requested to strafe it. At first it was unidentified and might have been Japanese reinforcements; however, the Air was requested to make a close reconnaissance before attacking. The next report was "Column contains jeeps and acted in friendly manner upon approach by P-38's". The Air Support was then instructed to watch the activities of the column, but not to attack. Movement of the column was reported as far South as a river 4 miles South of LIMAY where it stopped and then returned North. It later developed that the column contained GENERAL MacARTHUR and party visiting the town from which he sailed in 1942. At this time the road South of ORION was still infested with Japanese snipers.

On 16 February the remaining enemy on Highway 110 between MARIVELES and PARANG were mopped up, the tanks assisting. The 3d Battalion captured a field piece in vicinity of PARANG, and destroyed numerous supplies and caves, killing approximately 57 enemy. A patrol consisting of infantry mounted piggy-back on a tank, followed by motorized infantry, moved rapidly to CABCABEN and secured it.

The 3d Battalion 34th Infantry (Reinforced) was reembarked, and landed on SAN JOSE Beach on CORREGIDOR to assist the 503d Parachute Infantry Regimental Combat Team, who had dropped on the island in the morning.

17 February was occupied with extensive patrolling netting a number of Japanese. The I & R Platoon 151st Infantry proceeded towards BAGAC, on the West coast, and foot and motor patrols worked to LAMAO on the East coast. Other patrols worked the coves and draws along the coast from CABCABEN to GUAY BAY. Some of these patrols moved in LCMs.

On 18 February contact was established at LIMAY with elements of the EAST FORCE by a patrol from 3d Battalion 151st Infantry.

The activities of 19 February netted a number of enemy killed or captured, some believed to be escaping from CORREGIDOR. The I & R Platoon returned from observing BAGAC, reporting visual observation of an air strike on BAGAC that day, but no enemy activity on the route. The Platoon left BAGAC at 1330, arriving at MARIVELES at 2230, a distance in excess of 20 miles over a rough foot trail. At the same time the Platoon of the 24th Cavalry Reconnaissance Troop patrolled to the top of MT MARIVELES, but found no enemy activity.

Platoon of 151st Infantry approaching pill
box located in CORKSCREW Pass near MARIVELES.

Tanks were employed in CORKSCREW Pass
for destroying enemy pillboxes.

From 20 to 23 February, inclusive, routine patrolling was the major activity, catching and killing stray Japanese. On 21 February the I & R Platoon returned to BAGAC and made contact with the 1st Battalion 1st Infantry.

Company B 113th Engineer (C) Battalion on 23 February moved to CORREGIDOR to support the 503d Parachute Infantry in their operations.

The next day at 241145 February, the 2d Battalion 151st Infantry with 1 Platoon Cannon Company, and 1 Platoon Anti-tank Company landed on CORREGIDOR where they relieved the 3d Battalion 34th Infantry, and began the mopping up of the ROCK.

The Southern coast of BATAAN was now secure. Thereafter the 151st Infantry began active patrolling and mopping up and assaulted and captured CABALLO, EL FRAILE, and CARABAO Islands. These actions are covered in the following sections.

Reinforced pillbox destroyed by
151st Infantry vicinity PARANG

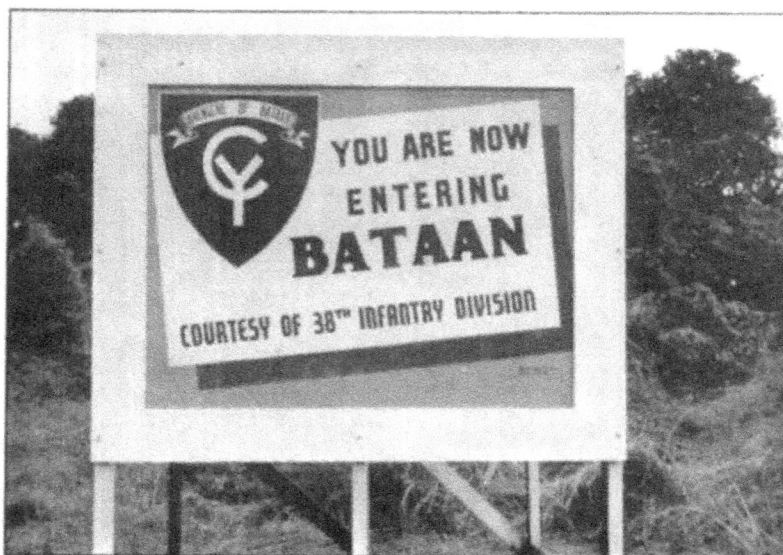

YOU ARE NOW
ENTERING
BATAAN

COURTESY OF 38TH INFANTRY DIVISION

ZAMBALES

TARLAC

ECIJA

TARLAC

$\frac{1}{XXX}$

XI

BAMBAM

SOUTH CHINA SEA

$\frac{152}{=} 149$

PAMPANGA

$\frac{149}{III}$
151

$38 \underset{XIV}{\times\times\times}$

BULACAN

38×6

$\frac{152}{III}$
151

$\frac{152}{III}$
149

ORANI

$\times\times$

SUBIC BAY

BATAAN

PAYSAWAN BAY

$\frac{149}{III}$
151

LIMAY

MANILA BAY

MANILA

RIZAL

CORREGIDOR IS.

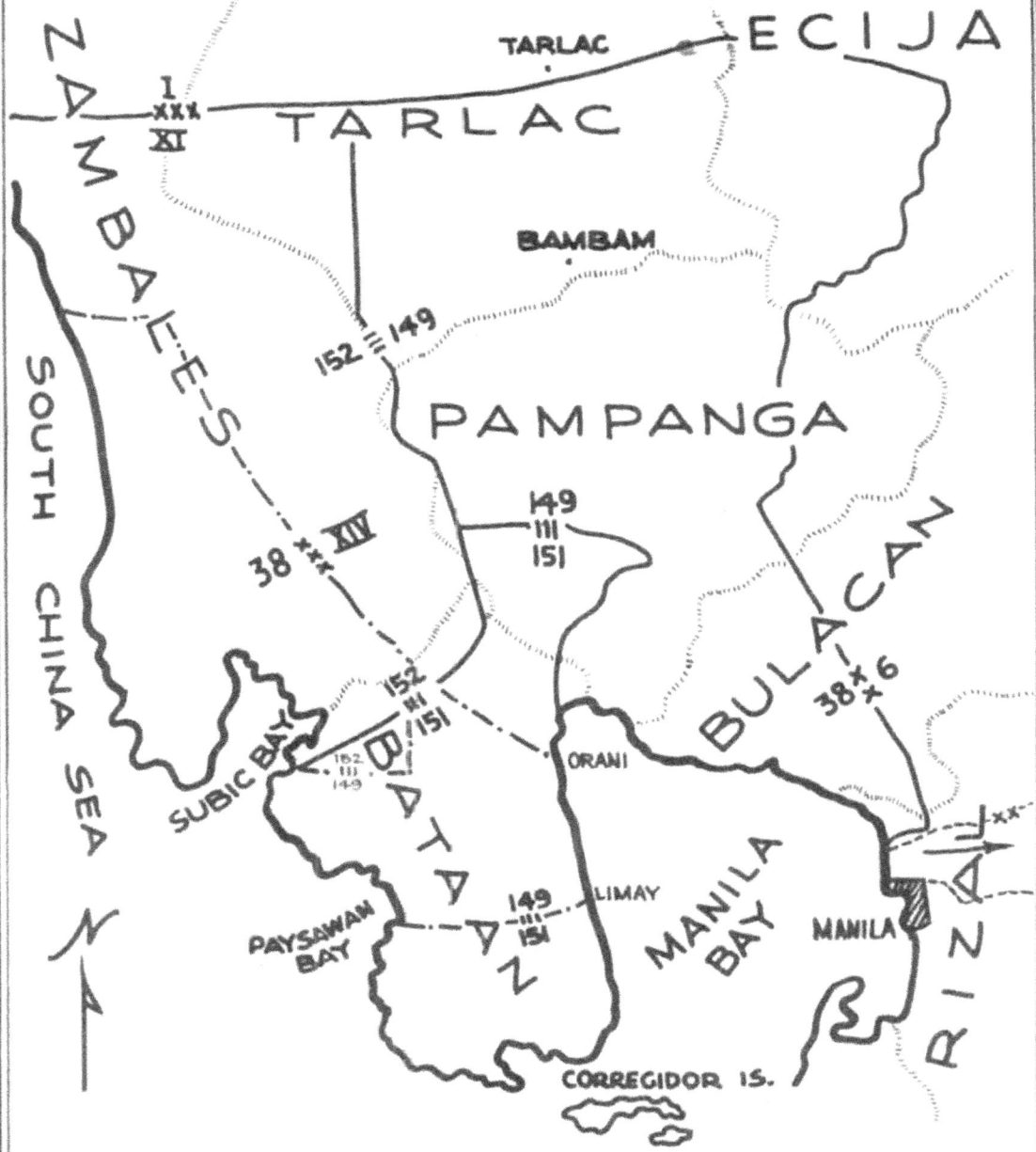

· THE AVENGERS' BATTLEGROUND ·

— · —	17 FEBRUARY 1945
———	7 MARCH 1945
- - - -	30 APRIL 1945

MOPPING UP PERIOD

There was no exact date when the "Mopping Up" period began. For the 152d Infantry it began at the end of the ZIG-ZAG Pass fight on 14th February, when they began to patrol and clean up the ZIG-ZAG Area. For the 151st Infantry this period began on 21 February when contact was established between the 1st Infantry and the 151st Infantry at BAGAC. For the 149th Infantry it began at the same time.

All units immediately began aggressive patrolling within their sectors. In the MARIVELES area the 151st Infantry was busy catching Japanese who were escaping across the bay from MANILA or swimming from CORREGIDOR. Sufficient clothing, food and medical supplies were found to initiate the rehabilitation and treatment of the natives who flocked down from MT MARIVELES forty-eight hours after the initial landing. These supplies were found in three localities, MARIVELES, PARANG, and CABCABEN. Of interest was the finding of three cemeteries used by American Forces in 1942. The patrolling operations cleared the territory South of the LIMAY-PAYSAWAN line.

The 152d Infantry initiated aggressive patrolling and cleaning up in the ZIG-ZAG Pass area. One area in the ZIG-ZAG deserves mention. This area contained a number of Japanese positions, unable to interfere with traffic on the Hwy, but still occupied. For several days the 152d Infantry leisurely and methodically wiped these positions out, killing a good number of Japanese. A large number of caves were destroyed, and tons of rice and other supplies turned over to the PCAU. Stray Japanese were found wandering around and were killed or captured. Within a few days the area was cleared of snipers and safe for souvenir hunters. The units at OLONGAPO promptly took advantage of this, and a few days later the battle field was as clean as a park.

In Northern BATAAN the 149th Infantry sent long range patrols North and South of Highway 7 from BALSIC and BULATE. These proved very profitable in the number of enemy killed. Patrols worked North from the PILAR-BAGAC road toward MT NATIB. On a trail looping North from the road a large number of buried Japanese dumps were found, containing food, clothing, ammunition and other supplies. Two 70mm mountain guns were found and destroyed. A number of Japanese were killed in that area and around ABUCAY HACIENDA.

The 38th Reconnaissance Troop established an OP on MT SAMAT and patrolled West from ORION, LIMAY and LIMAO, and South from the PILAR-BAGAC Road. These activities drove the Japanese around, and broke them up in small ineffectual groups. Sniping at bridge guards and unit perimeters was soon stopped.

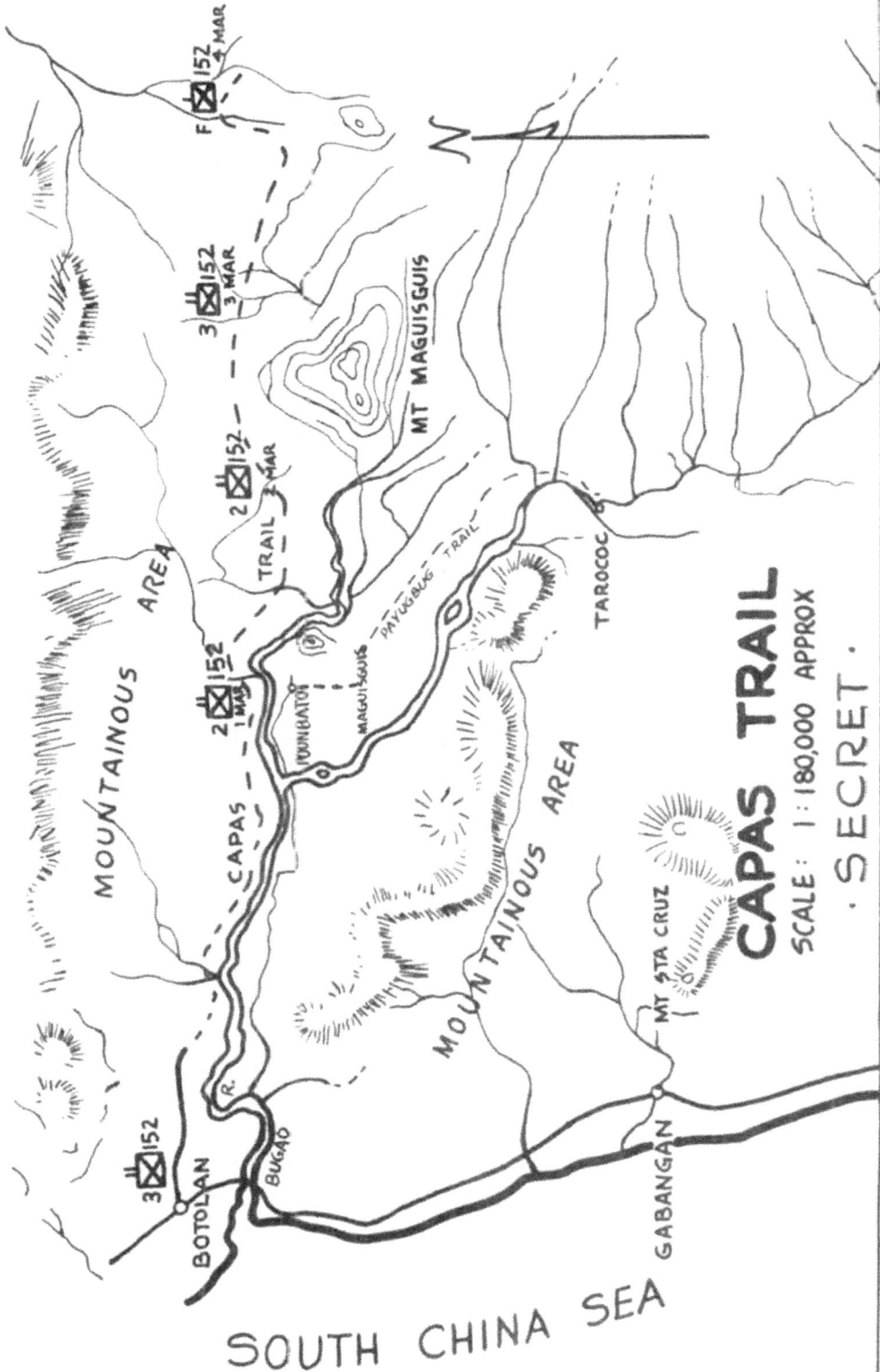

· SECRET ·

· SECRET ·

CAPAS TRAIL

SCALE : 1 : 180,000 APPROX

SOUTH CHINA SEA

MOUNTAINOUS AREA

MOUNTAINOUS AREA

MT MAGUISGUIS

MT STA CRUZ

CAPAS

TRAIL

PAYUGBUG TRAIL

MAGUISGUIS

PUUNBATON

TAROCOC

GABANGAN

BOTOLAN

BUGAO

R.

N

152 4 MAR
F

152 3 MAR
3

152 3 MAR
2

152 1 MAR
2

152
3

Minefield on beach at Corregidor lifted by
Company B 113th Engineer (C) Battalion during mopping up on the Rock. Note Q boat
launching tracks.

Clearing area of Malinta Hill.

Instructions were issued to all units, Division, Corps, and others, in the area that they would be responsible for their own local security, and that each unit would patrol daily every afternoon for at least 1000 yards around their location. Within forty eight hours all roadside sniping stopped, combat troops were not called upon to drive snipers from other units, and a fair number of Japanese killed.

Certain service units became so imbued with combat ideas that they had to be restricted in the interests of service. The most spectacular patrols were conducted by Company C 640th Tank Destroyer Battalion, who would dash across country in an M-10, the turret bristling with men carrying tommy guns. Surprisingly enough they produced results.

On 24 February the 3d Battalion 34th Infantry was relieved on CORREGIDOR by the 2d Battalion 151st Infantry, 1 Platoon Antitank Company and 1 Platoon Cannon Company 151st Infantry, and a platoon of Company B 113th Engineer (C) Battalion. They assisted the 503d Parachute Infantry in mopping up operations on the Rock, their sector being East on MALINTA Hill.

On 8 March the 503d Parachute Infantry was withdrawn from the Rock, and the entire island turned over to the 2d Battalion 151st Infantry. They continued cleaning up scattered Japanese until relieved on 13 April. During this time they furnished the troops for the CABALLO and EL FRAILE operations, which are covered in separate sections of this report.

On 10 April activity was observed around a cave on Battery Point. A patrol investigating this lost a man to enemy fire from the cave. It was decided to pour oil down one of the ventilators, and on 12 April this was started. Just as the first drum was emptied the Japanese blew up the entire cave. The explosion was terrific, smoke, dirt and rocks being thrown hundreds of feet in the air, leaving a crater over 100 feet in diameter and thirty feet deep. Nine men were killed, thirteen wounded, and four missing as a result of this.

On 7 March additional ground was given the 38th Division to clear. The Division area now included all of BATAAN, most of ZAMBALES and PAMPANGA, and part of TARLAC Provinces. The mission of destroying the Japanese forces West of FT STOTSENBURG and CLARK FIELD was assigned to the Division at the same time.

Regimental boundaries were redesignated, (see sketch) and the 149th Infantry given the mission to destroy all Japanese forces in the CLARK FIELD - FT STOTSENBURG area. This action developed into a full scale operation, and is described in a separate section of this report.

On 27 February, the 2d Battalion 152d Infantry, patrolling in the BOTOLAN-POONBATO-MAGUISGUIS area, was instructed to move East over the CAPAS-O'DONNELL Trail and contact units of the 43d Division at TIAONG. The 28th was spent in arranging for carriers and supply. The 2d Battalion moved out, F Company leading, on 1 March. On 4 March contact was made, effectively sealing the Northern side of the Division area. Further actions of this Battalion are covered in the account of the STOTSENBURG Operation.

As the 2d Battalion 152d Infantry moved East, the 3d Battalion took over the area. The 1st Battalion 152d Infantry remained in the SAN MARCELINO area, and the two units actively patrolled and cleaned out the scattered Japanese in the territory West of MT PINATUBO. A strong patrol from the 1st Battalion 152d Infantry was dispatched to CAVALRY Pass on the top of MT PINATUBO. This patrol initially was supplied by air drop. This stopped the movement of the Japanese over the pass and Southeast from MT PINATUBO towards SAN MARCELINO. The patrol was maintained until 23 April when the 6th Division took over the sector.

Many contacts were made by the 3d Battalion 152d Infantry and the 38th Reconnaissance Troop in the BOTOLAN-IBA area, and a good number of Japanese killed.

The 151st Infantry between 7 March and 26 April had furnished troops to garrison CORREGIDOR, and to conduct the CABALLO, EL FRAILE and CARABAO operations. On 20 March the road and bridge guards between SAN FERNANDO and MANILA were assigned them. This occupied such a large number of the strength of the 151st Infantry, that long range patrols on BATAAN could not be organized.

In the middle of April, PW's reported that the scattered Japanese in the MT NATIB area had assembled. The 3d Battalion 151st Infantry was assembled on the BAGAC-PILAR Road, the 2d Battalion in the ABUCAY HACIENDA-BALANGA area, both to advance toward MT NATIB, destroying all Japanese found. The movement of the units was slow due to difficult terrain and was continuing on 27 April when the 151st Infantry was relieved by elements of the 6th Infantry Division. Company K 151st Infantry remained North of the PILAR-BAGAC Road to maintain contact until the 2d Battalion 63d Infantry, 6th Infantry Division could resume the advance on MT NATIB, and was relieved 1 May.

Numerous lessons were learned in this movement in regards to supply. A suitable trail, even through heavy terrain, must be built right behind advancing troops. Also, in the use of guerrilla and native carriers, it is necessary to furnish

excellent Non-Com's to control them and ample guards to keep
them on the job.

The advance of the 149th Infantry up the SACOBIA River
and along the ridge North thereof, toward MT PINATUBO drove
many small parties of Japanese down from the mountain. This
was particularly true about the middle of April, when scattered groups appeared in the ANGELES-PORAC-FLORIDABLANCA area.
These groups were encountered and killed by patrols from
various Division units. The 38th Military Police Platoon and
38th Signal Company, whose duties took them over the area
daily, quickly developed a rivalry in the number of Japanese
killed. This continued up to the time the 38th Infantry
Division was relieved in that sector on 30 April.

During the period from 10 March until 30 April, the
pressure in the MT PINATUBO area forced a large number of
Japanese over the North West slopes of MT PINATUBO down into
the VILLAR-MAGUISGUIS-POONBATO area. These parties were
intercepted by patrols from the 2d and 3d Battalions 152d
Infantry. It was decided to plug this escape route at the
source, so the 3d Battalion 152d Infantry was directed to
move East along the MORUMAL River, and contact the 2d Battalion 149th Infantry and the 1st Battalion 149th Infantry,
who were closing in on the Japanese from the North and South
respectively. This action is covered in detail in the account
of the STOTSENBURG operation.

SECRET

CABALLO BAY

MANILA BAY

MORTAR PITS AND TUNNELS

ISLAND OF CABALLO P.I.

SCALE: 1:50,000 APPROX.

SECRET

2 151
27 MAR

G HILL 1

HILL 2
28 MAR

HILL 3
28 MAR

THE ASSAULT AND CAPTURE OF CABALLO ISLAND

FO # 10 Headquarters XI Corps dated 23 March 1945 assigned to the 38th Division the mission of seizing CABALLO Island and destroying all enemy forces thereon. G-2 XI Corps estimated the enemy strength on CABALLO Island at 522.

The 151st Infantry was assigned the mission, and the 2d Battalion 151st Infantry under command of Lt. Col. (then Major) Paul R. LeMasters was selected as the assault Battalion. Artillery support was furnished by the 163rd Field Artillery Battalion (105mm How) (less Battery B) from positions on CORREGIDOR and Battery A 150th Field Artillery Battalion (155mm How) from positions at CABCABEN on the mainland of BATAAN.

From 0650 to 0830 27 March 1945 a concentration of bombs was dropped on CABALLO Island. Supporting weapons (artillery and 81mm mortars) blanketed all likely targets from 0835 to 0855. Two DD's fired direct into enemy emplacements.

Company E 151st Infantry landed at 270900 March and immediately occupied Hill 1. Company G followed in column with the remainder of the 2d Battalion (less Company F). Company F remained on BLACK BEACH, CORREGIDOR, alerted to reinforce the assault forces if necessary. The advance continued to the foot of Hill 2 where Company E received heavy 20mm and knee mortar fire. Further direct advance up the hill was impossible as the face of the hill was covered by grazing fire from the West pit. Company E maneuvered to the South side of the island to attempt climbing the steep slopes. Supporting 60 and 81mm mortars attempted to silence the fire coming from two large pits on Hill 2.

At 1200 Company E was 25 yards from the crest of the hill. The route from their position to the crest of Hill 2 was a two foot ledge that the enemy covered by machine gun fire from the pits. It was decided to send a platoon under cover os smoke to the top of the hill, so supporting mortar fire was called for.

Considerable difficulty was encountered in resupply of Company E as all supplies had to be hoisted to the top of the edge ridge across which the men were to advance. However, enough had arrived to warrant sending the platoon across the ledge. The 163rd Field Artillery Battalion laid a smoke screen across the ledge and single file the troops advanced, the Japanese firing blindly into the smoke. At the end of the day all the top surface of Hills 1 and 2 were occupied by Companies E and G. The pits were contained by fire to prevent the enemy from escaping.

On the morning of 28 March the resupply and evacuation of Company E was again the foremost problem. One LCM was brought to the North side of the island and with use of a rope gun, a rope was catapulted to the top of Hill 2. One rope was not enough to meet the situation so an air drop of rope and water was attempted. After several trials the drop was successful, which relieved the situation considerably.

Company E continued to move the remainder of the Company across the ledge under cover of smoke, and the forward elements pushed up towards Hill 3, occupying the ground for the night.

On the morning of 29 March Company E sent patrols to the West of the island with no enemy contact. This secured all the island except the mortar pits and tunnels on Hill 2, which contained the remaining Japanese garrison. The remainder of the destruction of the pit on Hill 2. Until the final destruction of the pits all supplies for the troops on top of Hill 2 and 3 were hoisted up from the beach at the foot of the North cliff.

The final reduction of CABALLO Island was made difficult by an impasse occasioned by the occupation of the Japanese garrison of the mortar pits, where weapons were so sited as to command all approaches to the pits (see sketch), with the exception of one vent which was most difficult of access. Troops approaching the craters on the slopes were exposed to intense small arms and 20mm cannon fire. Access from the top of Hill 2 was denied due to grazing fire constantly placed by Japanese forces up the slope to the crest. It was possible to put mortar fire into the pit; however, when this was done, the Japanese merely withdrew to the safety of the tunnels and, of necessity, our Infantry was forced to withdraw down the outer slope to avoid their own fragmentation. The Japanese were able to come out of the tunnels upon cessation of our mortar fire in time to prevent our Infantry from moving up the slope and into the pit where they might block out the tunnel entrances. The siting of Japanese weapons in the tunnel entrances were so arranged that they were mutually supporting.

Investigation later showed that the Japanese had constructed two sandbag blast walls in each tunnel, so constructed that weapons could fire over them (see sketch).

Tanks were brought over to CABALLO on 3 April, and a road constructed by the 113th Engineers to enable them to reach the edge of the pits. It was found that the tank guns would not depress sufficiently to bear on the tunnels. If the tanks ad-

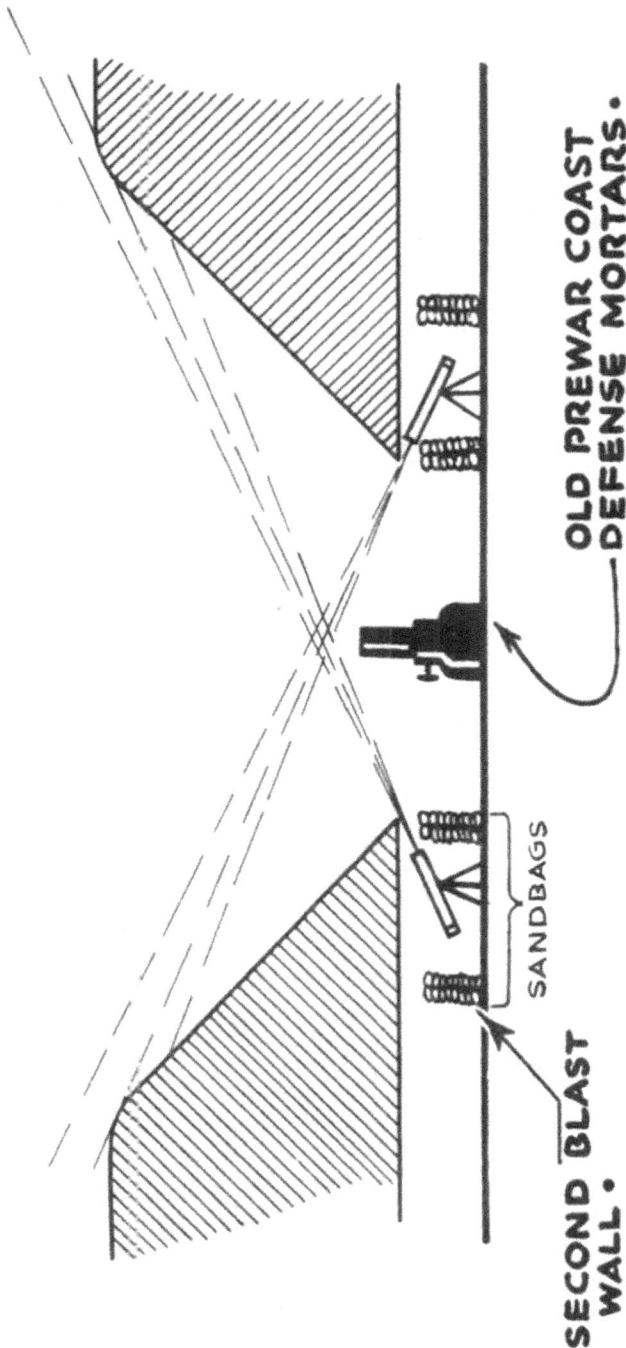

SECRET·

CROSS SECTION OF MORTAR PITS
ON CABALLO ISLAND

OLD PREWAR COAST
DEFENSE MORTARS.

SANDBAGS

SECOND BLAST
WALL·

·SECRET·

vanced far enough to tilt down the slopes, they began to slide down into the pits. For this reason the tanks were withdrawn.

That night a banzai attack was made against the 2d Battalion 151st Infantry resulting in 86 Japanese killed.

Lt. Col. Lobit, regimental commander of the 151st Infantry, conceived the idea of pouring diesel oil down the one vent to which there was access and igniting it. In order to accomplish this, a long and painfully laborious system of pulling oil drums up the steep slope by the use of ropes and pulleys was employed. Sufficient oil could not be taken up on the slope, nor stored on the top of the slope to permit sufficient volume at any one time to produce the desired effect.

Then the idea was conceived of placing oil into the pits by the use of pumps from a vessel of considerable gallonage capacity. It was at first hoped that a large Navy or Army fuel barge could be obtained for the purpose. When this was found not obtainable, the idea was modified to the mounting of Navy pontons on an LCM. The technical details of design were turned over to the Division Engineer.

On preliminary survey, the Division Engineer obtained the following equipment:

> One LCM
> Two Navy Cubes
> One AvGas pump of 110 hp capacity with the necessary pipe and fittings
> Sufficient lengths of AvGas pipeline to reach the top of the mortar pit from the waterline.

The device familiarly became known as the "Rube Goldberg" (see sketch). On the initial try-out 5 April 1945, the Division Engineers, assisted by personnel from an Engineer Petroleum Distribution Company, connected the pipe line with flexible joints, ran it up the slope, hooked it up to the pump in the LCM, tried out the pump with sea water first, and when it was found it would work, proceeded to pump a mixture of diesel oil and gasoline into the mortar pit. Capacity was limited, of course, totaling not more than 2,600 gallons of fuel. When the cubes had been emptied, Infantry elements lobbed WP mortar shells into the pit, thus igniting the mixture. The results were most gratifying. A tremendous volume of flame came out of the pit and, subsequently, the explosion of small arms ammunition could be heard, followed by seven explosions, apparently of a picric acid base explosive. A drain whose existance had not been known blew out, and some of the oil escaped and burned on the North beach.

Fastening pipe together to pump oil into the
mortar pits on CABALLO Island.

Mortar pits burning on CABALLO Island.

The next day small arms fire was received from the West tunnel entrance, so it was decided to repeat the "hot oil" treatment, after carefully plugging the drain.

On 6 April additional oil was pumped into the pits and ignited, followed by intense fires and the explosion of small arms ammunition. During the evening there were several muffled underground explosions.

On 7 April the oil was pumped into the pits again. At the same time a 500 pound and a 250 pound demolition bomb were lowered down the ventilator. A 500 pound charge was also placed at the East tunnel entrance. The oil, the bombs and the charge were successively ignited resulting in an enormous volume of flame and smoke, followed by a terrific explosion. The fire burned into the night, during which time additional explosions were heard and felt.

On 13 April, after the pits had cooled, a patrol entered, counted 50 dead Japanese, and reported complete destruction within the pits.

When, to continue the mopping up phase, the 2d Battalion was relieved by the 1st Battalion, the total enemy was 229 killed, 50 found dead and 3 Prisoners of War. This was a grand total of 279 killed and 3 Prisoners of War.

THE "RUBE GOLDBERG"

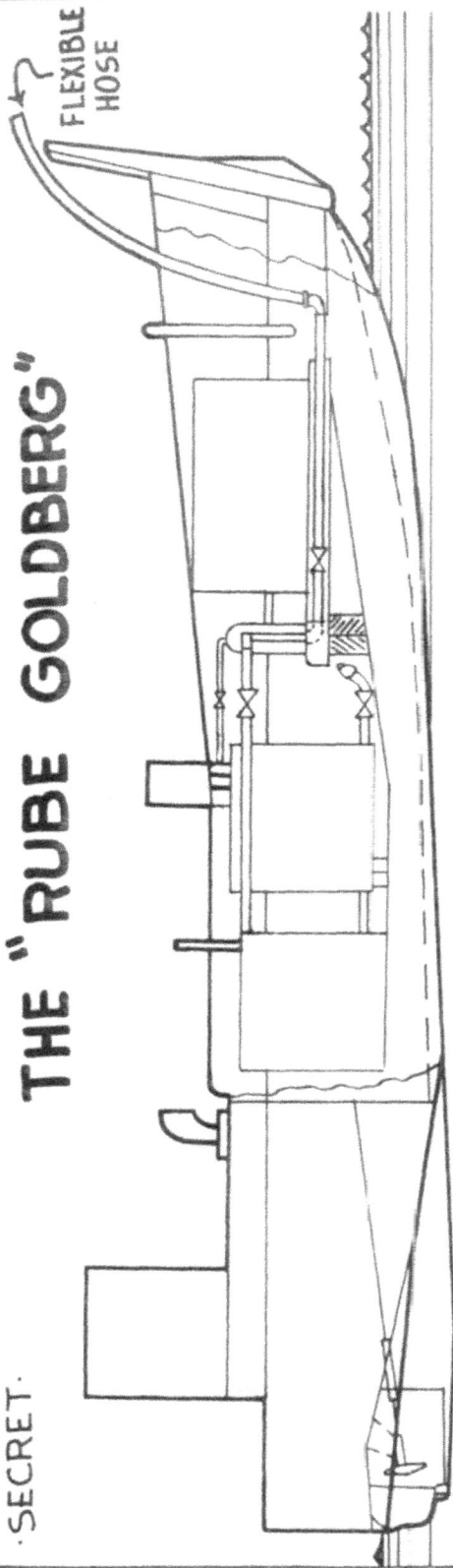

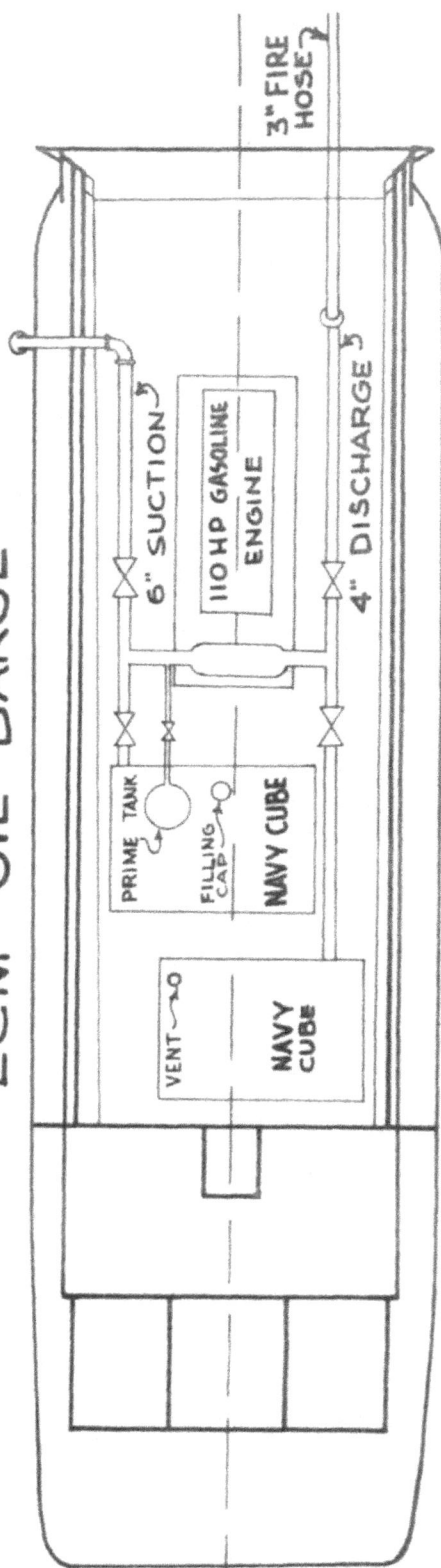

LCM OIL BARGE.

FLEXIBLE HOSE

3" FIRE HOSE

6" SUCTION

110 H.P. GASOLINE ENGINE

4" DISCHARGE

PRIME TANK

FILLING CAP

NAVY CUBE

VENT

NAVY CUBE

THE ASSAULT AND DESTRUCTION OF EL FRAILE (FT. DRUM)

FO 314, Headquarters XI Corps, 19 April 1945, directed the 38th Division to seize EL FRAILE Island (Fort Drum) and destroy all Japanese forces therein.

FORT DRUM is a concrete block in the shape of a ship, built on a reef, EL FRAILE, in the entrance to MANILA BAY. It was built between 1912 and 1922 of reinforced concrete, and mounted two turrets with two 14" guns each and double 6" guns in casemates on each side. These had been rendered inoperative when the American forces surrendered in 1942.

The walls were 18 to 30 feet thick, and the deck 15 to 18 feet. The inside was divided into three decks, connected by stairways.

The only entrance was through a sally-port which extended from side to side on the stern (East) end. This connected with a gallery that ran longitudinally into the rooms inside. A naval patrol investigating the Fort several days previous was fired on by a machine gun and several men in the sally-port were killed or wounded.

It was decided the best means of attack would be the "Rube Goldberg" oil pumping device. Plans of the Fort were studied (see sketches) and every available source of information canvassed to learn the arrangement of the rooms, powder rooms, doors, stairways and ventilators. Invaluable information was received from Col. J. R. Burns, Sixth Army CWO, who had been in the Fort in 1941 to plan the proposed gas proofing and air conditioning equipment.

From Col. Burns it was learned that there were ventilator vents on the top, from which ducts lead to all parts of the interior. Based on this, Lt. Col. Lobit, Commanding Officer 151st Infantry, decided that the best means of attack would be to land on the top, secure it, pump oil down the vents, ignite the oil and withdraw.

This posed the question of how to reach the deck, forty feet above the water line. The wall was vertical except for the last five feet which sloped inward at a 60 degree angle, making the use of scaling ladders almost impossible.

A joint conference was held with representatives of the Navy, the Assistant Division Commander, G-3, G-4 and Col. Lobit. At this meeting it was suggested that a ladder be placed on a landing craft capable of reaching the top, but in scaling it off, it was found that the men would still be too far away

FORT DRUM
EL FRAILE ISLAND P.I.

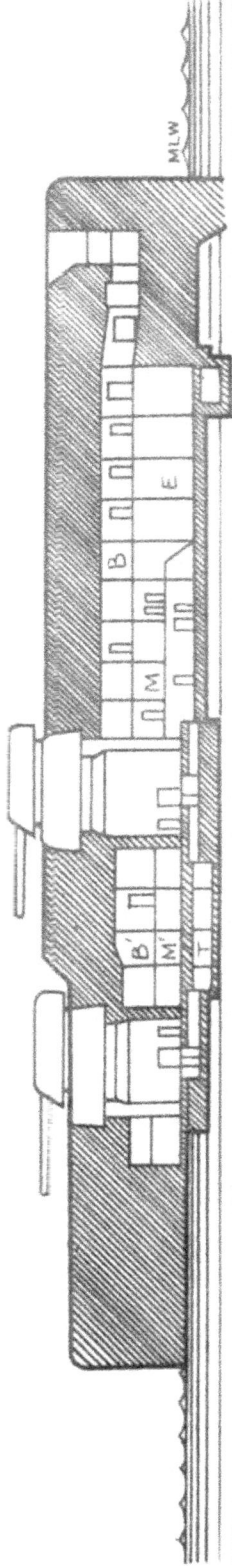

B - BARRACKS ELEV FLOOR   16' 9"   B'- BARRACKS   11' 2"
M - MESS ROOM   7' 3"   M'- MAGAZINE   2' 3"
E - ENGINE ROOM   2' 0"   T - TANK ROOM   6' 9"

SCALE : I INCH = 50 FEET   SHEET # 1

FORT DRUM

SECRET.

SECRET.

N

SHEET #2

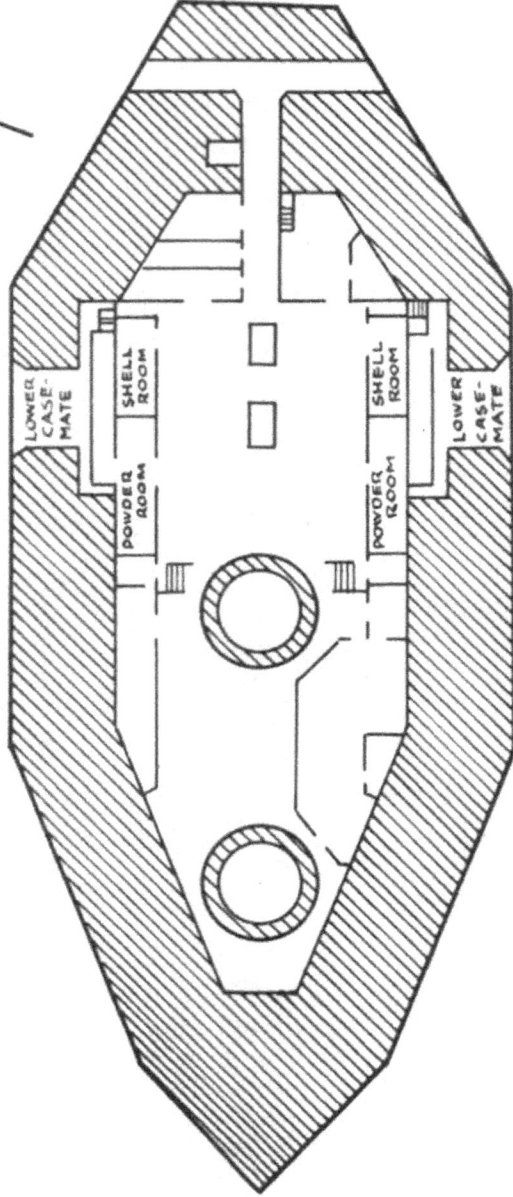

SCALE: 1 INCH = 50 FEET

LOWER CASE- MATE

SHELL ROOM

POWDER ROOM

SHELL ROOM

POWDER ROOM

LOWER CASE- MATE

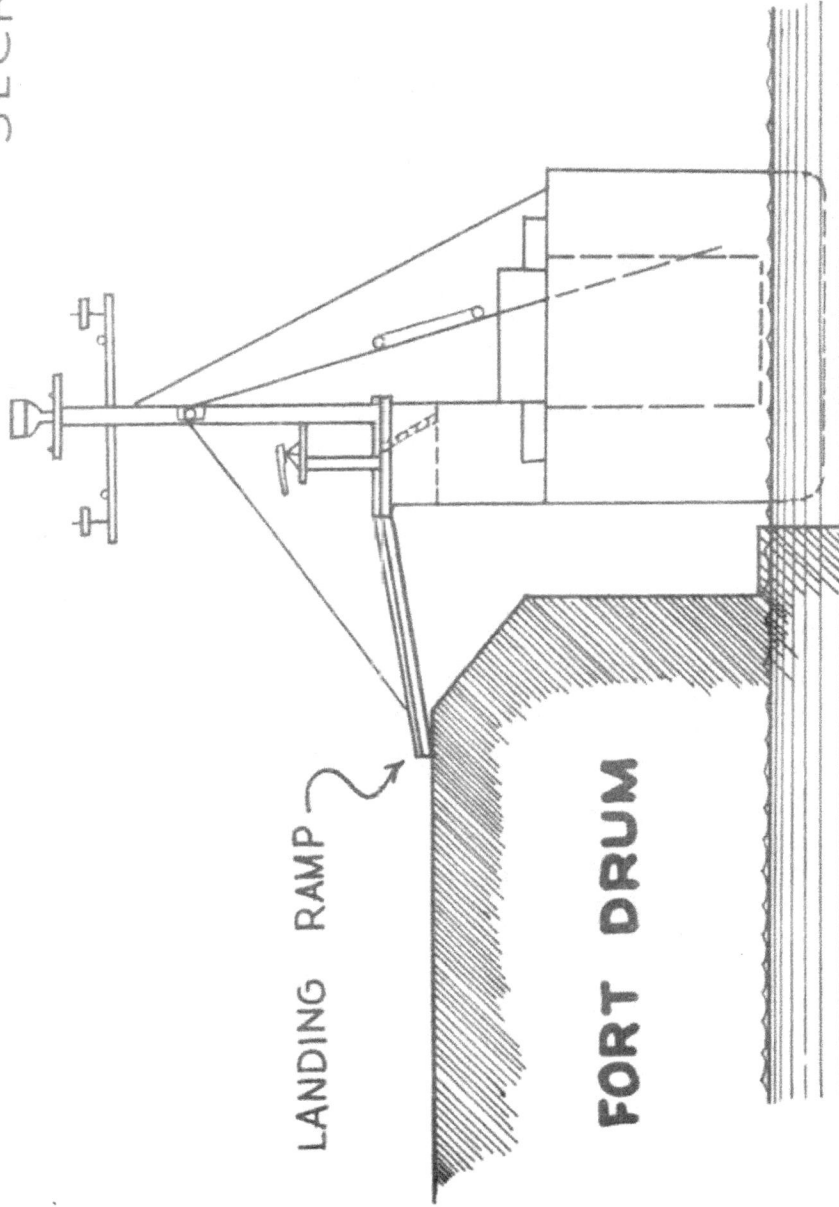

LANDING RAMP

FORT DRUM

EL FRAILE (FORT DRUM) OPERATION
"THE TROJAN HORSE"   SCALE 1" = 16'

Assault party landing on top of FT DRUM.

Effect of cruiser gun fire on casemate. Japanese fired
rifles from these holes upon assault party until silenced
by automatic fire from LSM. Note escape ropes.

from the top. It was then decided to make a draw bridge, on the top of an LSM, which would be lowered to the top of Fort Drum, thus enabling the assault crew to land on the top (see sketch).

Lt. Comdr. Pattie, USN, was directed by the Comdr. 7th Amphibious Force to assist in constructing this device. A large part of its ultimate success was due to his enthusiastic cooperation. The 113th Engineer (C) Battalion was directed to construct the draw bridge, and the 1st Platoon of Company A moved to SUBIC to do the work.

This new model assault landing ship was promptly dubbed the "Trojan Horse". It was completed and moved to CORREGIDOR, arriving the morning of 12 April in time for a rehearsal that afternoon. The assault team was composed of the 1st Platoon Company F 151st Infantry and a Platoon of Company A 113th Engineer (C) Battalion.

On the morning of 12 April, Fort Drum was shelled by a cruiser to see if a hole could be knocked in the wall to permit better entrance of the oil or explode the magazines. This was unsuccessful, although the casemates were punctured.

On the morning of 13 April at 0934 the "Trojan Horse" LSM accompanied by the "Rube Goldberg" LCM moved alongside the Fort. Ineffective small arms fire was received from the holes in the casemates. The draw bridge was lowered, the covering party rushed over the top deck, secured it, followed by the engineers with the oil line and a 600 pound demolition charge.

At 1000 the pumping was started, the demolitions were set in an opening found in the deck in the rear, the fuse ignited and the assault party withdrew.

After pumping 400 gallons of oil the hose line burst. The broken section of hose was cut out while at the same time the Engineer Officer, the Commander of the 2d Battalion 151st Infantry and several enlisted men rushed back on the Fort and cut the fuse. Since it was noted that some of the oil was escaping from the 6" gun casemate, the oil line was shifted to a ventilator on the opposite side of the deck (see sketch) and the nozzle sandbagged down. The ignition charge and fuse were replaced, the pumping renewed and the party withdrew. The demolitions were set to explode at 1048.

At the scheduled time large volumes of black smoke came from the Fort indicating that the oil was burning fiercely. This changed to white and then yellow smoke, followed by a

Ready to start pumping oil.

Placing hose nozzle and connecting demolitions.

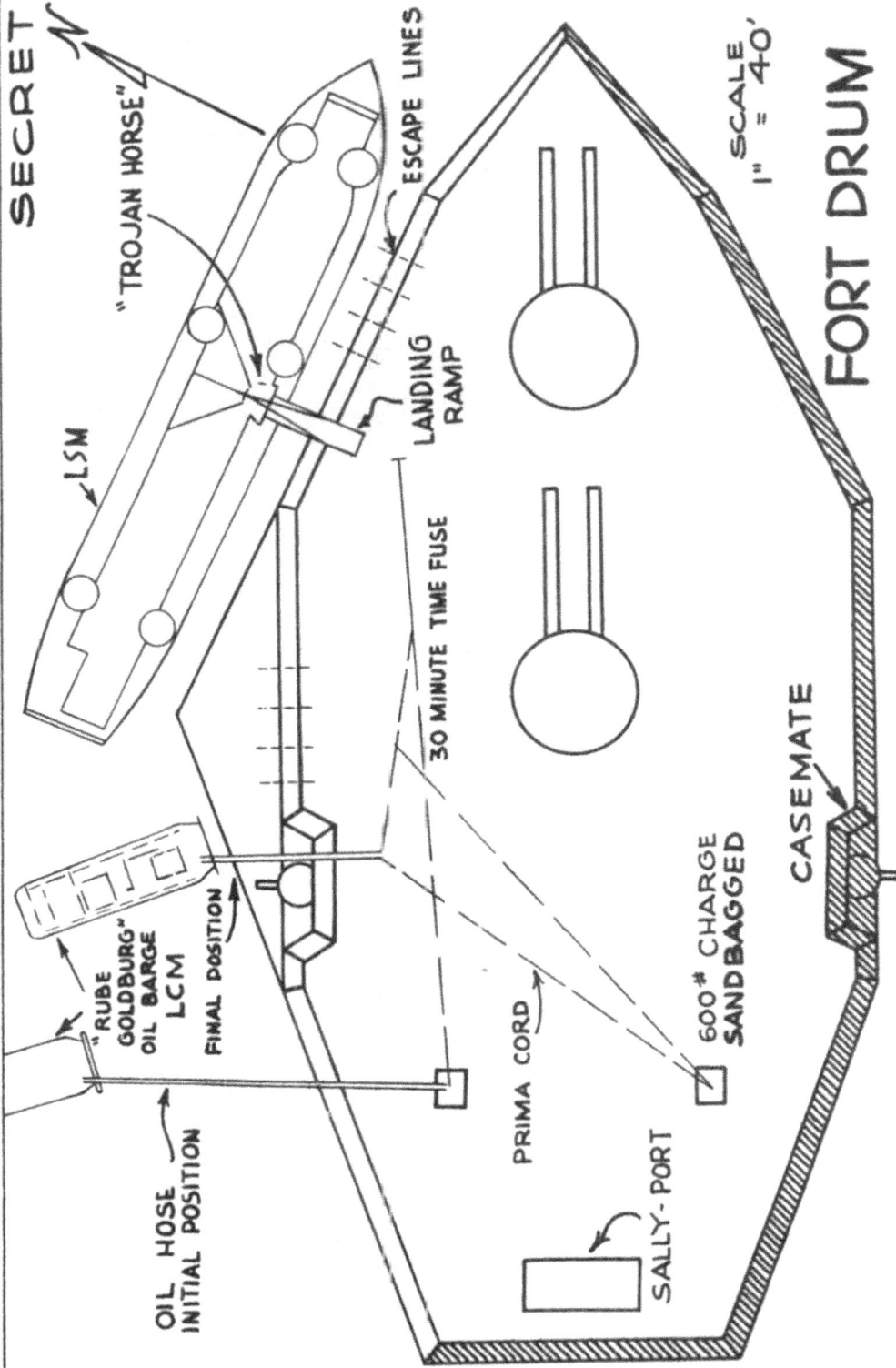

N

"TROJAN HORSE"

LSM

ESCAPE LINES

LANDING RAMP

30 MINUTE TIME FUSE

"RUBE GOLDBURG" OIL BARGE LCM
FINAL POSITION

OIL HOSE
INITIAL POSITION

PRIMA CORD

SALLY-PORT

600# CHARGE
SANDBAGGED

CASEMATE

SCALE
1" = 40'

FORT DRUM

Before

After

violent explosion which rent the deck of the Fort, sent steel plates hundreds of feet in the air and caused smoke to issue from every vent, gun muzzle and opening.

For four days the interior was too hot to permit entrance; on the fifth, smoke prevented any descent below the first deck. On the 18th of April patrols completed the investigation of the interior finding 60 burned and suffocated Japanese.

This highly successful operation was executed with only minor injuries and at a minimum of effort, due to careful detailed planning, close coordination and the effective use of these two novel amphibious assault crafts.

CARABAO ISLAND OPERATION

16 April 1945

To attack, seize and occupy CARABAO Island, and to destroy all hostile forces thereon, was the mission assigned the 38th Infantry Division by FO #13, Headquarters XI Corps, 3 April 1945. The G-2 estimate of the defense force strength was 336, the majority of which were believed to be enemy machine gun units.

Information of recent excavations was partially confirmed by PT boat and aerial reconnaissance on 9 April. Several emplacements on the West side of the island were thought to be occupied although movement was not conspicuous.

C-Day and H-Hour was designated 160930 April 1945. The 151st Infantry was given the mission and the 1st Battalion under command of Maj Morton K. Sitton, was selected as the assault battalion. Attached supporting troops for the assault force were: 1 Platoon Company C 113th Engineer (C) Battalion, Detachment Company B 113th Medical Battalion, 18th Support Aircraft Party, 239th JASCO, Artillery Forward Observer and Liaison Party, and 1 oil pump and crew with LCM from the 592d Engineer Boat and Shore Regiment. The 592d Engineer Boat and Shore Regiment furnished and manned the assault landing craft, and furnished amphibious evacuation and supply for the operation.

The Supporting Weapons Group was composed of the 139th Field Artillery Battalion (105mm How), Battery A 150th Field Artillery Battalion (155mm How) with 1 Platoon 50 Caliber Machine Guns, 81mm mortar platoons from Companies D and M 151st Infantry, 1 Platoon Antitank Company 151st Infantry, 2 Platoons Cannon Company 151st Infantry, Detachment 113th Engineer (C) Battalion, and 1 Platoon Company C 82d Chemical Battalion (4.2" Chemical Mortars). Direct support was furnished by this Supporting Weapons Group from positions vicinity TERNATE on the mainland South of MANILA BAY.

Air support from C-6 to C-Day consisted of daily bombardment with medium bombers and fighter craft dropping 1000 lb bombs and executing strafing attacks. On C-4 moderate but inaccurate anti-aircraft fire was received by the attacking planes. Devastating air strikes were made covering the entire surface of the island. The earth was torn and crumbled to the extent that great land slides closed up many tunnel entrances.

The use of C-47s, out of which were dropped 55 gal drums of NaPalm, was highly successful. Guns and emplacements were

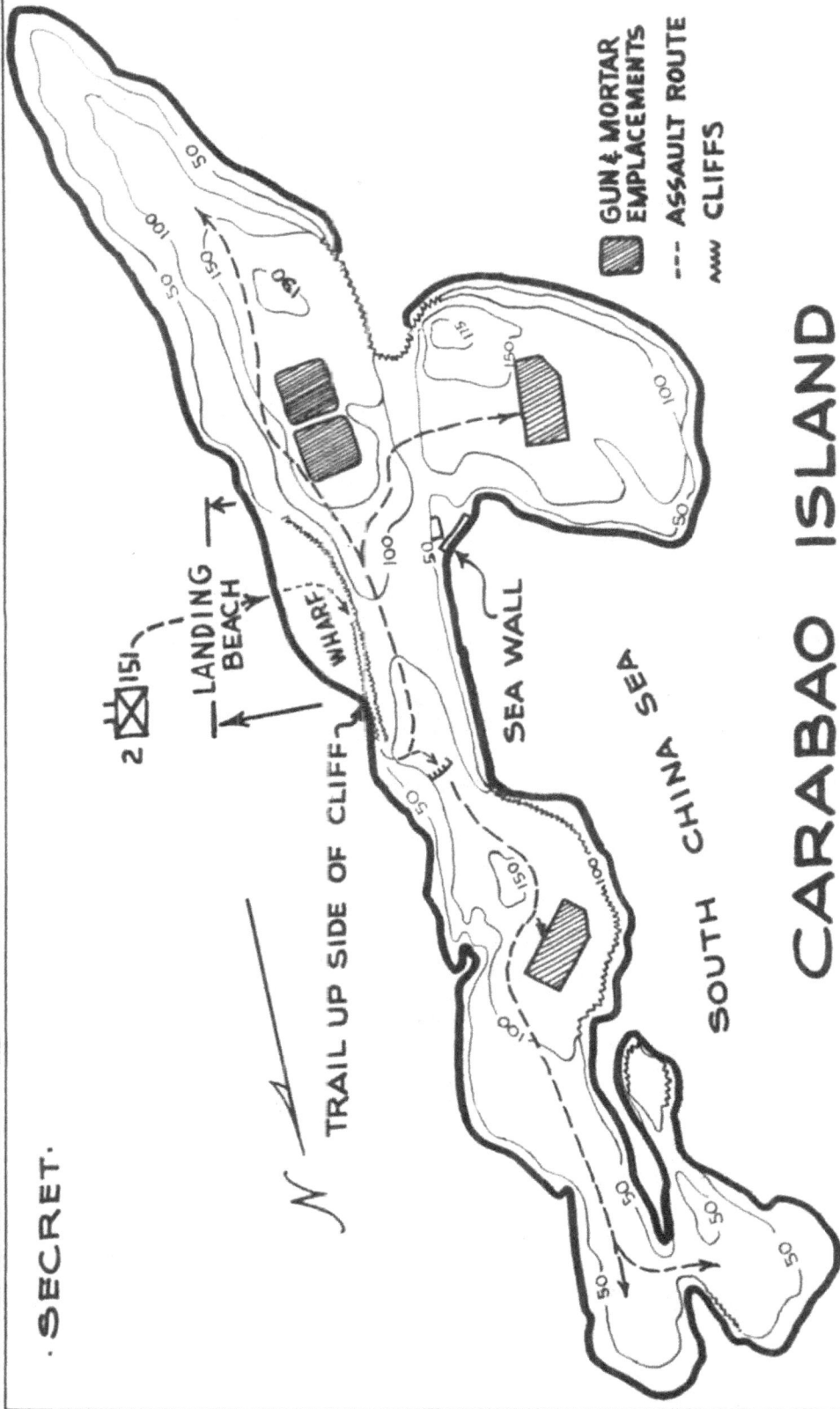

CARABAO ISLAND

SCALE 1:36,000 APPROX.

GUN & MORTAR EMPLACEMENTS

--- ASSAULT ROUTE

CLIFFS

2 ⊠ 151

LANDING BEACH

WHARF

TRAIL UP SIDE OF CLIFF

SEA WALL

SOUTH CHINA SEA

N

destroyed, much of the foliage and vegetation removed, and the island left scorched and barren.

Reconnaissance was conducted to locate positions for the Artillery on the mainland, possible enemy shore positions, landing beaches, walls, and enemy works on CARABAO, including mines, underwater obstacles, and wire; and to determine if the sea wall had to breached to permit bulldozers, tanks, and SPM's to be landed and moved across beach. PT boats accompanied the reconnaissance party. On C-3 Artillery and 81mm mortars landed on the selected positions on the South shore of MANILA BAY. The Artillery registered in, then fired on targets of opportunity and night harassing fires from C-2 to H-1.

The landing beach selected was mid-way on the eastern coast and consisted of a flat stretch of ground 200 yards long by 75 yards deep. A vertical sea wall five feet high ran along the waters edge. This flat stretch was surrounded by vertical shale cliffs, in the face of which were four large caves. In the face of one cliff a sloping road had been cut out prior to the war. The beach on the North end of the island where a landing might have been attempted was well covered with mutually supporting emplacements, barbed wire and natural obstacles. High walls had been constructed at the waters edge at the entrance of all accessible ravines. Tunnels and emplacements built at the waters edge commanded the approaches. Precipitous cliffs a hundred feet high rose out of the sea at other points making assault impossible.

Naval gunfire C-1 and C-Day breached the sea wall and closed all possible caves that could furnish opposition to the landing. The coordination of Naval gunfire, fire from Rocket Boats, and the supporting Artillery was minutely planned and very well executed.

Between 0830 - 0900 C-Day air strikes with strafing were conducted to destroy emplacements and drive the enemy into caves. From 0900 - 0920 Naval gunfire bombarded the landing beach and the cliffs adjacent thereto. Between 0920 - 0930 Naval Rocket Fire gave close support while Artillery and Naval Fire neutralized all parts of the island.

Assault waves reached the hostile shore on schedule without opposition. The plan of attack called for two platoons to land, advance across the flat, and while one platoon secured the beachhead, the other to advance rapidly up the inclined road, and secure the top of the ridge where the road reached the top. Following units were to throw a block across the island on the North side of the connecting ridge, while the remainder of the Battalion secured the Southern end of the island.

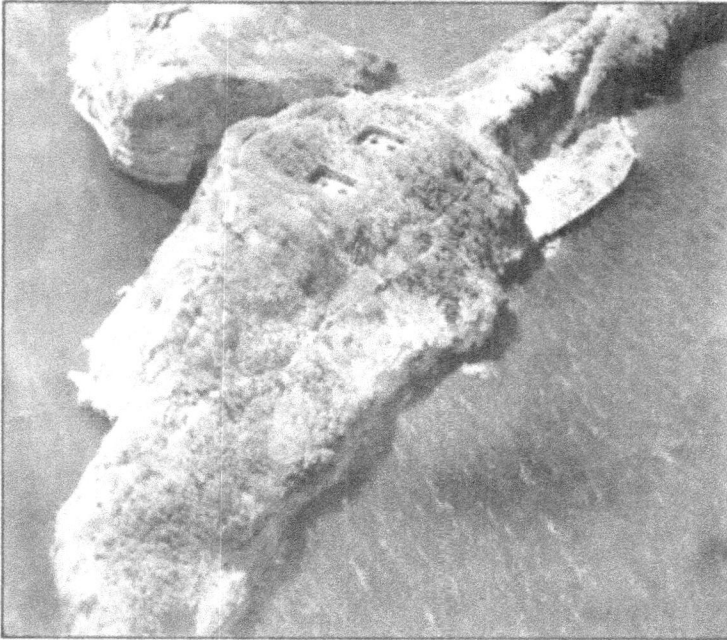

CARABAO Island, showing confined landing
beach, the road up the side of the cliff
and old emplacements.

Assault Team advancing up steep road from
landing beach.

Then the Western peninsula, followed by the Northern end, was to be secured. This was followed out to the letter and by 1140 the entire surface of the island was secured.

No enemy was encountered. The Engineers brought a bulldozer up to the high ground with winches and cables. The troops then proceeded to demolish all emplacements, covered all tunnel entrances, and ignited several enemy ammunition dumps resulting in large underground explosions.

On the second day an investigation of all remaining emplacements, tunnels, and caves, disclosed the fact that CARABAO Island had not been occupied by the enemy for several days.

STOTSENBURG AREA

The 40th Division as one Division in the M-1 Operation had seized CLARK FIELD and FT STOTSENBURG on the drive via TARLAC and SAN FERNANDO into MANILA. The Japanese forces who had attempted to defend CLARK FIELD and FT STOTSENBURG had been pushed West into the foothills of MT PINATUBO.

Approximately two weeks prior to the 38th Division participation in the attack West of STOTSENBURG, the 43d Division relieved the 40th Division in that sector and came under the control of XI Corps. Field Order 8, headquarters XI Corps, dated 7 March 1945, extended the boundaries of the 38th Division to include the STOTSENBURG area. Leaving the 169th Regimental Combat Team, Companies B and C 640th Tank Destroyer Battalion, and Company B 82d Chemical Battalion, the 43d Division was withdrawn for other operations in the Corps sector.

Prior to this on 24 February the 152d Infantry was given the mission to advance elements North on highway 7, from vicinity SAN ANTONIO and SAN FELIPE on the West coast of the ZAMBALES Province, into the BOTOLAN - IBA - PALAUIG BAY sector. They were also given the mission of guarding CLARK FIELD with one rifle company. Beginning on 25 February 1945 the 2d Battalion 152d Infantry, 163d Field Artillery Battalion (less B Battery), and the 38th Reconnaissance Troop moved into BOTOLAN with only slight resistance. On 27 February the 2d Battalion 152d Infantry was directed to proceed East and contact elements of the 43d Infantry Division in the vicinity of TIAONG, and prevent the enemy from moving North from the PINATUBO area. Followed by the Field Artillery and proceeded by 1 Platoon 38th Reconnaissance Troop as far as POONBATO, and MAGUISGUIS, the Battalion began a long and laborious march East over the CAPAS Trail from POONBATO on 1 March. This trail from BOTOLAN over the CABUSILAN Range to TIAONG, O'DONNELL, and CAPAS was an old prewar cavalry trail and training ground. As the trail was so rugged and steep that only lightly equipped small bodies of troops could move over it, the Battalion had to be supplied by native carriers and carabao carts. At 1510 on 4 March Company F, the Battalion leading element, contacted patrols of the 43d Reconnaissance Troop at TIAONG. Company G arrived TIAONG next day and the remainder of the Battalion on 6 March.

This proved to be a surprise move on the part of our forces, as a great number of enemy were found along the river draws and were killed as they were cooking meals or sleeping in preparation for movement by night. Contact with the 43d Reconnaissance Troop and elements of 2d Battalion 172d Infantry

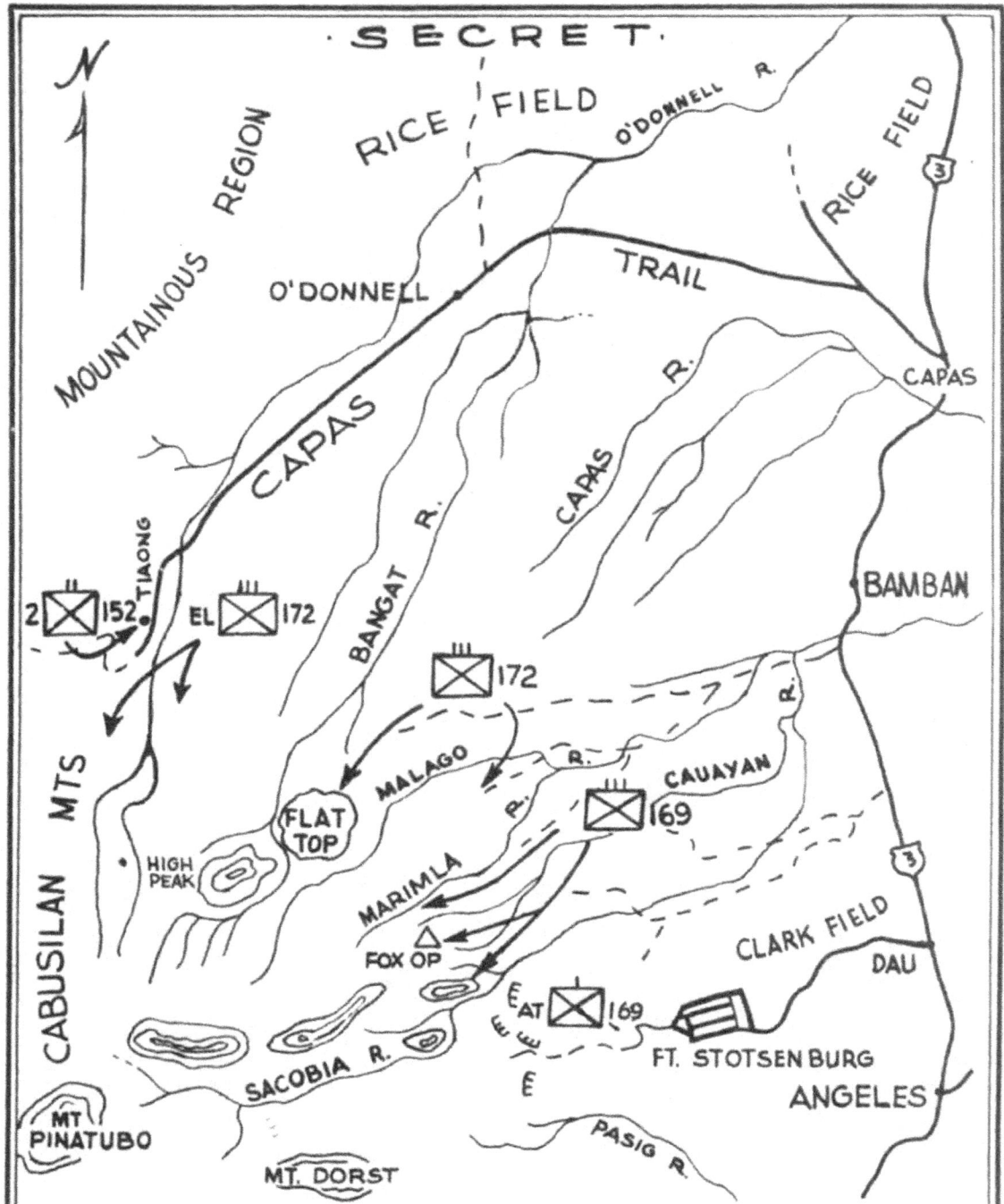

STOTSENBURG AREA
SITUATION PRIOR TO RELIEF OF 43rd DIV.
SCALE 1:180,000 APPROX.

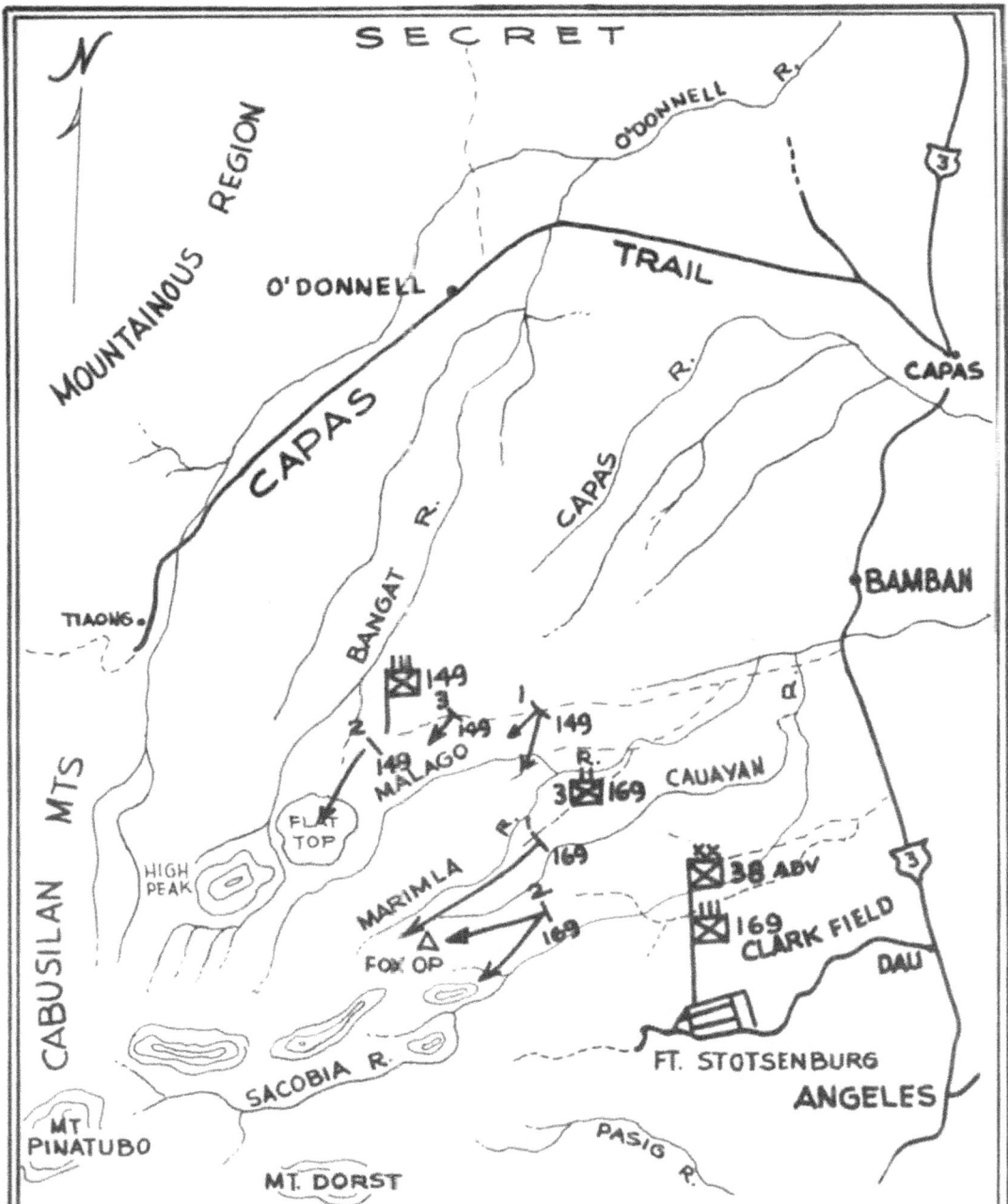

STOTSENBURG AREA
SITUATION ON RELIEF OF 43rd DIV
10 MARCH 1945
SCALE 1:180,000 APPROX.

was established in the vicinity of TIAONG thus entirely blocking the CAPAS Trail from mass movement of the enemy out of the
STOTSENBURG area.

With the mission to press the attack against enemy forces
in STOTSENBURG area, the 149th Regimental Combat Team (less 2d
Battalion), the 139th Field Artillery Battalion, the 150th
Field Artillery Battalion, and the 38th Reconnaissance Troop
were moved to vicinity STOTSENBURG and BAMBAN. These units
plus those attached from the 43d Division were placed under the
command of Brigadier General William Spence, Commanding General
38th Division Artillery. The Division Artillery Staff assisted
by a detachment of officers and men from the Division Headquarters became the 38th Division Advance (Task Force). The CP
opened at FT STOTSENBURG at 1800, 10 March 1945.

Upon organization of the 38th Division Advance (Task Force)
the 2d Battalion 152d Infantry and Company C 152d Infantry who
were guarding CLARK FIELD, were attached and remained to assist
in the destruction of enemy forces in that area. Company E
remained South of TIAONG in the CAPAS Trail area to block the
enemy's escape routes. The 2d Battalion 149th Infantry had
previously been sent into the FISHPOND area South of SEXMOAN,
MASANTOL, HAGONOY, and MALOLOS. Using small boats, barges, and
land patrols, numerous small enemy parties were contacted and
destroyed as they were trying to escape from the fight in
MANILA.

Composition of the 38th Division Advance (Task Force) with
indicated attachments was as follows:

        Detachment 38th Division Headquarters
          38th Division Artillery Headquarters and Headquarters
          Battery
          139th Field Artillery Battalion (105mm Howitzer)
          150th Field Artillery Battalion (155mm Howitzer)
          2d Battalion 152d Infantry attached Company C 152d
          Infantry
          1 Platoon 38th Quartermaster Company
          Company B 82d Chemical Battalion (Tactical control
          only)
        149th Regimental Combat Team
          149th Infantry
          138th Field Artillery Battalion
          Company E 152d Infantry
          Company A 113th Engineer Battalion
          Company A 113th Medical Battalion
          Company C 640th Tank Destroyer Battalion
          38th Cavalry Reconnaissance Troop

149th Regimental Combat Team (Continued)
1 Platoon Company B 82d Chemical Battalion
1st Platoon Company D 113th Medical Battalion
169th Regimental Combat Team
169th Infantry
169th Field Artillery Battalion
Company B 118th Engineer Battalion
Company B 640th Tank Destroyer Battalion
Collecting Company 118th Medical Battalion
3d Platoon Company D 118th Medical Battalion
1 Platoon Company B 82d Chemical Battalion

The terrain in the STOTSENBURG area was unlike any thus far fought over in the M-7 Operation. Small streams flowed between high ridges and individual hills covered with coogan grass. Bamboo thickets and scrubby trees covered numerous paths and caves along the streams used as supply and evacuation routes by the enemy. Overlooking these paths were chalk cliffs containing caves and tunnels from which the enemy fired upon our advancing troops and then took cover in as artillery and mortar fire was dropped upon them.

On certain of these caves only direct fire by artillery, self-propelled cannon, and antitank weapons would neutralize them. Assault teams could find no approach to them because of the bare slopes covered by fire from caves in adjacent ridges.

Caves containing riflemen, machine guns, and 20mm and 40mm dual purpose weapons also contained stores of food, clothing, ammunition, and explosives. For water supply, small parties descended winding paths down the cliffs into the small streams at night. Thus the enemy was able to exist almost indefinitely.

Some 17000 yards West of BAMBAN and to the rear of these bare ridges and knolls were higher and steeper ridges forming the foothills of MT PINATUBO. Thick forests and dense undergrowth afforded the enemy natural camouflage for observation posts, command posts and well dug in strong points. In this area abundant camouflage materials were available.

Supply roads became more difficult to construct and maintain as our forces advanced. More and more engineers were required to push the supply routes well forward and to furnish demolition teams for destroying the caves and tunnels taken by the forward elements. The advance of the infantry was dependent to a great extent on the advance of supply roads by the engineers. A great number of caves containing large amounts of explosives had to be blown after advancing troops and supporting units were clear of the area.

Engineers building supply road
West of FT. STOTSENBURG

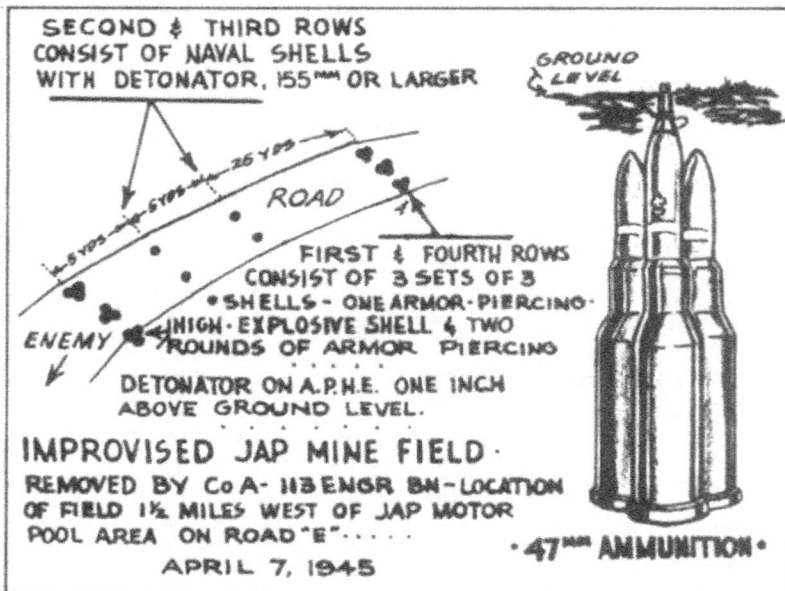

SECOND & THIRD ROWS
CONSIST OF NAVAL SHELLS
WITH DETONATOR, 155ᴹᴹ OR LARGER

GROUND LEVEL

ROAD

FIRST & FOURTH ROWS
CONSIST OF 3 SETS OF 3
SHELLS - ONE ARMOR-PIERCING-
HIGH-EXPLOSIVE SHELL & TWO
ROUNDS OF ARMOR PIERCING

ENEMY

DETONATOR ON A.P.H.E. ONE INCH
ABOVE GROUND LEVEL.

IMPROVISED JAP MINE FIELD.

REMOVED BY Co A- 113 ENGR BN - LOCATION
OF FIELD 1½ MILES WEST OF JAP MOTOR
POOL AREA ON ROAD "E".....
        APRIL 7, 1945

·47ᴹᴹ AMMUNITION·

Details of mine field neutralized
at the West end of Jap Motor Pool.

Supply road in STOTSENBURG Area. This shows type
of terrain over which troops had to advance.

Moving farther back into the mountains advancing elements found steeper ridges, commonly called hogbacks, extending between the heads of small streams and rivers. Stream beds headed up into dead-end gorges. Often leading elements came face to face with sheer cliffs and blank walls so precipitous as to afford no further advance.

At this point engineers with bulldozers were no longer able to construct supply roads. Native carriers were then employed extensively as carrying parties to provide the fighting men with food, water, and ammunition. Near the point where the enemy's supply lines became shorter and their ability to concentrate upon a stiffer resistance became greater, our supply and evacuation routes were narrow rough carrier paths some 4000 yards in length. Some routes crossed valleys 500 feet deep and less than half a mile from crest to crest. Carrier parties moved slowly, as a foot slip along the slopes often gave the individual serious bodily injuries.

Altogether, the terrain in the STOTSENBURG area formed numerous defensive zones capable of withstanding our concentrated and coordinated assaults for days.

When the 38th Division troops completed the movement into the STOTSENBURG area on 10 March, the 169th Infantry with attached troops remained in place, and the 149th Infantry with attached troops relieved the 172d Infantry who were disposed as shown on sketch. The 43d Division Engineers had constructed and improved supply routes to these points.

The TIAONG area had been occupied by the 2d Battalion 152d Infantry. Company E, with elements at TIAONG and on the ridge 3500 yards to the South, remained in that area. The remainder of the Battalion was moved to the vicinity of FT STOTSENBURG and became the Task Force Reserve.

On 11 and 12 March the 149th Regimental Combat Team had advanced elements of the 1st Battalion 3500 yards along the MALAGO River to the base of SUGAR LOAF Hill against light resistance, the 3d Battalion assisted by Tank Destroyers moved 1600 yards South along the West fork of MALAGO River and the East branch of the BANGAT River. Moderate resistance was met by the 3d Battalion as they destroyed a great number of caves. One company back tracked around the left (East) flank to clean out the draws and destroy the bypassed areas. The 2d Battalion 169th Infantry had captured FOX OP and the East end of SACOBIA RIDGE on 9 March, from FOX OP they now cleaned out the draws to the North. Elements of the antitank Company 169th Infantry held the hills of OPs 2, 3, 5, and 7 facing the JAP MOTOR POOL area. Company E 152d Infantry held the ridges 3500 yards South of TIAONG, sending a Platoon in an unsuccessful effort to contact 149th Infantry.

For the next three days, 13, 14 and 15 March, all elements made advances 400 - 500 yards per day against increasing resistance. More noticeable gains were made by the 1st and 3d Battalions 169th Infantry. Company G 152d Infantry on 13 March was attached to the 2d Battalion 169th Infantry for a coordinated attack with their Company G along the draw between SACOBIA RIDGE and FOX OP Hill. This combined attack gained approximately 2000 yards on 14 March. In a coordinated attack the 3d Battalion 169th Infantry moved along the CAUAYAN River draw to the North base of SPENCE RIDGE while the 1st Battalion gained the draws leading into the ridge on the East. SPENCE RIDGE was not taken. Company B took an East nose of the ridge but was forced to withdraw because of the heavy enemy resistance and the lateness of the day. On 14 March the 2d Battalion 152d Infantry (less Company E), was ordered into the area of FLAT TOP Hill and was attached to the 149th Infantry. This Battalion moved South on the BANGAT River to the base of HIGH PEAK (BM 26). Over 1240 Japanese were killed during these three days, the greatest accumulation being 403 by the 149th Infantry on 13 March. Our own casualties were light.

Artillery and mortars played a great part in this action so far. With one light Battalion in direct support of each of the two Regiments and one light and one medium Battalion in general support, they had selected positions where massed concentrations could be delivered upon any slope of these narrow ridges. •As an example of the artillery ammunition expended, 2632 rounds were fired on the 13th, 2498 rounds on the 14th, and 3504 rounds on the 15th.

81mm Mortar Platoons firing in battery found excellent positions on the reverse slopes of the many hills and ridges from which they poured round upon round into the enemy defenses. On 13, 14, and 15 March over 1025 rounds of ammunition was expended, 5% of which was white phosphorous. Numerous brush fires were started by the white phosphorous shells, burning off the underbrush and camouflage over the Japanese emplacements, and allowing our troops to locate their positions.

Again on 16 and 17 March appreciable advances were made toward MT PINATUBO. Greater gains were made in the 149th Infantry sector as the 3d Battalion 169th Infantry on the 169th Infantry's right (North) flank was slowly being pinched out. The mission of the 1st Battalion 169th Infantry had been taken over by the combined advances of the 1st Battalion 149th Infantry and the 2d Battalion 169th Infantry. The 1st Battalion was then ordered to exploit the Task Force Southern flank

STOTSENBURG AREA
SITUATION 15 MARCH – 17 MARCH
SCALE 1:180,000 APPROX

South of the JAP MOTOR POOL. Company A moved on this mission while the remainder of the Battalion consolidated and reorganized in position. Company B 82d Chemical Battalion, who had been supporting the Task Force with one Platoon to each of the two Regiments, was now ordered to reconsolidate and support the 1st Battalion 169th Infantry. On 17 March they were in place and delivered 366 rounds in massed concentrations for that Battalion.

The Battalions of the 149th Infantry pushed into the beginning of the thickly overgrown area of the MARIMLA, MALAGO, and BANGAT Rivers, while elements of the 2d Battalion 152d Infantry were sent around the North side of HIGH PEAK. For all Battalions the total enemy killed now mounted to 2167 and 27 Prisoners of War.

The enemy by this time had settled into highly organized positions South and West of the JAP MOTOR POOL, on LEWIS Ridge, SACOBIA Ridge, SAWTOOTH Ridge and SPENCE Ridge. Only by assistance of heavy artillery and mortar barrages were the infantry able to move into these entrenchments, neutralizing them with fragmentation and white phosphorous hand grenades. Engineer demolition teams followed with prepared charges to blow them and prevent reoccupation by the enemy. 3970 rounds of artillery ammunition were fired on these two days.

To overcome a difficult supply problem, the Engineers, who by this time consisted of the greater portion of 113th Engineer (C) Battalion and Company B 118th Engineer (C) Battalion constructed roads into the forward areas capable of carrying the heaviest traffic. Bulldozers followed the assaulting units, sometimes appearing to be an organic part of the Companies.

Signal units composed of a detachment of the 38th Signal Company and the organic communication personnel of the Regiments had by this time assumed enormous responsibilities in maintaining wire and radio communications into the forward zones. By constructing laterals and by continuous maintenance of all lines, communications were never out.

The hills and ridge lines in the STOTSENBURG area decrease in ruggedness and elevation as you go North and Northeast from MT PINATUBO. Streams flowed in this direction into the O'DONNELL and MORIONES Rivers, thence into the area of rice paddies at CAPAS and TARLAC. These stream lines formed natural escape routes for small enemy parties. Starting with limited rations the Japanese infiltrated through our front lines at night and into the O'DONNELL River area. There they rested and replenished supplies from the rice fields among the many

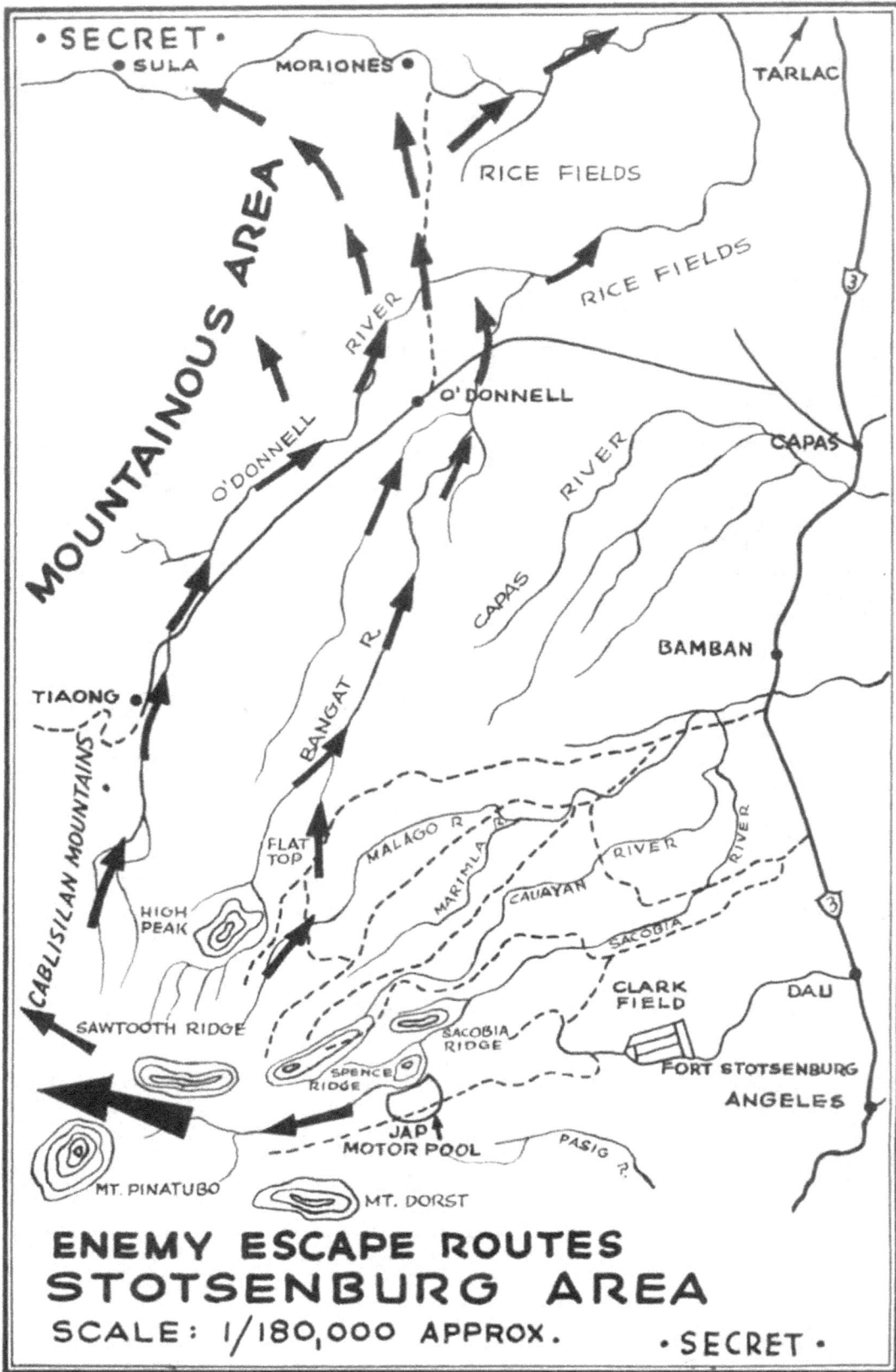

ENEMY ESCAPE ROUTES
STOTSENBURG AREA
SCALE: 1/180,000 APPROX.

evacuated barrios. Prisoners of war taken in this area stated
that they were from the STOTSENBURG area and that they were trying to rejoin their forces at BAGUIO. Captured maps and documents indicated trails in that direction.

Here, the 38th Cavalry Reconnaissance Troop enters the
picture. Attached to 149th Infantry, the Troop was ordered to
patrol the areas along the CAPAS Trail and O'DONNELL River to
TIAONG and the MORIONES River area West from TARLAC. This
was an ideal mission for a Reconnaissance Troop with its highly
mobile fire power. Co C 169th Infantry moved to O'DONNELL to
assist the Reconnaissance Troop, but was returned when the reported enemy force failed to materialize. Stream beds and
barrios were searched daily resulting in many light contacts
and many enemy killed in this sector.

March 18, 19, and 20 found all Battalions of the Force in
constant contact with the enemy. The 2d Battalion 149th Infantry had accomplished its mission in the Fishpond area and
on 20 March took over the FOX OP - SPENCE RIDGE part of the sector of the 2d Battalion 169th Inf. The 2d Battalion 169th Infantry concentrated on the sector between FOX OP and SACOBIA
RIDGE. The 1st and 3d Battalions 149th Infantry made limited
advances encountering heavy resistance in the extremely rugged
terrain at the base of SAW TOOTH and SPENCE RIDGES. The 3d
Battalion 169th Infantry patrolled and destroyed caves to the
rear along the CAUAYAN River upon being relieved.

Company E 152d Infantry relieved the 38th Reconnaissance
Troop in the MORIONES River area on 19 March, placing one platoon at TIAONG, one platoon at O'DONNELL, and one platoon at
MORIONES. The remainder of the 2d Battalion 152d Infantry,
against moderate resistance, pushed deep into the river draws
2000 - 3000 yards Southeast of HIGH PEAK. The 38th Reconnaissance Troop moved to CONCEPTION 5 miles E of BAMBAN and was
given the mission to investigate reports of enemy stragglers
along Highway 7.

The 1st Battalion 169th Infantry was ordered to move Southeast along the SACOBIA River with its objective the JAP MOTOR
POOL, at that time under constant surveillance by their Antitank Company. An enveloping move by this Battalion gained part
of the palteaus South of the JAP MOTOR POOL; but, handicapped
by the terrain in this area, repeated attempts to penetrate into the MOTOR POOL were unsuccessful. On 18 March Company B
82d Chemical Battalion fired 1325 rounds (18% white phosphorous)
in support of this action. At 191200 March it was detached from
the 38th Division, reverting to Battalion control in place.

On 20 March orders were received from XI Corps to relieve

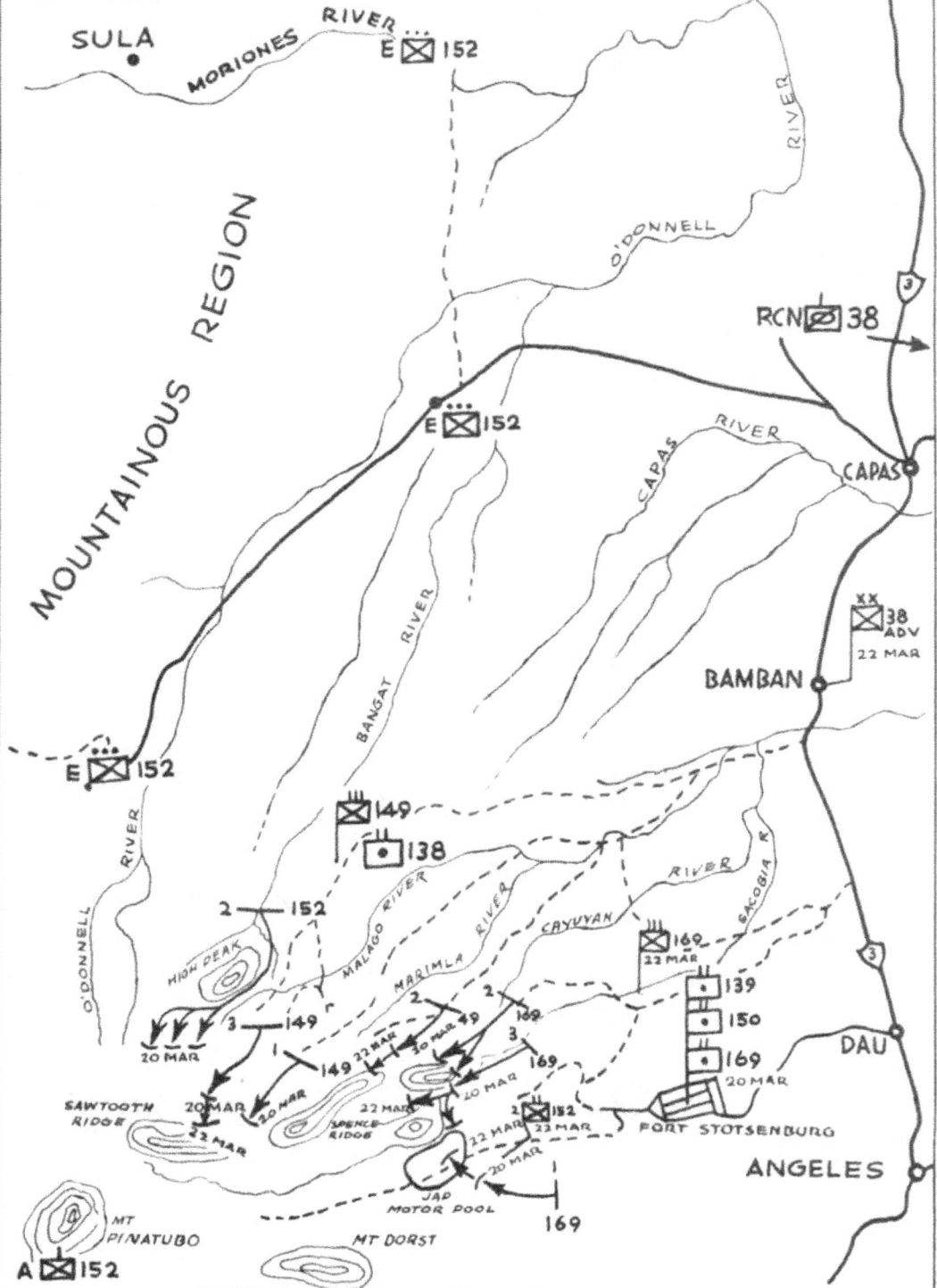

STOTSENBURG AREA
• SITUATION   20 MARCH ~ 22 MARCH •
SCALE: 1/180,000 APPROX

the 169th Regimental Combat Team and to concentrate their units by 222400 March for movement.

Both Regiments had a definite mission on 21 March. The 1st Battalion 149th Infantry after an artillery and mortar preparation attacked South with its objective to secure SPENCE RIDGE in that sector. Companies A and B, as leading elements, advanced approximately 500 yrads against increasingly heavier resistance. Gains were made only after a hard coordinated attack on each successive hill or ridge.

The 2d Battalion 149th Infantry patrolled forward from vicinity FOX OP and cleaned out the adjacent river draws. Enemy contact developed late in the period at the East end of SPENCE RIDGE. In addition to artillery and mortar fire the Battalion Headquarters Company fired a .50 Cal preparation from FOX OP that was very effective. Company G gained a high point on the East nose of this ridge and held it under harassing grenade and mortar fire from the enemy. Enemy emplacements were definitely located and supplies were brough forward in preparation to attack these positions on the following day.

Company I led the assault of the 3d Battalion 149th Infantry during this day. After a preparation of 100 rounds 155mm Artillery and 150 rounds 105mm cannon from the Cannon Company, Company I made repeated attempts to capture SAWTOOTH Ridge. On each successive terrain feature the enemy occupied well dug in emplacements, well camouflaged and so arranged as to afford interlocking fires. 60mm and 81mm mortars were fired to blanket certain strong points while others, one by one, were being neutralized. Results of the days attack showed a gain of approximately 800 yards.

During the period 600 rounds of 60mm mortar, 200 rounds of 81mm mortar and 1730 rounds of artillery (105mm and 155mm) were fired by the Task Force, a major portion of it in support of the 149th Infantry.

The operation of the 169th Infantry on 21 March was as follows: The 1st Battalion, with Company A leading, again tried to move around the flank of the JAP MOTOR POOL positions. At the close of the day they were about 1200 yards from the objective. Two factors handicapped the progress of this Battalion; first, it was understrength, Company A could muster approximately 40 riflemen; and second, the extremely difficult and rugged terrain.

Near SACOBIA RIDGE the 2d Battalion 169th Infantry held positions on the East end of the ridge, a small nose on the North side, and the draw North of SACOBIA RIDGE. The days

57mm AT gun firing across 2d Battalion
149th Infantry flank on SACOBIA Ridge
(skyline on left). Direct fire destroyed 7 enemy machine guns and 3 20mm dual
purpose AA guns located along ridge to
the right of the hump in the skyline.

principle activity for this Battalion consisted mainly of "flushing out" the draws and destroying caves in that vicinity.

The 3d Battalion 169th Infantry, on the previously assigned mission to move Southwest on the JAP MOTOR POOL, advanced about 2000 yards against light opposition. By the end of the period they had cleaned out the draws along SACOBIA River and about 300 yards on the North fork between LEWIS and SACOBIA RIDGES.

In preparation for the forthcoming relief of the 169th Regimental Combat Team the 2d Battalion 152d Infantry moved by truck to the East entrance of the JAP MOTOR POOL. The move was completed late in the afternoon and the Battalion prepared for attack the following day.

Early in the morning of this day a report from the 632d Tank Destroyer Battalion (I Corps troops) of several Japanese in the vicinity of TARLAC was received. Upon investigation by elements of 38th Reconnaissance Troop an estimated force of 40 entrenched enemy was engaged North of TARLAC River and 2000-3000 yards West of TARLAC. The Japanese position was a clump of bamboo and trees North of a deep swampy creek. Their machine guns controlled the road and the rice paddies on both sides of the stream; while the bridge was too weak to carry the M-8 Armored Cars. Men could advance to the edge of the stream by crawling along the paddy dikes, but could not cross the waist deep mud in the stream. A guerrilla party attempting this was driven back with some losses.

When it became apparent that dismounted men could not cross the creek, fire from 60mm mortars and the 37mm's on the Armored Cars was placed on the thicket. At the same time several cars made a circuit of four miles, crossed the creek at another bridge, and came in from the rear. On signal fire was lifted, and the men came in from the rear. After a short encounter, twenty-seven whole dead Japanese were counted, and an estimated thirteen in pieces.

Several elements were engaged in this action of TARLAC which occupied most of the day. In addition to the 38th Reconnaissance Troop, an Artillery Liaison plane played an interesting part. The Artillery Air Officer and the Task Force S-4, investigating the situation from the air, dropped a quantity of fragmentation and white phosphorous hand grenades on the entrenched enemy. Results were negligible and some small arms fire was received but with no damage to the plane or occupants.

At 212000 March 1945 the 169th Regimental Combat Team was issued orders to concentrate in the vicinity of FT STOTSENBURG not later than 222400 March. They were to be prepared to move on XI Corps order.

The results of 13 days (10-22 March) of combat duty with the 38th Division Advance (Task Force) netted the 169th Regimental Combat Team approximately 800 enemy killed, or found dead from artillery and mortar fire. Their casualties for this period were 40 KIA and 177 WIA, a ratio of approximately 4 Japanese killed to every friendly casualty.

The 1st and 2d Battalions 169th Infantry and the 169th Field Artillery Battalion continued their mission until 1200, 22 March. Company A pressing Northward on the JAP MOTOR POOL encountered an enemy strongpoint approximately 600 yards from the objective. Company B entered the JAP MOTOR POOL from the Southeast and, with the assistance of Cannon Company self propelled mounts, operated in that area until noon destroying numerous caves and enemy positions. Companies I, K and L maneuvered on the South fork of SACOBIA River neutralizing several strong points that held up their previous days advances. During this one-half day 15 Japanese were killed and 4 found dead from artillery and mortar fire. The 169th Regimental Combat Team then assembled vicinity FT STOTSENBURG as ordered. Continuance of the mission against the JAP MOTOR POOL was taken over by the 2d Battalion 152d Infantry (less Company E) who were already in position and advancing through the East entrance.

The remaining assault elements of the 38th Division Advance (Task Force) on 22 March continued an aggressive attack. With the 1st Battalion 149th Infantry gains were measured in hard fought yards. Companies A and B lead the attack, Company A forward and Company B enveloping on the Battalion right (West) flank gaining approximately 500 yards. Extremely difficult terrain, more often with only one approach to the target, was the greatest handicap. Enemy resistance consisted of heavy sniper, automatic weapons and knee mortar fire. Caves some of them 30 to 40 feet deep were destroyed by the combined effort of assault infantrymen and heavy artillery and mortar concentrations.

On the East end of SPENCE Ridge the 2d Battalion 149th Infantry concentrated maximum effort to gain a firmer foothold. Company G from a vantage point on the Northeast nose attacked frontally, Company F flanked the same position from the East, both were supported by heavy 155mm and 105mm artillery and 81mm mortar preparations. A Japanese 37mm Antitank gun less sight was dismantled and hand carried to the top of FOX OP where the 1st Sergeant of the Battalion Headquarters Company bore sighted and fired direct into enemy emplacements confronting Companies F and G. Lt Col Silas B. Dishman, the Battalion Commander, was the observer and Lt Col Carl O. DeBard, Commanding Officer of the 139th Field Artillery Battalion, was the assistant gunner.

The objective of Company G was a large enemy strong point
on a steep sided hill just below the Eastern end of SPENCE
Ridge. Several attacks were made on this hill during the morning. From the development of the enemies positions, Company G
rearranged its plan of maneuver. Late in the afternoon after
a mortar and artillery preparation, a bayonet charge was made
up the hill. Seventy-three Japanese were killed with bayonets
and grenades, and the hill secured. Over 30 caves were closed,
the majority of which were known to contain from 1 to 3 Japanese. This objective was overlooked by a higher fortified
knoll to the rear afterward known as DISHMAN Hill. Company E
occupied positions on the North slopes of SACOBIA Ridge.

The 3d Battalion again on this same day pressed onward to
the objective, SAWTOOTH Ridge. Company I, again leading,
attacked along a steep "hogback" extending North from the ridge.
Only one approach was available to this Company and it was well
fortified and continually swept by enemy automatic weapons fire
from the adjacent ridges. By the end of the period Company I,
assisted by a left (East) flank attempted by Company L, was
firmly entrenched on high ground commanding all but the South
side of SAWTOOTH Ridge. Company K advanced to occupy an adjoining high point to the West.

On 22 March approximately 700 rounds and 29 concentrations
were fired by the Artillery and over 1200 rounds of 81mm and
800 rounds of 60mm mortar ammunition were fired in close support
of the Task Force. Wire communications were uninterrupted.
The Engineers concentrated their maximum effort to the forward
elements. Even the Engineer's excellent support left the leading elements with a supply problem of hand carrying food, water
and ammunition 2000 to 3000 yards over very rough trails.

During the night of 22-23 March the enemy harassed all
Battalions of the 149th Infantry with grenades and mortars.
All elements held their hard won positions. This produced no
friendly casualties, however, and did not hinder preparations
to continue the attack on the following day.

Early in the morning of 23 March the Task Force Artillery
and 81mm mortars fired preparations for the 1st, 2d and 3d
Battalions of the 149th Infantry. The 1st Battalion attacked
at 0930, the 2d Battalion at 0905 and the 3d Battalion at
0900.

The 2d Battalion 152d Infantry (less Company E), supported
by one self propelled mount, began to feel out the likely
approaches into enemy positions in the JAP MOTOR POOL area.
Company E 152d Infantry during the day was relieved of its mission in the TIAONG - O'DONNELL - MORIONES area by a Provisional Company composed of one Provisional Platoon from each of the

138th, 139th and 150th Field Artillery Battalions. Company E rejoined the Battalion at noon on 24 March.

The 1st Battalion 149th Infantry under a rolling mortar barrage gained very little distance but eliminated an enemy strongpoint which was the outpost of a highly organized forti- fied area estimated to contain 300 to 400 enemy.

Captured enemy weapons silenced several Japanese automatic weapons for the 2d Battalion. Several caves and emplacements were sealed while the Battalion reorganized and resupplied for the next attack.

For the 3d Battalion 149th Infantry the situation was much the same as the 1st Battalion. Local assaults captured two enemy strongpoints on SAWTOOTH Ridge, entrenchments embedded in rock and eliminated only by the assistance of heavy 81mm mortar concentrations. Several Japanese weapons including machine guns and knee mortars were captured and then used successfully against the enemy.

Gains in the 149th Infantry sector were not noted in ground distance this day. The amount of supporting 60mm and 81mm mortar ammunition expended will indicate the type of work done and the quality of the enemy's resistance. 4250 rounds of 60mm and 3371 rounds of 81mm were fired. This was more than three times as much as was fired on the previous day.

There is, however, an explanation as to why the ammunition expenditure was so much greater. Brig Gen William Spence, Task Force Commanding General, and Brig Gen Robert H. Soule (then Colonel), the Assistant Division Commander, saw how effective massed mortar fires were in this type terrain. Knowing that this was the major activity of the 38th Division at this time they requested two extra 81mm Mortar Platoons. The request was granted and a Platoon from the 151st Infantry and one from the 152d Infantry were dispatched. The one from the 151st Infantry arrived on 23 March in time to participate in the action of the 149th Infantry. As the Platoon from the 152d Infantry had to be moved from the vicinity of SAN MARCELINO Airfield, it did not arrive until late in the period. This Platoon was attached to the 2d Battalion 152d Infantry upon arrival.

The 113th Engineer (C) Battalion was greatly responsible for the advance of assault infantrymen during the past days, although the terrain by now had become so difficult that it was almost impossible to further extend the existing supply roads. The situation was overcome to some extent by constructing laterals or by building an entirely new road where the terrain would permit.

118 Japanese were killed by the four Battalions on 23 March. Enemy resistance remained heavy in all sectors.

At the Task Force Commanders conference the evening of 23-24 March it was decided to place the 2d Battalion 149th Infantry and the 2d Battalion 152d Infantry under the tactical control of Brig Gen Robert H. Soule (then Colonel), the Assistant Division Commander. He was to coordinate the attacks of these two Battalions along SACOBIA and SPENCE Ridges and along the SACOBIA River into the JAP MOTOR POOL. The two remaining Battalions of the 149th Infantry were to remain under Regimental control and continue the occupation of SAWTOOTH Ridge and the West end of SPENCE Ridge. Two air strikes on SPENCE and SAWTOOTH Ridges were planned; artillery and 81mm mortar preparatory fires were scheduled. The 38th Reconnaissance Troop was ordered to reconnoiter for Southern approaches into the JAP MOTOR POOL in anticipation of employing Company E 152d Infantry upon its return to the Battalion.

At 1035 on the morning of 24 March the air strikes were completed and all Battalions moved forward. The 2d Battalion 152d Infantry and the 38th Reconnaissance Troop probed the Southern approaches into the JAP MOTOR POOL. Several light contacts were made but patrols from Companies F and G accompanied by a 105mm Self Propelled Mount entered the POOL from the East at 1400. The Battalion Antitank Guns, from positions on high ground overlooking this area, assisted this advance by direct fire into caves and emplacements.

To the Northwest the 2d Battalion 149th Infantry on SPENCE Ridge made slow advances against heavy opposition. A series of enemy strongpoints from which the battalion had received fire from the past two days was attacked. At the close of the period a number of the forward emplacements had been neutralized.

With the 1st and 3d Battalions 149th Infantry the situation was much the same as the previous day. A pocket of an estimated 300 to 500 Japanese confronted the 1st Battalion. Well dug in entrenchments were so placed as to afford only one approach and these were covered by automatic weapons fire. The 3d Battalion was fighting the terrain and deeply entrenched enemy in its sector. Ground distance again was not a measure of gains made by these Battalions. Gains were indicated by the number of Japanese killed, the number of strongpoints neutralized, the number of caves closed and by the quantity of captured enemy equipment and supplies salvaged or destroyed.

In the TIAONG - O'DONNELL - MORIONES area Company E 152d Infantry on 24 March was relieved by what was henceforth called

the Division Artillery Provisional Company. Provisional
Platoon - 138 was placed at MORIONES, Provisional Platoon -
150 and the Provisional Company Headquarters at O'DONNELL
and the Provisional Platoon - 139 in the vicinity of TIAONG.
A more thorough reconnaissance of the area convinced the
Company Commander to request permission to move the Provisional Platoon 139 from TIAONG to the junction of the BANGAT
and O'DONNELL Rivers. This request was granted and the move
accomplished on 26 March. Patrols locally around O'DONNELL
on 24 March killed 6 Japanese stragglers which were the first
enemy contacts.

The total enemy casualties to date for the 38th Division
Advance (Task Force) now mounted to 3201 killed, 273 found
dead from air strikes, artillery or mortar fire and 14
Prisoners of War.

Activities for the Task Force were light during 25 March.
The 1st and 2d Battalions 149th Infantry consolidated gains of
the previous day, cleaned out and destroyed the enemy caves
and emplacements in the vicinity of their positions, patrolled
the adjacent draws, improved supply routes and accumulated
sufficient supplies to continue the attack.

Advances up to 1000 yards were made by the 3d Battalion
on SAWTOOTH Ridge. The day before, this Battalion had gained
a high point which enabled them to move forward. Opposition
was light as the attacks of previous days had considerably
disorganized the Japanese defenses.

Advances against light opposition were made by the 2d
Battalion 152d Infantry in its effort to capture the JAP MOTOR
POOL. High ground on the Southeast overlooking the objective
was gained, thus permitting the Battalion to plan for a continued attack. Company E rejoined the Battalion and prepared to
move on the objective by routes previously reconnoitered by the
Reconnaissance Troop.

On 26 March the 2d Battalion 152d Infantry moved through
the JAP MOTOR POOL Company G meeting automatic weapons and rifle
and machine gun fire 500 yards to the South. Company E because
of the difficult terrain on the South was as yet unsuccessful in
finding a route to the high ground overlooking the objective.
Elements of the 38th Reconnaissance Troop which had been assisting Company E was relieved of its mission and rejoined the Troop
which relieved Company C 152d Infantry guarding the main CLARK
FIELD air strips.

The 2d Battalion 149th Infantry, the other element of Brig
Gen Soule's command, attacked DISHMAN Hill, the highest ground

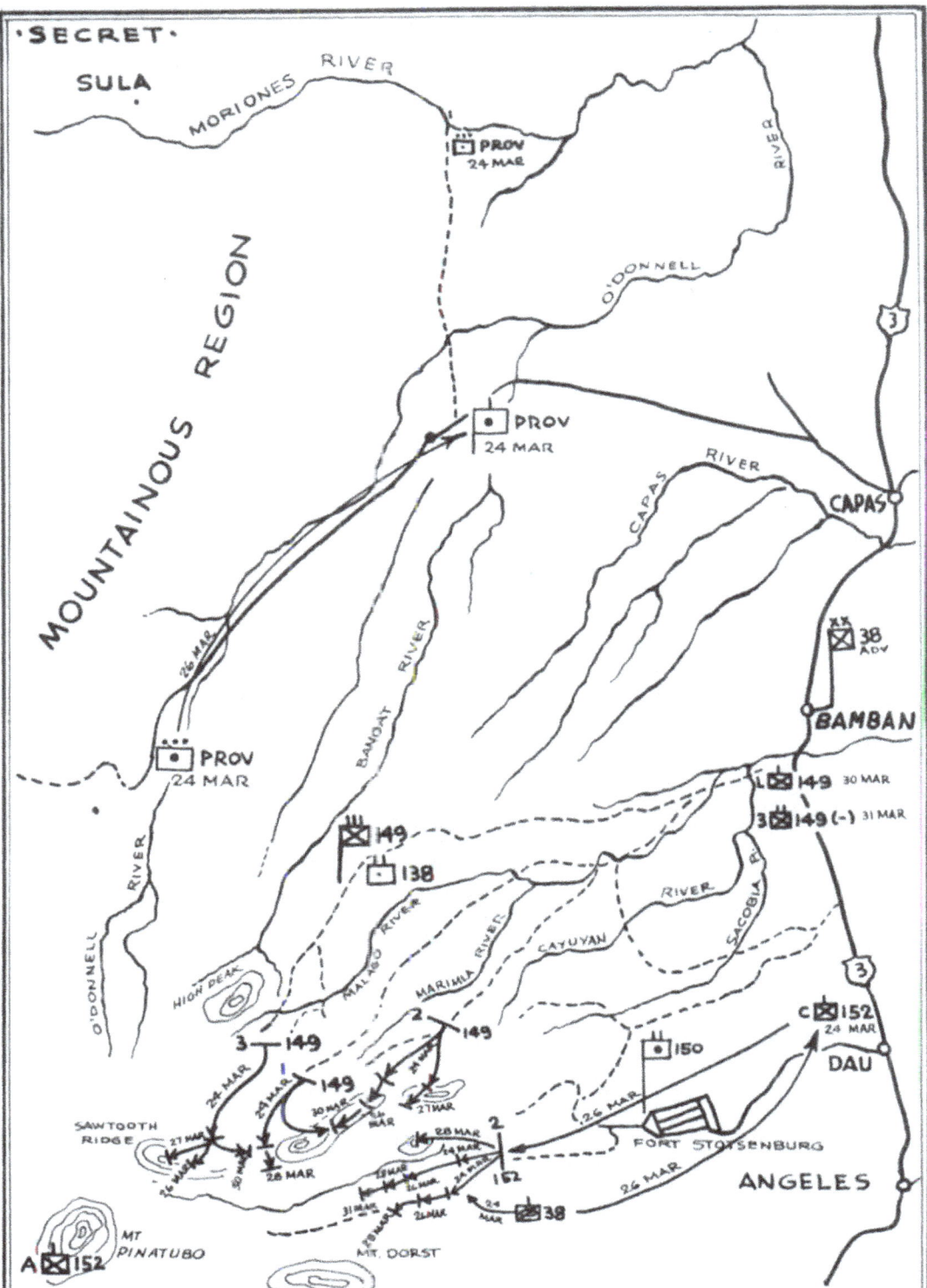

SECRET

SULA

MORIONES RIVER

MOUNTAINOUS REGION

O'DONNELL

RIVER

3

PROV
24 MAR

PROV
24 MAR

CAPAS RIVER

CAPAS

XX 38
ADV

BAMBAN

BANDAT RIVER

PROV
24 MAR

O'DONNELL RIVER

149

138

L 149 30 MAR

3 149 (-) 31 MAR

RIVER

SACOBIA R.

CAYUYAN

3

HIGH PEAK

MALABO RIVER

MARIMLA RIVER

3 149

2 149

C 152
24 MAR

DAU

149

150

FORT STOTSENBURG

SAWTOOTH RIDGE

152

38

ANGELES

A 152

MT PINATUBO

MT. DORST

STOTSENBURG AREA
SITUATION   24 MARCH – 31 MARCH
SCALE: 1:180,000 APPROX

SECRET

at the East end of SPENCE Ridge. Thorough preparations and coordination of all supporting weapons had been made the day before. After heavy artillery and mortar preparation, companies E and G advanced up an extremely steep slope to seize the top of the hill. Over 200 dead enemy were counted at the close of the day. Numerous caves were blown, some of which exploded violently after using white phosphorous and fragmentation hand grenades. The enemy again put up a fanatical resistance but were killed to the last man. Dug-in OP's with seven telephones and numerous wire lines indicated this was an important command OP. Two 20mm automatic weapons were captured and destroyed.

The 1st Battalion 149th Infantry continued to reorganize and resupply. It was no longer possible for the Engineers to construct roads further behind the 1st and 3d Battalions 149th Infantry. The only means of supply was a slow laborious hand carry.

In a coordinated attack by Companies I and L the 3d Battalion on 26 March advanced South, encountering only light resistance. Another hill in this chain on SAWTOOTH Ridge was captured.

This had been a long and hard fight by the 3d Battalion. The ridge was not completely occupied but the heaviest enemy opposition was apparently breaking. Each strong point had been a battle within itself. The numerous hills, ridges and precipitous peaks had enabled the enemy to construct interlocking positions of a magnitude not heretofore encountered by this Battalion. More than once the situation arose in which only one approach to the enemy's entrenchments was possible. These were continually swept by enemy automatic fire. Caves, some estimated capable of housing 200 men, were located and destroyed. Some of these caves contained enormous stores of food, small arms and ammunition. The capture of these supplies often proved to be a considerable value to our own forces as their supply lines were so extended. Only by the excellent support of massed artillery and 81mm mortar fires were these slow gains possible.

An official count of enemy casualties for the day, 26 March, was as follows: 334 killed by the 149th Infantry, 8 killed by the 2d Battalion 152d Infantry and 20 killed by the Task Force Artillery and the Provisional Company on the MORIONES and O'DONNELL Rivers.

Successful advances were again made by the 38th Division Advance (Task Force) on 27 March. The 2d Battalion 152d Infantry encountered sniper and automatic weapons fire from the plateau South and West of the JAP MOTOR POOL. Company E

moved back to Battalion Reserve having been unsuccessful in
entering the MOTOR POOL from the South. Battalion patrols
located the enemy positions while the remainder of the Battalion prepared for attack the following day.

400 yards were gained by the 2d Battalion 149th Infantry
along SPENCE Ridge. Opposition was light as the enemy had
apparently abandoned their positions and reorganized farther
to the rear. SACOBIA Ridge from which the Battalion had been
receiving enemy machine gun fire was entirely occupied by
Company F. A large number of fresh graves were found, and two
20mm guns, and several machine guns found destroyed by artillery and mortar fire.

With its objective the remaining high ground overlooking
a gap between SPENCE and SAWTOOTH Ridges, the 3d Battalion
attacked following heavy artillery and mortar preparations.
The objective was occupied late in the period thus securing
all three peaks of SAWTOOTH Ridge.

The 1st Battalion completed preparations for a coordinated
attack on 28 March.

There was a reason why resupply was important. Artillery
and mortar ammunition supply for Sixth Army were very low.
Upon advice from higher headquarters every effort was made to
conserve these stocks. As our own supply lines were long and
difficult at this time, it was decided to use the day's allowance to support attacks of one or two Battalions allowing the
others to consolidate gains and prepare for future operations.
This was a successful plan as it concentrated the available
artillery and mortar support in one or two Battalion fronts
rather than four. To illustrate the decline in ammunition
allowances the following 81mm expenditures were reported by
the 149th Infantry. 5729 rounds were fired on 26 March, 4986
rounds on 27 March, 4068 rounds on 28 March, 234 rounds on
29 March and 665 rounds on 30 March. Expenditures of artillery and 60mm ammunition were similar in quantity.

616 Japanese were killed by the Task Force on 28 March.
This was the greatest number for any one period throughout
the STOTSENBURG action. The accumulated score was now 4471
counted dead.

28 March was the day for which the 1st Battalion 149th
Infantry had so long prepared. At 0952, after a preparation
of massed artillery and mortar fires, the Battalion attacked
to secure SPENCE Ridge within its zone. Immediately upon
jumping off an enemy fortification in the form of a horseshoe was encountered. There was only one approach along lines
of interlocking automatic weapons fire. The thick undergrowth

was so thick it was impossible to see more than a few yards ahead. After being repulsed in the first attempt, more and heavier artillery and mortar concentrations were fired. At 1330 the Battalion again attacked and again they were repulsed. At 1530 after another artillery and mortar preparation they seized this highly organized position, and advanced about 750 yards over the organized terrain to completely occupy the objective. Reports were that in excess of 300 enemy were killed. On recounting in daylight the next day 430 Japanese were dead on the field. Only one minor strong point remained between this objective and positions overlooking SACOBIA River.

In the 3d Battalion sector a strong point, partially reduced the previous day was gained. Inspection of the area found many abandoned caves and emplacements containing an undetermined quantity of food, arms and ammunition. Except for mopping up and the reduction of a few minor strongpoints the 3d Battalion had captured all peaks in the chain named SAWTOOTH Ridge. They now held positions on the high ground overlooking LEWIS Ridge and the area confronting the 2d Battalion 152d Infantry.

The 2d Battalion 149th Infantry and the 2d Battalion 152d Infantry also made limited advances on 28 March. Sharing in the Task Force ammunition allowance the 2d Battalion 149th Infantry continued the attack on the East end of SPENCE Ridge. Within 100 yards of their objective, a nose extending Southeast from the ridge, they were strongly counterattacked. Artillery and mortars enabled them to successfully hold the ground gained thus far. The Battalion was still engaged near the end of the day as they tried to maneuver around the enemy positions.

One Platoon of Company E 152d Infantry patrolled LEWIS Ridge without opposition while the remainder of the Battalion encountered well dug-in enemy positions about 1200 yards beyond the entrance to the JAP MOTOR POOL. Company G secured the high ground on the South. Preparations were made to attack these positions on the following day.

Artillery Air Observers discovered considerable enemy activity along the SACOBIA River as far West as the slopes of MT PINATUBO. An estimated 200 to 500 Japanese moving to the West with horses and at least 3 vehicles were taken under fire by two Artillery Battalions. Many were reported killed and the evacuation apparently disorganized. An air strike on the following day was arranged as the more Western activities were beyond Artillery range.

The Provisional Company at O'DONNELL and MORIONES killed their share of the enemy on 28 March. A total of 30 Japanese dead was the result of their extensive patrolling in that area.

Activities of 29 March consisted mainly of consolidation of the gains made on the previous day, replenishment of supplies and probing forward to locate new enemy defenses.

In the 1st Battalion 149th Infantry zone Company B over-ran a position confronting them at the close of the last period. Patrols into the areas in the vicinity of the Battalion positions destroyed or salvaged an enormous quantity of enemy arms and equipment. Some of these arms were yet unpacked.

Enemy contacts with the 2d Battalion 152d Infantry high-lighted the period. Company G advanced slightly against stiffening enemy opposition from entrenchments about 2000 yards West of the JAP MOTOR POOL, positions which withstood heavy artillery and mortar fire.

By this time in the STOTSENBURG action the enemy opposi-tion with some exceptions was broken. The exception was the group confronting the 2d Battalion 152d Infantry West of the JAP MOTOR POOL. The 3d Battalion 152d Infantry in the POON-BATO - MAGUISGUIS area encountered an increasing number of small enemy parties. Prisoners of War revealed that they were endeavoring to reach the coastal area of BOTOLAN and IBA. Receipt of this information prompted the Division Commander to move the Battalion deeper into the MT PINATUBO area in order to more completely cut off the enemy's escape routes.

On 30 March the 2d Battalion 149th Infantry attacking with heavy Artillery and mortar support reduced an enemy strongpoint encountered the previous day. They continued their advance against slight opposition along SPENCE Ridge to within 700 yards of the 1st Battalion. Patrols from the two Battal-ions made physical contact before the day ended.

The 2d Battalion 152d Infantry aggressively attacked their objective 2000 yards West of the JAP MOTOR POOL supported by the Task Force Artillery, the Battalion Antitank guns, one self propelled mount and an extra 81mm mortar platoon from the 1st Battalion 152d Infantry. Information from the previous days patrols estimated the enemy to be 75 well entrenched riflemen with a minimum of 6 machine guns and 1 20mm duel purpose anti-aircraft weapon. Several times during the day elements of the Battalion supported by heavy artillery and mortar barrages attempted to take this position. It developed that interlocking cross fires repulsed every effort. An air strike of 500 pound demolition bombs on this position was then planned for the following day.

With the 1st and 3d Battalions activity was considerably lighter than the previous days. Operations consisted of mopping up in the position areas, salvaging or destroying the captured enemy equipment, and eliminating the remaining small enemy strong points. The 1st Battalion near the end of the day encountered a heavier strongpoint. Preparations were made to attack on 31 March. Company L, weary and almost exhausted from the mountain fighting, was moved to a rest camp near the Regimental Command Post in the vicinity of BAMBAN.

On the morning of 31 March the objective of the 2d Battalion 152d Infantry was subjected to an airstrike of 500 pound demolition bombs, heavy artillery and mortar preparations and .50 and .30 caliber supporting fires from the 2d Battalion 149th Infantry on SPENCE Ridge. With Company G leading the Battalion attacked through the draws on the enemy's right (South) flank. High ground overlooking the objective on that flank was gained, but heavy automatic weapons fire prevented digging in to hold it. Other elements of the Battalion investigating further along the draws encountered two enemy light tanks. A direct hit by bazooka fire was reported to have been made on one of them. The tanks withdrew. At the end of the day the Battalion was still engaged.

All three Battalions of the 149th Infantry continued mopping up and cleaning out the few scattered enemy positions on SPENCE and SAWTOOTH Ridges. One reinforced Company was left to hold positions on SAWTOOTH Ridge while the remainder of the 3d Battalion was withdrawn and assembled near BAMBAN.

The 38th Reconnaissance Troop investigated reports of enemy stragglers East and West of Highway 3 killing 11 enemy and capturing 1 Prisoner of War. The Provisional Company at O'DONNELL patrolled West and Northwest making several minor contacts in the mountainous region.

On 1 April it was decided to relieve the 2d Battalion 152d Infantry in the JAP MOTOR POOL area, moving the 2d Battalion 149th Infantry to continue the drive West on the SACOBIA River. One reinforced Platoon was left on SPENCE Ridge; the 2d Battalion 149th Infantry then completed the relief during the day. The 2d Battalion 152d Infantry before relieved continued patrolling to find new approaches into the enemy installations with very little results because of the very difficult terrain and the limited routes available.

Activity in the 1st and 3d Battalions 149th Infantry was very light, the 1st Battalion continuing the mopping up and evacuation of captured supplies and equipment on SPENCE Ridge. Company I, the remaining element of the 3d Battalion on

STOTSENBURG AREA

SITUATION   1 APRIL—9 APRIL

SCALE: 1:180,000 APPROX ·

SAWTOOTH Ridge, aggressively patrolled that area with no contact. Company K relieved the 38th Reconnaissance Troop as guards on the CLARK FIELD Airstrips. The Reconnaissance Troop then was detached from the 38th Division Advance (Task Force) and attached to the 152d Infantry in the vicinity of SAN MARCELINO.

In order to furnish closer support to the attacks and to enable long range fires to be placed deeper on SACOBIA River the 138th Field Artillery Battalion was moved near the Eastern entrance of the JAP MOTOR POOL. Extensive air reconnaissance enabled this Battalion to successfully fire on targets at the base of MT PINATUBO.

Considerable enemy activity was noted daily on the SACOBIA River as far West as the North base of MT PINATUBO. Elements of the 1st and 3d Battalions 149th Infantry on SPENCE and SAW-TOOTH Ridges overlooking these trails established trail blocks using long range .50 caliber machine gun fire. Efforts were made to send a Platoon down the steep and precipitous Southern slopes of these two ridges. The terrain was found to be too difficult.

On 2 April the 2d Battalion 149th Infantry 2000 yards West of the JAP MOTOR POOL again attempted to develop both flanks of the enemy positions. Small arms, machine gun and knee mortar fire prevented accomplishment of this mission. The enemy had well dug-in entrenchments along a V-shaped cliff which dropped about 300 feet to the river. All approaches were well covered by these interlocking positions. Heavy mortar and artillery fire did'no appreciable damage to the forward slopes of the position while concentrations fired on the reverse slopes merely dropped into the gorge to the rear. At least one enemy tank was known to be in that area but the Engineers had mined all approaches into our front.

Air and ground observers reported considerable enemy activity in a box canyon about 5000 yards West of the JAP MOTOR POOL. An air strike of 500 pound demolition bombs was placed on this area causing several landslides and the destruction of a possible Japanese Command Post.

The remaining elements of the Task Force on 2 April patrolled locally for security and rested from their recent heavy tasks on SPENCE and SAWTOOTH Ridges.

It is worthy to note at this time that the enemy's resistance had apparently collapsed, that the opposition in the JAP MOTOR POOL area was only to delay our advances. An increasing number of stragglers were contacted by the 3d Battalion 152d

Infantry West of MT PINATUBO in the POONBATO - MAGUISGUIS area.
Captured documents, interpretation reports from prisoners of
war and aerial observation showed several trails leading West
through the Northern slopes of MT PINATUBO. Prisoners of War
taken by the 3d Battalion 152d Infantry stated that they were
trying to reach IBA on the West coast of ZAMBALES Province.
For this reason the 3d Battalion 152d Infantry was given the
mission to block that movement.

For the period 3 and 4 April friendly operations in the
Task Force sector consisted mainly of patrols around local
positions, mopping up the scattered and defeated enemy on
SPENCE and SAWTOOTH Ridges, and reconnaissance patrols in the
JAP MOTOR POOL area. In keeping with the tactical plan artillery and mortar ammunition was conserved for an all out attack
on SACOBIA River. Supplies were assembled, the 2d Battalion
was reorganized and regrouped while the air struck all along
the SACOBIA River to disrupt the enemy's withdrawal and to
prevent construction of new defenses.

On the morning of 5 April the 2d Battalion 149th Infantry
found that continuous pressure and harassment on the Japanese
positions confronting them had paid excellent dividends. With
only light resistance the high ground was occupied and several
large caves closed trapping the few remaining Japanese. It
was thought that the main force had withdrawn along the river.
The 1st Battalion was then ordered to relieve the 2nd
Battalion and continue the advance toward MT PINATUBO. Company
I relieved the elements of Company C and the elements of the
2nd Battalion holding SPENCE Ridge as part of the Task Force
plan to regroup and consolidate. Company I assumed complete
responsibility of SPENCE and SAWTOOTH Ridges.

The Provisional Company at O'DONNELL continued to aggressively patrol the MORIONES and O'DONNELL River area. By this
time the total enemy casualties from the many straggler contacts
had risen to over 130 killed and found dead.

For the period 6 to 9 April inclusive the main operations
in the STOTSENBURG area was a 3000 yard advance West on SACOBIA
River with little opposition. One partially disabled light
tank was captured on 8 April. It was thought that other armored vehicles of some type were yet in this area. Also on 8
April the 139th Field Artillery Battalion relieved the Provisional Company at O'DONNELL. The Provisional Company was dissolved to revert to their respective organizations. The 150th
Field Artillery Battalion (less Battery A) was attached to XI
Corps Artillery and moved to the IPO area.

On 9 April the heaviest contact since relieving the 2d

Battalion 152d Infantry was made by the 1st Battalion 149th
Infantry. Hastily prepared enemy positions yielded to our
forces determined advance to accumulate another 140 enemy
killed or found dead, 5 Prisoners of War and numerous fresh
graves discovered. The 138th Field Artillery Battalion (105mm
How) plus Battery A 150th Field Artillery Battalion (155mm How)
from positions in the JAP MOTOR POOL gave excellent close support in this attack.

The advance continued on 10 and 11 April against only
light resistance. Company E relieved Company K on CLARK FIELD
guard. Company I left one reinforced Platoon on SPENCE Ridge,
the remainder of the Company rejoining the Battalion. As the
139th Field Artillery Battalion was to furnish artillery support for the CABALLO operation it was assembled 11 April in
the vicinity of CLARK FIELD. 3d Battalion 149th Infantry moved
to O'DONNELL area to relieve 139th Field Artillery Battalion.
Battery C 138th Field Artillery Battalion displaced to the
vicinity of O'DONNELL to support the 3d Battalion.

The mission of the 38th Division Advance (Task Force) to
destroy all Japanese forces in the STOTSENBURG area was now
virtually accomplished. Over 5500 enemy had been counted dead
and a total of 42 Prisoners of War captured. All resemblance
of an organized and effective defense was completely disrupted.
Their food, ammunition and supplies were almost exhausted as
was stated by Prisoners of War.

The only escape from the aggressive pressure applied by
our forces was to withdraw North and East along the trails on
the North slopes of MT PINATUBO. Trails on the South slopes
had for many days been blocked by Company B 152d Infantry.
The 3d Battalion 152d Infantry supported by the Cannon Company
was effectively blocking the West as was indicated by the increasing number of enemy casualties East of POONBATO and
MAGUISGUIS.

On 11 April the 38th Advance (Task Force) was dissolved.
The 38th Division Headquarters staff was returned to the
Command Post near FLORIDABLANCA, the 38th Division Artillery
assuming tactical control of the task to complete the enemy's
destruction in the STOTSENBURG Area. On 14 April, however,
tactical control was taken from the 38th Division Artillery.
The 149th Infantry then became a normal element of the 38th
Division.

The 1st Battalion 149th Infantry on 12 April advanced
another 800 yards West on the North fork of SACOBIA River.
Patrols moved 600 yards along the South fork with no enemy
contact. Small holding forces from hastily dug positions and

log pillboxes, were encountered by the North force. These were quickly neutralized.

On 13, 14 and 15 April due to the extreme ruggedness of the terrain gains by the 1st Battalion were slow. Scattered resistance only was offered by the enemy but innumerable times the attacking Battalion penetrated the dense jungle for a short distance to find the way blocked by steep cliffs. On 14 April the 2d Battalion again entered the operation moving to assist the 1st Battalion on their left (South) flank.

Boundaries were changed within the Division on 14 April. The 151st Infantry on the BATAAN Peninsula required more troops to control CABALLO Island and EL FRAILE Island (FORT DRUM), to carry out the CARABAO Island mission and to patrol the increasing enemy activity around MT NATIB. The 149th Infantry's highway and railway bridge guard duties from TARLAC to SAN FERNANDO were extended to include Highway 3 all the way to the Northern outskirts of MANILA. To assume this respon- sibility the 38th Reconnaissance Troop relieved the 3d Batal- lion 149th Infantry in the O'DONNELL - MORIONES area. The 3d Battalion (less Company I) then relieved the 3d Battalion 151st Infantry from SAN FERNANDO to MANILA. There it remained until relieved by elements of the 63d Infantry about 3 May. Company I remained in the TIAONG area to patrol that sector for Jap- anese stragglers.

The 1st and 2d Battalions advanced approximately 2500 yards on 16, 17 and 18 April against light to moderate re- sistance. Artillery and mortar concentrations assisted in the overrunning of several hastily constructed strongpoints. Several supply and evacuation installations were captured including a Japanese field hospital. Physical contact was also made by the 1st Battalion with Company B 152d Infantry on the Southern slopes of MT PINATUBO. Company I 149th Infantry at TIAONG patrolled West to make physical contact with Company L 152d Infantry. Only one light contact was reported.

The 3d Battalion 152d Infantry, to within 5000 yards of MT PINATUBO on the West, was literally having a field day. Trail blocks and ambushes were set up which captured or killed an average of 50 enemy per day.

On 18 April the 2d Battalion 149th Infantry was with- drawn from the SACOBIA River sector and moved to TIAONG to apply pressure on the MT PINATUBO area from the North. Company I which was at TIAONG was attached to the 2d Battalion to assist in the attack.

For a clearer understanding of the box like attack at this

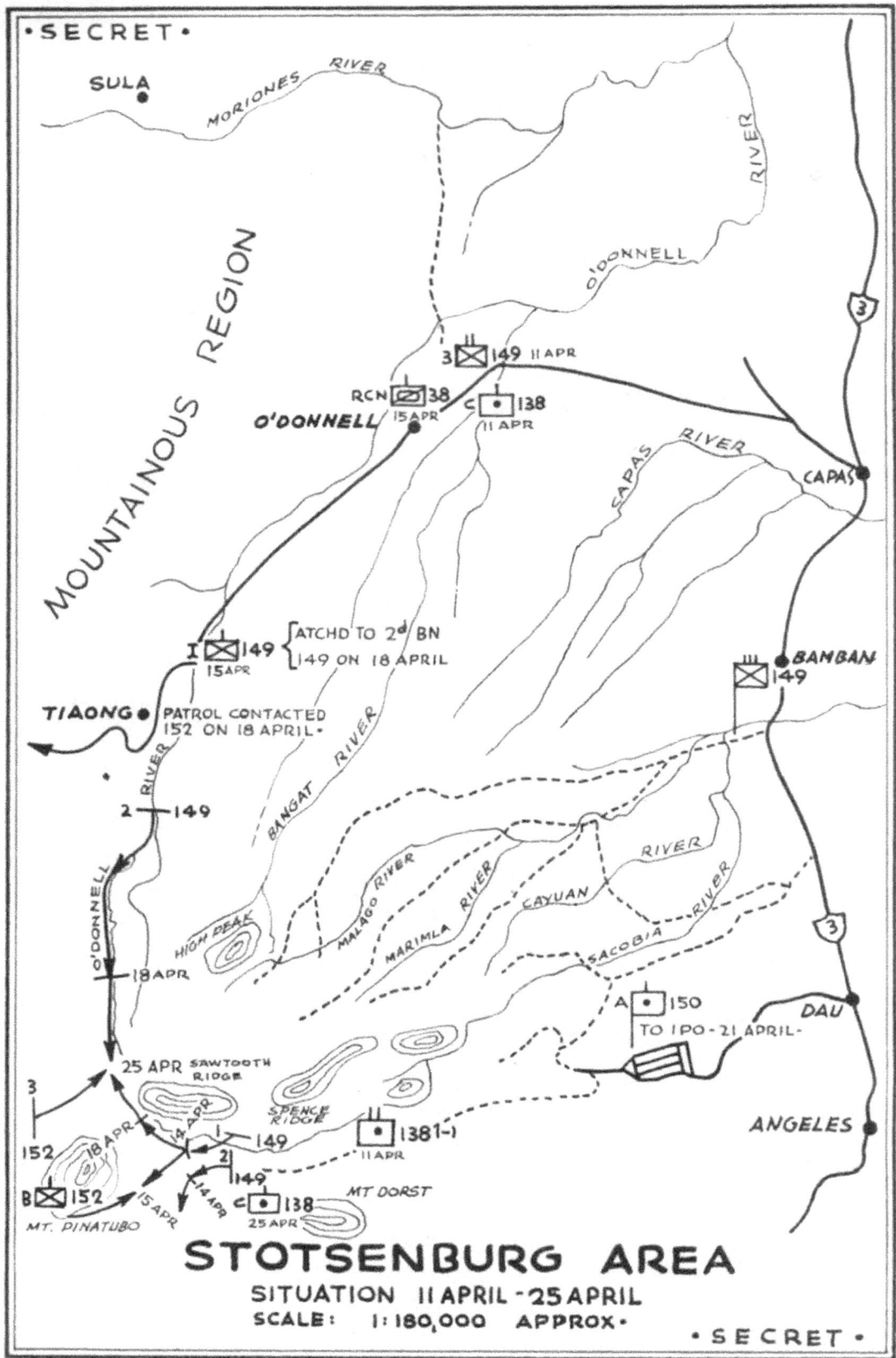

SULA

MORIONES RIVER

MOUNTAINOUS REGION

O'DONNELL RIVER

RIVER

3

3 |×| 149 11 APR

RCN |⊡| 38 15 APR

O'DONNELL

C • 138 11 APR

CAPAS RIVER

CAPAS

1 |×| 149 15 APR

{ ATCHD TO 2ᵈ BN 149 ON 18 APRIL

III |×| 149 BAMBAN

TIAONG • PATROL CONTACTED 152 ON 18 APRIL ·

BANGAT RIVER

2 — 149

O'DONNELL RIVER

18 APR

HIGH PEAK

MALAGO RIVER

MARIMLA RIVER

CAYUAN

RIVER

SACOBIA RIVER

A • 150 TO IPO - 21 APRIL ·

DAU

25 APR SAWTOOTH RIDGE

SPENCE RIDGE

1 — 149

C • 138I-1 11 APR

ANGELES

3

152 18 APR

2 — 149

14 APR

B |×| 152 MT. PINATUBO

15 APR

C • 138 25 APR

MT DORST

STOTSENBURG AREA
SITUATION 11 APRIL - 25 APRIL
SCALE: 1:180,000 APPROX·

time, picture MT PINATUBO, approximately 5000 feet elevation, being converged upon from four different directions. The 2d Battalion 149th Infantry plus Company I, was on the North, the 1st Battalion 149th Infantry on the East, the 1st Battalion 152d Infantry on the South and 3d Battalion 152d Infantry on the West. The 1st Battalion 152d Infantry on the South was more of a holding force although it did make several minor contacts with enemy stragglers drifting back into the area of ZIG-ZAG Pass. Artillery support was available to all four attacking forces. Here the squeeze play was applied until the 38th Division was relieved by the 6th Division on 30 April.

Between 18 and 22 April 578 Japanese were killed, 379 found dead from artillery and mortar fires or from wounds and sickness and 13 Prisoners of War captured by the 3 Battalions on the East, West and North. Several log pillboxes made the advance of the 1st Battalion 149th Infantry very slow while the 2d Battalion 149th Infantry on the North pushed forward rapidly, gaining an average of 2000 yards per day. The beaten Japanese only opposed their movement when forced to do so.

Field Order # 14, Headquarters XI Corps, 19 April 1945 directed the 38th Infantry Division to exchange sectors with the 6th Infantry Division, the exchange to be completed by 5 May.

The 1st Battalion 149th Infantry on 22 April physically contacted patrols of the 3d Battalion 152d Infantry on the Northern slopes of MT PINATUBO. This same day the 2d Battalion 149th Infantry advanced 2000 yards South to make radio contact with the other two Battalions. Radio channels were then adjusted to enable a closer coordination of all attacks.

According to the plan of relief by the 6th Division the 152d Infantry less the 3d Battalion was relieved by the 1st Infantry less 1 Battalion on 23 April. The 3d Battalion 152d Infantry was attached to the 149th Infantry to continue the attack and mopping up in the MT PINATUBO area until relieved by the remaining Battalion of the 1st Infantry.

By this time, 24 April, the 1st Battalion 149th Infantry had gained a mountain saddle at the North foot of MT PINATUBO. The 2d Battalion 149th Infantry was about 2500 yards to their North. To the West of MT PINATUBO the 3d Battalion 152d Infantry was only 1800 yards from the 1st Battalion 149th Infantry. All Battalions were pushing patrols forward to make physical contact with each other. The enemy lightly opposed this pincer action from hastily constructed entrenchments and log pillboxes, but these were overcome as rapidly as the extremely difficult terrain would permit.

On 25 April each Battalion attacked with the mission to contact the other two. Physical contact was made between 1st and 2d Battalions 149th Infantry about 1200 and later in the day the 3d Battalion 152d Infantry reported their mission accomplished against moderate opposition. That afternoon the 3d Battalion 152d Infantry was ordered to assembly in the vicinity of POONBATO, mopping up and patrolling as they withdrew.

At 1715 on 26 April the 3d Battalion 1st Infantry relieved the 3d Battalion 152d Infantry who then moved, on the returning trucks, to the vicinity of MONTALBAN. With the 1st and 2d Battalions 149th Infantry scattered enemy opposition resulted in over 260 Japanese killed or found dead. These Battalions were to remain in the STOTSENBURG area to continue the mopping up until about 3 May. The 149th Infantry was to be the last Regiment relieved in the exchange of sectors with the 6th Division. They did, however, begin on 27 April to withdraw Companies into the base camp at BAMBAN.

On 28 April the 1st Battalion on the SACOBIA River at MT PINATUBO was relieved by a reinforced Platoon of Company F. Company F (-) assumed responsibility for the TIAONG area while the remainder of the 2d Battalion moved to the vicinity of BAMBAN.

From now until 30 May, the day on which commands of the two areas was to change, activity and enemy resistance in the STOTSENBURG Area was very light. There was conclusive evidence now that organized opposition by the Japanese forces in that area was completely broken. Nearly 8000 of them had been killed and approximately 75 captured since the 38th Division was ordered to destroy all enemy forces West of CLARK FIELD and FT STOTSENBURG.

On 30 April 1945 the 38th Infantry Division had killed 14,149 Japanese and taken 389 prisoners. This total includes the ZIG - ZAG Pass, the MARIVELES landing, the PILAR - BAGAC Road, the STOTSENBURG, the FORT DRUM and the CABALLO Operations, and the mopping up activities of all the Divisional units in the various provinces up to this time.

OPERATIONS EAST OF MANILA

On 20 April FO 15 XI Corps directed that the 38th Infantry Division relieve the 6th Infantry Division and the 172d Infantry of the 43d Infantry Division in place. These units were in contact with an estimated force of 5000 Japanese East of MANILA.

By agreement between the Divisions, the relief was effected by regiments and battalions, command passing when the major portion of each Division was in the new area. This was accomplished by 301800 April when the Commanding General 38th Infantry Division assumed command. For location of units see sketch map.

The 145th RCT of the 37th Infantry Division had been attached to the 6th Infantry Division for the assault on MT PACAWAGAN. Prior to 30 April, the 145th Infantry in a brilliantly executed and courageous assault, had taken most of the top and all of the Western slopes of MT PACAWAGAN. The Engineers of the 6th Infantry Division had constructed a trail up the Southwest shoulder of MT PACAWAGAN during the assault. This unit was detached from the 6th Infantry Division and attached to the 38th Infantry Division in place.

The 38th Infantry Division also took over other attachments of the 6th Infantry Division. At the outset 1 May the attachments were as follows:

```
38th Infantry Division
    Less:   149th Inf (Attached 6th Inf Div)
            3d Bn 152d Inf (Attached 6th Inf Div)
            1st Bn 151st Inf (Attached 6th Inf Div)
            Btry A, 138th FA Bn (Attached 6th Inf Div)

    Attached:  145th Inf Regt
               135th FA Bn (105mm How)
               80th FA Bn (155mm How)
               Co C 754th Tk Bn (Medium)
               Co's B and C (less 2d Plat) 32d Cml Bn
                 (4.2" mortars)
               3d Bn 63d Inf
               236th Cml Serv Plat
               Btry D 161st AAA Gun Bn

    In support:  4th SAP (Support Air Party)
```

For an understanding of the action that follows, a brief description of the terrain follows: With few exceptions, the hills West of the MARIQUINA – BOSO BOSO Rivers were open and covered with grass. There were a few scattered trees on the hill tops, while the draws were outlined with the usual bamboo and brush thickets. The slopes toward the MARIQUINA River and BOSO BOSO Rivers were steep and wooded. The gorges between PACAWAGAN, BINICAYAN and SUGAR LOAF were steep sided rock masses covered with thick brush and trees.

On the South the BOSO BOSO River runs through a wide plain, with banana trees and rice paddies in the bottom. Surrounding it are bare grassy hills, with some trees and bamboo along the bottom of the slopes.

East of the MARIQUINA River the mountains were heavily wooded, except for some slopes near the top of MT PURRO, the valley between PURRO and the ridge composing the Western bastion of MAPATAD, and the extreme Eastern peak of MAPATAD.

North of the MARIQUINA River, MT HAPONANG BANOY, MT PAMITINAN, and MT AYAAS were heavily wooded. MT ORO was grassy, with thickets in the draws. West of HAPONANG BANOY and MT ORO the foothills were covered with trees and thickets. Immediately North of HAPONANG BANOY, and in the saddle between it and AYAAS were very heavy dense bamboo thickets.

The larger streams ran through gorges with rocky precipitous sides.

The Japanese had a number of 150mm mortars (four were captured later in good order, and in addition base plates and bipods for several others), a large number of 90mm mortars, and an equally large number of field pieces in the 75mm gun, and 77mm mountain howitzer class. In addition fire from 25mm and 20mm automatic weapons and 37 or 47mm AT guns was received spasmodically.

The bare North and East slopes of MT PACAWAGAN were under direct observed fire from weapons emplaced North of the MARIQUINA River. Any movement, of even an individual, was promptly followed by observed fire.

The bare tops of all the ridges West of the MARIQUINA - BOSO BOSO Rivers were registered in with 150mm mortars, 90mm mortars and field pieces. The seizure of any ridge by our troops was immediately followed by intense mortar and artillery fire before the men could dig in.

This counterattack by fire persisted until most of the weapons were located and destroyed by our artillery. However up to 25 June the Japanese would drag a mountain howitzer or a mortar out of some cave and fire a few rounds on some unit.

This did not cause many casualties, but was annoying.

It is interesting to note that while a number of the 150mm mortars, field pieces and mountain guns were captured, no 90mm or 81mm mortars were found except one or two totally destroyed by our artillery or mortar fire. It is believed that the destruction or capture of the ammunition supplies for these two weapons was responsible for the cessation of fire from them, and that the Japanese hid or carried away the weapons.

The initial plan of operation follows: The 145th Infantry was to continue to advance, secure the high ground of MT PACAWAGAN, destroy all enemy found, and clear out all draws and caves in MT PACAWAGAN between the MARIQUINA River and the MANGO River. The 151st Infantry (less 1st Battalion) was to hold present positions and mop up within zone South of the MANGO River. The 152d Infantry (less 3d Battalion) was to clear draws, destroy caves and destroy all enemy found in zone; to protect the Division right (South) flank; to patrol to the North and East to determine enemy strength, locations and dispositions; and to prepare to attack North down WOODPECKER Ridge to Regimental Objective Hill. The 149th Infantry, 3d Battalion 152d Infantry, and 1st Battalion 151st Infantry were attached to the 6th Division in place. Upon relief they were to move to the new area of the 38th Division.

On 1 May the units of the 151st Infantry patrolled their zone with only minor contacts. The 1st Battalion 151st Infantry moved from CORREGIDOR to the 151st Infantry zone. In the 152d Infantry sector the 1st and 2d Battalions patrolled to the North with numerous contacts. It became apparent that the enemy was quite strong in the vicinity of WOODPECKER Ridge. Numerous machine guns and defensive positions were definitely located by the patrols, and artillery fire was placed on these positions.

The 145th Infantry continued its advance on the high ground of MT PACAWAGAN against light resistance and by late afternoon troops were on the crest of the Mountain.

Throughout the day enemy mortar and artillery fire harassed the troops in all sectors, concentrations being especially heavy on MT PACAWAGAN. Three air strikes were conducted on probable enemy artillery and mortar positions.

The 3d Battalion 149th Infantry arrived in the 149th Infantry assembly area.

At 0800, 2 May, the 1st and 2d Battalions 152d Infantry, after a heavy artillery preparation, launched a coordinated attack against WOODPECKER Ridge toward Regimental Objective

SUGAR LOAF
1000

MARIQUINA
500
RIVER

RETURNED 13 MAY
F Co.

RIVER

1000

500

TWIN PEAKS 2 —152
23 MAY 152
REGIMENTAL OBJECTIVE HILL
1000
152
22 MAY

24 MAY
152
23 MAY
152
152
11 MAY 152
152
WHITE HILL
4 MAY 152
4 MAY
152
3 MAY
152

2 —152
2 —152
4 MAY
2 —152

WOODPECKER
152
RIDGE
18 MAY 152
B Co.
6 MAY

2 MAY

1000

1500

2 — 152

3 — 152

1 — 152

1000

MT. BAYTANGAN

3 ⊠ 152

2 ⊠ 152   1 ⊠ 152

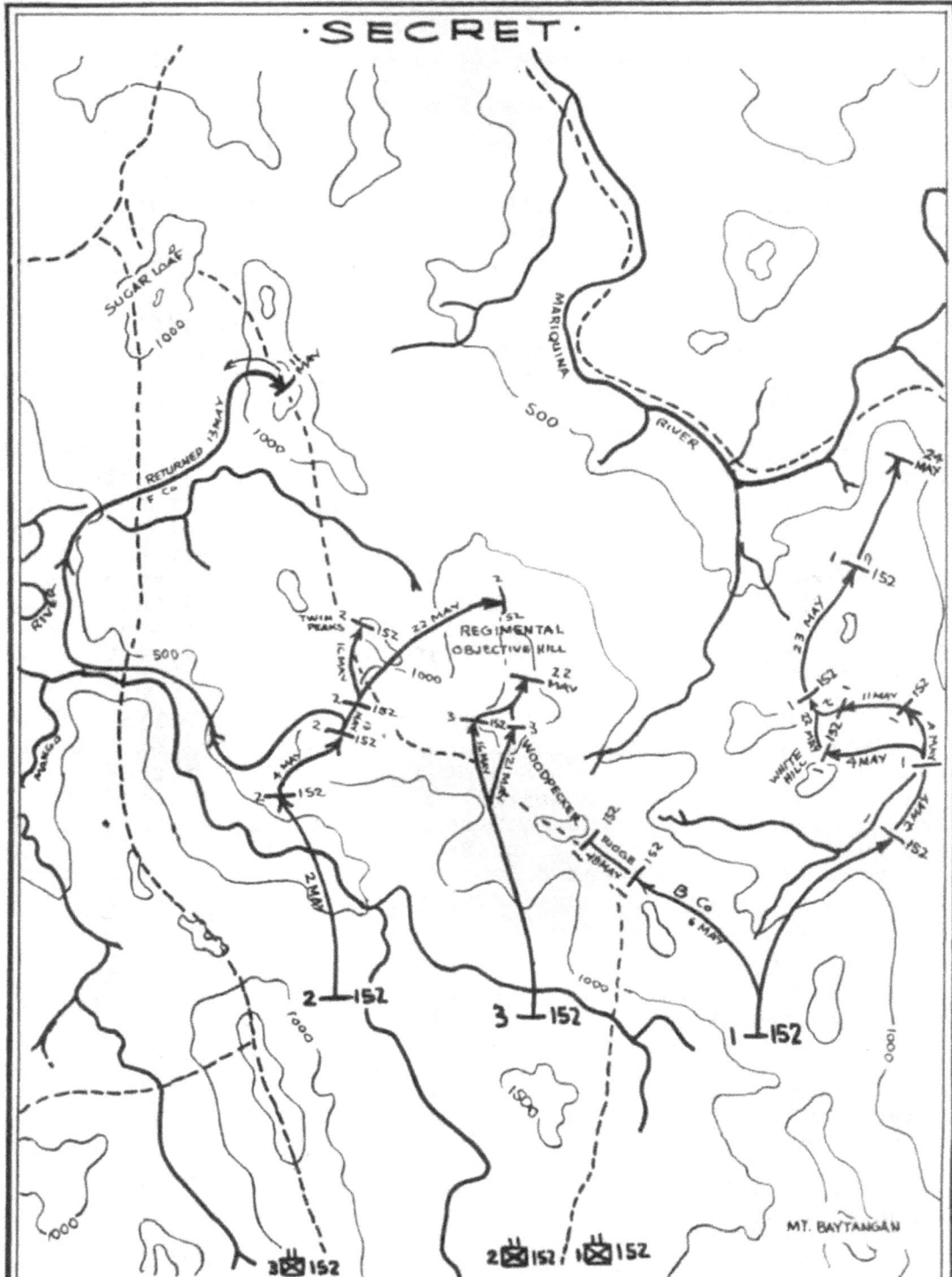

WOODPECKER   RIDGE
OPERATIONS OF 152nd INF   2-24 MAY 1945
SCALE   1:25,000

Hill. The 1st Battalion encountered heavy resistance on the
right of the Regimental sector consisting of very effective
mortar, machine gun, and rifle fire from well dug-in positions.
Late in the afternoon a general advance of approximately 500
yards had been made after a period of bitter fighting. Elements
of the 2d Battalion made a limited advance on the left of the
1st Battalion to a position on left flank of WOODPECKER Ridge,
meeting heavy resistance throughout the sector. Tanks of
Company C 754th Tank Battalion supported the attack of both
Battalions with direct fire on caves and emplacements, aiding
greatly the advance of the assault troops. However, the movement of the tanks forward was limited by a huge tank trap on
the South slope of WOODPECKER Ridge. One tank was knocked out
during the assault. A total of 73 Japanese were killed in the
152d Infantry sector during the day.

In the numerous caves and draws of the MT PACAWAGAN area
the 145th Infantry found over 100 dead Japanese killed by our
artillery fire. To supply the troops on the mountain proved
to be very difficult. The trail to the top was extremely
steep and all rations, water and supplies had to be hauled up
by tractor and trailer. The 113th Engineers did a remarkable
piece of work in maintaining and improving this trail throughout the operations in this sector.

On 3 May the 1st Battalion 152d Infantry reorganized,
strengthened positions, and brought up ammunition and supplies
in preparation for an attack 4 May. The 2d Battalion 152d
Infantry patrolled to the North locating enemy positions with
possible routes of approach for the next days attack. Throughout the day heavy artillery concentrations were laid on
possible enemy positions and six air strikes were made on areas
approximately 1000 yards to the front of the assault troops.
The 150th Field Artillery Battalion was released from XI Corps
Artillery and rejoined the Division at SAN MATEO on 3 May.

On this day changes were made in the positions of the
Battalions. The 1st Battalion 151st Infantry relieved the 1st
Battalion 145th Infantry in place, the 2d Battalion 151st
Infantry was attached to the 152d Infantry in place, the 1st
Battalion 149th Infantry joined the 3d Battalion 149th Infantry
in Division reserve, and the 3d Battalion 152d Infantry relieved
the 172d Infantry in place on the South flank.

On 4 May the 1st and 2d Battalions of the 152d Infantry
began their attack to the North to secure the high ground of
Regimental Objective Hill. The 1st Battalion, advancing on
the right of the Regimental sector to the Northwest, met heavy
enemy resistance which consisted of an abundance of mutually
supporting automatic weapons and mortars covering the numerous

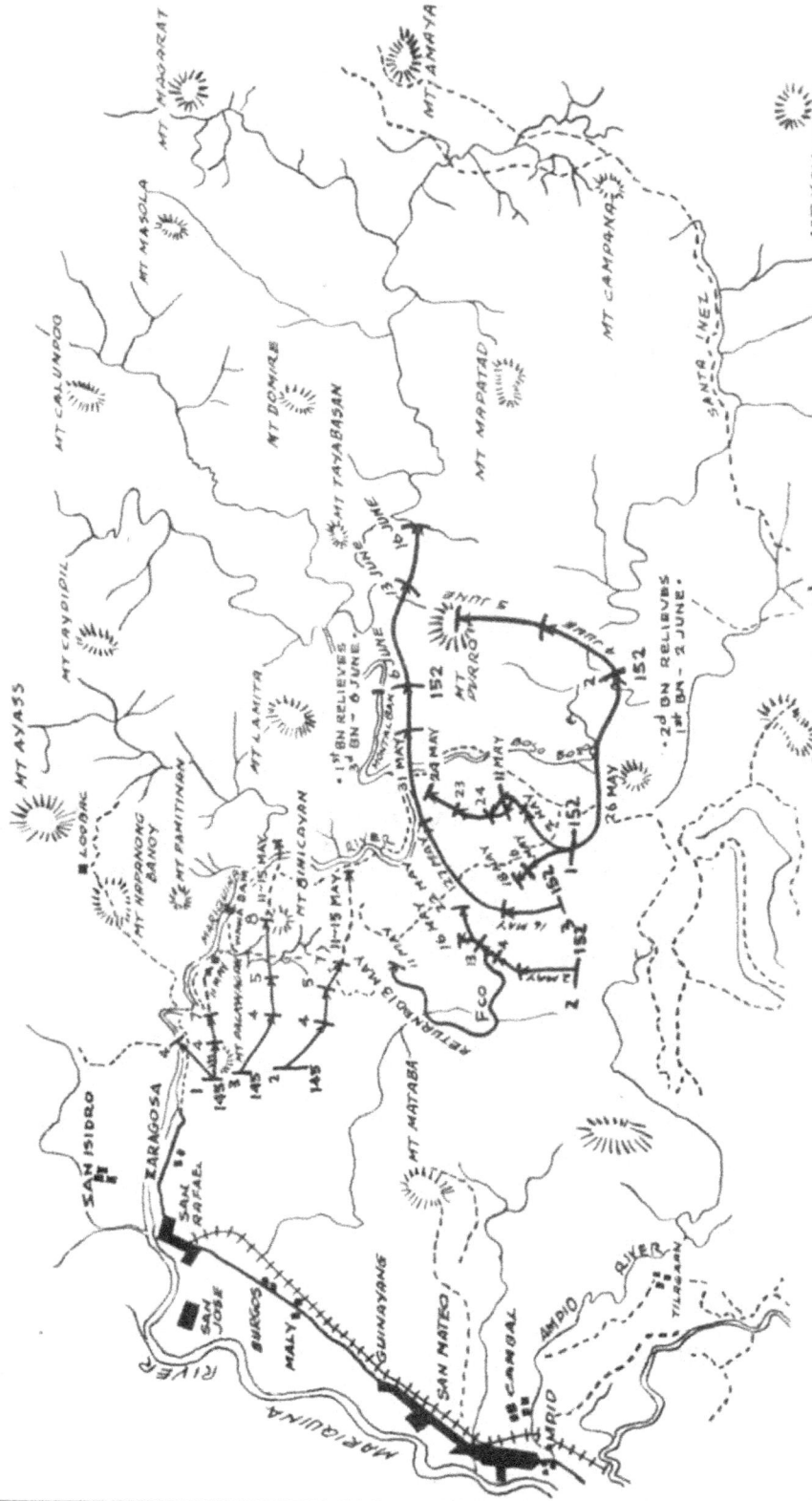

ACTION OF 145TH INF & 152d INF
FROM 1 MAY TO 16 JUNE 1945

SCALE: 1:100,000

· SECRET ·

152d INFANTRY

1ST BN DIV RES	1 JUNE
2d BN DIV RES	27 MAY
3d BN DIV RES	6 JUNE

hills, draws and ridges in the sector. During the morning, elements of the 1st Battalion repulsed a strong enemy counter-attack in the vicinity of the South slope of Regimental Objective Hill, and advanced to a position on the South slope of White Hill. The 2d Battalion advanced in the left of the Regimental sector against heavy machine gun and rifle fire to a position Southeast of TWIN PEAKS, a gain of from 400 to 600 yards. A total of 66 Japanese were killed during this advance.

The 145th Infantry on the North advanced with 3 Battalions abreast at 0500 with the mission of securing the MARIQUINA River line in its sector. The 1st Battalion on the left initially met small arms fire and then ran into heavy resistance from enemy positions tunneled into MT PACAWAGAN, after advancing about 50 yards down the East slope toward WAWA. The 3d Battalion advancing in the center, met no resistance, but the extremely difficult terrain and the fact that the 1st Battalion was held up on its left flank prevented any movement further than the forward elements of the 1st Battalion. The 2d Battalion, on the right, advanced against slight resistance until an enemy strong point was encountered consisting of 5 pillboxes containing a number of heavy and light machine guns. An attempt to flank this position was halted because the difficult terrain prevented completion of the movement by darkness. Although the assaulting troops were unable to advance a great distance they did account for 81 Japanese killed.

On 5 May the 152d Infantry reorganized after the previous days attack, and mopped up the numerous draws in their sector, sealing and blowing many caves.

In the 145th Infantry sector the 1st Battalion on the left made slight gains down the East slope of MT PACAWAGAN against heavy enemy resistance eminating from the tunneled-in positions in the side of the mountain. The 3d Battalion, on the right of the 1st Battalion, made considerable advance to the East against moderate resistance to positions near the Southwest base of MT BINICAYAN. The 2d Battalion on the right advanced to the Southeast against light resistance and at 1500 visual contact was made between Company G 145th Infantry and a patrol from Company F 151st Infantry on the right flank.

Battery D 161st AAA Gun Battalion was detached from Division Artillery and attached to the 152d Infantry.

On 6 May the action in the 152d Infantry zone consisted of a number of local offensive actions against enemy strong points in the immediate vicinity. Elements of Company C 754th Tank Battalion, supporting the 1st Battalion 152d Infantry destroyed 3 enemy machine gun positions in vicinity of WOOD-

PECKER Ridge. The 2d Battalion 151st Infantry attached to the 152d Infantry patrolled MT MATABA with no contacts.

The 145th Infantry continued its advance to secure the MARIQUINA River line. Elements of the 2d Battalion 145th Infantry reached SUGAR LOAF Hill. Strong enemy resistance was encountered at this point and the hill was not secured at the close of the day. The 1st Battalion 145th Infantry was gradually cleaning out the tunneled-in positions on the East slope of PACAWAGAN. Patrols from the 3d Battalion 145th Infantry approaching the top of BINICAYAN reported approximately 40 Japanese in caves along the crest of the mountain. The 3d Battalion 149th Infantry was attached to the 145th Infantry and occupied positions formerly held by 145th Infantry on MT PACAWAGAN.

Four air strikes were conducted during the period along the MARIQUINA River in the MT PURRO area and two strikes were made in the MT ORO - PURAY River area.

Battery B 198th AAA AW Battalion was attached to the Division.

On 7 May the 152d Infantry attacked at 1050 after an air strike and heavy artillery and mortar preparations. The 1st Battalion on the right attacked to the Northwest toward WOODPECKER Ridge while the 2d Battalion attacked North to TWIN PEAKS. Immediately after the jump-off, heavy resistance from mortars and machine guns was received which continued for the remainder of the day. All rifle companies were actively employed in working out the numerous draws and gaining footholds on the many well defended knolls. All supporting weapons, including a Platoon of Company C 754th Tank Battalion and the .50 caliber machine guns of 2d Platoon Battery B 198th AAA AW Battalion, were used to the maximum in an attempt to drive the enemy from his strong points. All units showed gains of from 200 to 300 yards after a day of bitter fighting.

The 1st Battalion 145th Infantry, advancing toward WAWA, continued cleaning out the caves and dug-in positions on the East slope of PACAWAGAN. The 3d Battalion 145th Infantry remained in position, operating patrols in vicinity of MT BINICAYAN in preparation for an attack on BINICAYAN the following day. The 2d Battalion 145th Infantry continued its attack to the Southeast over extremely difficult terrain and reached the high ground of SUGAR LOAF HILL.

The 2d Battalion 149th Infantry joined the 1st Battalion 149th Infantry in Division reserve.

The 152d Infantry on 8 May patrolled locally, feeling out approaches into enemy positions. Elements of the 1st Battalion cleaned out local draws, in many instances employing flame throwers and demolition teams.

After a heavy mortar and artillery preparation the 3d Battalion 145th Infantry attacked the Southern slopes of MT BINICAYAN. Difficult terrain and enemy machine gun fire made the advance slow, and at the close of the day two companies were part of the way up the slope of the mountain.

At 1330, 9 May, the 1st Battalion 152d Infantry attacked to the Northwest. One company gained a foothold on White Hill against moderate resistance where they held and sent patrols to the North. The 2d Battalion in its previous advances to the North had suffered so many casualties in attempting to secure TWIN PEAKS, that it was decided to send a company around to the left of it in an enveloping movement. With Company E holding its present position, Company F advanced to the left of TWIN PEAKS against moderate resistance to a point Northeast of TWIN PEAKS.

The 1st Battalion 145th Infantry continued cleaning out enemy positions on the North and Northeast slopes of MT PACAWAGAN. The 2d Battalion mopped up against scattered resistance in the SUGAR LOAF area. The 3d Battalion continued its attack up the South and East slopes of BINICAYAN at 0830, following an artillery, mortar, M7 and 40mm AAA preparation. At 1200 Company K gained the shoulder of the mountain from the South slope and the company dug in on the mountain for the night.

The 3d Battalion 149th Infantry patrolled over the entire Eastern arm of MT PACAWAGAN.

On 10 May the 1st Battalion 152d Infantry continued cleaning out enemy positions on the East slope of White Hill. Enemy positions proved to be well located on the slopes of draws surrounding the high ground. Three machine guns were destroyed during the period in the 2d Battalion area. Company F 152d Infantry followed by Company F 151st Infantry continued to advance against moderate resistance in its enveloping movement around the regimental left flank.

In the 145th Infantry area the 1st Battalion continued its mission of eliminating enemy strong points on North and Northeast slopes of PACAWAGAN. Patrols worked down to the WAWA area and reported no contacts. The remainder of the regiment patrolled local areas.

During the period from 11 May to 15 May inclusive the
1st and 2d Battalions 152d Infantry continued aggressive
patrolling and probing of the well organized area facing them
in an attempt to find possible approaches for an attack on 16
May. The enemy terrain in this sector consisted of a series of
barren hills, studded with dug-in, well camouflaged machine
gun positions, and accompanying entrenchments for riflemen.
Excellent fields of fire and the lack of concealment for
assaulting troops made each hill a major obstacle in itself.
These hills were mutually supporting and attempts to isolate
and occupy one met effective fire from those on the flanks and
front.

The shortage of 81mm mortar ammunition and the limited
amounts of artillery ammunition did not permit the neutralizing
of adjacent hills long enough to allow troops to dig in when
a hill was taken.

The 3d Battalion 152d Infantry was relieved in the NEW
BOSO BOSO area by the 2d Battalion 151st Infantry. Thus, on
16 May, the regiment was able to attack with three Battalions.

During the night 13-14 May a determined infiltration was
made on a platoon perimeter of Anti-tank Company 152d Infantry
in the Southeast part of the area by a sizeable enemy force.
Five Japanese officers and numerous men were killed in this
banzai attack.

Positions of the 2d Battalion 151st Infantry were taken
over by elements of the 2d Battalion 152d Infantry.

The 1st Battalion 145th Infantry continued to wipe out
the remaining enemy resistance on the Northeast slope of MT
PACAWAGAN. Patrols reached the town of WAWA reporting
numerous Japanese trucks, equipment, and supplies in the area.
No contact with the enemy was made but enemy positions were
observed on the heights North of the river. The 2d and 3rd
Battalions 145th Infantry patrolled East toward MARIQUINA River
reporting minor contacts.

The 1st Battalion 151st Infantry, during this period,
patrolled the MT ORO-TANOG River and PURAY River areas with
nil contact.

At 1300 16 May the 152d Infantry attacked with three
Battalions. Operations were supported by artillery, tanks,
40mm and 90mm AAA units, and 4.2 chemical mortars. Resistance
was extremely stubborn and heavy, and intense fighting resulted
throughout the afternoon. Grazing machine gun fire and
exceptionally accurate mortar fire along the entire front made

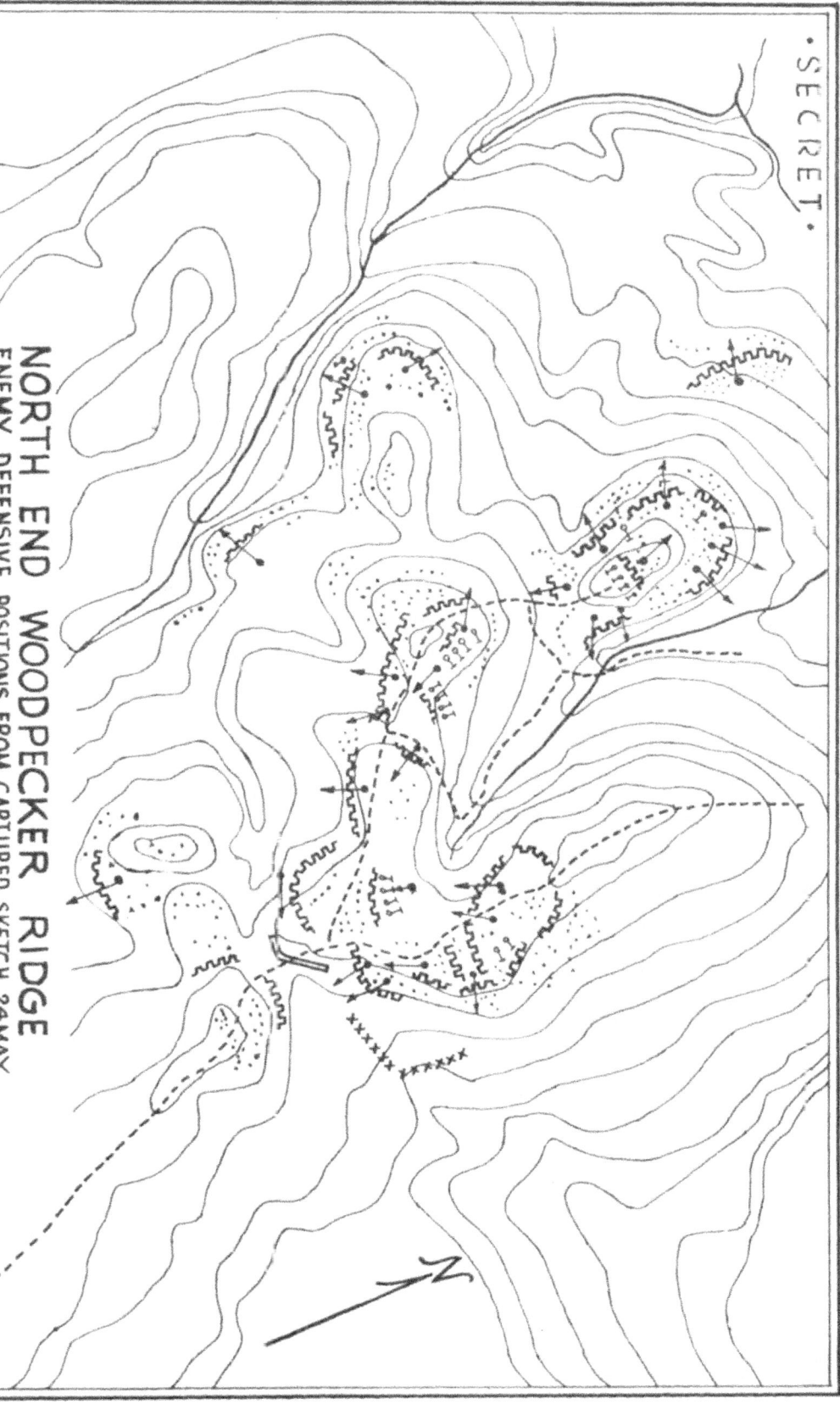

NORTH END WOODPECKER RIDGE
ENEMY DEFENSIVE POSITIONS, FROM CAPTURED SKETCH 24 MAY
NOTE: THIS PROVED TO BE REMARKABLY ACCURATE
SCALE 1:12,500

advances slow and very costly. On the left the 2d Battalion advanced and seized the West side of TWIN PEAKS after an extremely stiff fight. The 3rd Battalion in the center, fought its way to the Military Crest of WOODPECKER Ridge where mortar and machine gun cross fire caused the loss of 3 company commanders, 4 other officers, and many men. This caused them to dig in on the West slope of the ridge to reorganize. The 1st Battalion on the right made slow progress in the WOODPECKER Ridge area against the cross fire of numerous machine guns. Assault detachments knocked out many machine gun emplacements. At the close of the day the 152d Infantry had accounted for 210 dead Japanese.

In many instances the enemy attempted to infiltrate through the positions which the 152d Infantry had gained. Some of these attempts were practically full-scale attacks but in every case the enemy was repulsed, losing many men and much equipment. Small "Banzai" charges were made during the day as well as at night but these attacks proved disastrous to the enemy forces.

In the 145th Infantry sector the 1st and 3rd Battalions conducted aggressive patrolling. The 2d Battalion 145th Infantry was relieved by the 2d Battalion 149th Infantry.

In the period from 17 to 19 May inclusive the 152d Infantry continued to eliminate enemy strong points on TWIN PEAKS, WOODPECKER Ridge and WHITE HILL. Numerous caves in the area were closed and neutralized by assault detachments. Tanks of Company C 754th Tank Battalion knocked out many enemy emplacements by direct fire.

On 18 May the 149th Infantry relieved the 145th Infantry in the MT PACAWAGAN-MT BINICAYAN area. 145th Infantry went into Division reserve.

The 1st Battalion 151st Infantry maintained position 4000 yards North of MONTALBAN and sent patrols to TANOG-PURAY River and MT ORO areas with no contacts.

On 20 and 21 May the 2d Battalion 152d Infantry working around the North side of TWIN PEAKS met heavy resistance from enemy machine gun fire. The 3d Battalion still advancing in the Regimental Objective Hill area closed many caves and knocked out numerous enemy positions. A road was pushed well forward in the 3d Battalion area and tanks were brought up with excellent results. The 152d Infantry after 10 days of bitter fighting against a strong enemy force seemed to be cracking the enemy's defenses throughout the zone. During these 2 days of heavy fighting the regiment killed 250 Japanese

ACTION OF 149TH INF & 151st INF

FROM 19 MAY TO 26 JUNE 1945

SCALE: 1:100,000

MARIQUINA RIVER

and found 80 dead.

The assault troops of the 152d Infantry were greatly
aided by the multiple 50 caliber M-51 half tracks. They
provided an excellent base of fire for maneuvering elements
of the infantry and in many instances the half tracks were
actually ahead of the front line troops. They proved an
excellent means of cleaning out the many draws throughout
the area.

The 1st Battalion 151st Infantry patrolled aggressively
in the MT ORO-TANOG River-PURAY River area with minor contact.
On 21 May the 3d Battalion 151st Infantry attacked in the area
between the MARIQUINA and PURAY Rivers after a very heavy and
effective NaPalm air strike. A total of 168 planes dropped
336 x 165 gallon NaPalm bombs on targets Northwest of HAPONANG
BANOY. Enemy artillery, mortars, trenches, caves and supply
dumps were hit during the very effective strike and fires
continued to burn several minutes after the last wave of planes
left. This strike greatly helped the 3d Battalion 151st Infantry take its initial objectives, HILLS BLUE 1 and RED 1.

During the night of 20-21 May the enemy launched a
strong attack supported by machine gun and mortar fire against
elements of the 2d Battalion 151st Infantry in the NEW BOSO BOSO
area. The enemy force was estimated to be 60-100 strong and
was repulsed with heavy losses.

A flamethrower Detachment 13th Armored Group was attached
to the Division. This consisted of three flame throwing tanks.

On 22 May all Battalions of the 152d Infantry supported
by medium and flamethrower tanks, 40mm, 90mm, 50 caliber AAA,
and 4.2" mortars, in addition to normal support weapons,
advanced in a well coordinated attack. The 1st Battalion on the
right advanced against strong resistance on the North slope of
White Hill. The 2d Battalion blew many caves and cleaned out
the numerous draws in the TWIN PEAKS area. The 3d Battalion
made the main effort which broke the interlocking fires and
mutually supporting weapons on WOODPECKER Ridge. At the close
of the day the American flag was flying on REGIMENTAL OBJECTIVE
HILL.

Throughout the operation in the REGIMENTAL HILL-WOODPECKER
Ridge area the movement of troops could be viewed by the enemy
who had positions on the high ground of MT PURRO. To minimize
the advantage held by the enemy, the 4.2" chemical mortars of
Company B 82d Chemical Battalion were used extensively to
screen the movement of the troops. The smoke screen from the
white phosphorous shells proved to be very effective and greatly

57mm AT gun firing in support of 1st Battalion
152d Infantry in attack on WOODPECKER Ridge.

Artillery tractor hauling supplies up MT PACAWAGAN. All
supplies and vehicles had to be hauled up in this manner.

Terrain over which the advance was made by 152d Infantry
toward WOODPECKER Ridge. Road bulldozed under fire by
113th Engineers enabled tanks to advance to positions to
support the attack 22 May of the 152d Infantry.

aided the 152d Infantry in securing its objective in this area.

Flamethrower tanks aided greatly in the days advance. Numerous caves occupied by the enemy which could not be reached by the assault troops were burned out by the tanks. One ridge was successfully cleared by an assault team composed of a bulldozer followed and covered by a medium tank, followed by flame throwing tank, followed by a platoon of infantry. The bulldozer scraped a road on the knife edged ridge for the tanks to follow, Japanese riflemen being driven to cover by tank and mortar fire. When the flame thrower opened up, the Japanese started running in all directions, and over thirty were killed in as many seconds.

In the 149th Infantry sector a Japanese OP was observed on MT PAMITINAN and was destroyed by direct fire from the Cannon Company.

Battery D, 198th AAA Battalion and Company D 754th Tank Battalion were attached to 38th Division.

On 24 May the 2d Battalion 149th Infantry began mopping up enemy positions on the Northeast slope of MT BINICAYAN.

This position, which had resisted attack for three weeks, was found to be an OP, with telephones and wire leading down to the MARIQUINA River. The top of the hill could only be approached from the South by climbing to the top of a fifteen foot stone ledge. The top of this ledge was as flat and smooth as a table and was about thirty yards across. Beyond this was a jumble of rocks and brush rising twenty to thirty feet and extending North to the cliff overlooking WAWA Dam.

Machine guns and rifle pits dug in the soft limestone swept this open ledge, while the vertical cliffs on the East and West prevented flanking movement.

Surprise fire from artillery, SPM's, 57 AT guns, 50 Cal MG's and mortars decimated the defenders until the position was finally assaulted and taken by Company G 149th Infantry. 79 Japanese were killed or found dead in this position.

The 1st Battalion 151st Infantry advanced against moderate resistance and reduced enemy caves and pillboxes on the North slope of Blue 2. The 3d Battalion advancing to the North to join the 1st Battalion met moderate resistance.

The 1st Battalion 152d Infantry advanced to the high ground North of the junction of the BOSO BOSO - MARIQUINA

Mopping up on WOODPECKER Ridge

Rivers and immediately patrols were sent to the junction.
The 2d and 3d Battalions sent patrols to the MARIQUINA River.
Many caves were demolished and much enemy equipment found in
the deserted enemy positions.

The Japanese OP and machine gun nest of REGIMENTAL
OBJECTIVE HILL, which had withstood continued bombardment by
our artillery and mortars, was found to be Built between
several very large boulders. Access was gained by ladders in
a vertical shaft twenty feet deep, connecting with a large
cave over fifty feet in length. This cave in turn was connected by a shell proof cut and cover trench to a second cave
thirty feet lower down the hill. From the telephones, wires
and other equipment found in the rooms of these caves, it was
apparently an important installation.

In a coordinated movement of the 1st and 3d Battalions,
the 151st Infantry on 25 May secured the high ground 800
yards East of Blue 2. The 1st Battalion moved in from the
North advancing against slight resistance. The 3d Battalion
from the South advanced Northeast against moderate resistance
and joined with the 1st Battalion.

The 152d Infantry secured the MARIQUINA River line in
its zone and neutralized the remaining organized resistance.
A patrol from the 2d Battalion which crossed the MARIQUINA
River destroyed much abandoned enemy equipment. As the 152d
Infantry reached the river line it became apparent that our
artillery had done much to defeat the enemy in this area.
Hundreds of dead Japanese had been found killed by artillery
fire.

Battery C 227th Searchlight Battalion (less 1 Platoon)
was attached 38th Division.

On 26 May a reinforced Platoon from 1st Battalion 149th
Infantry reached WAWA, advancing against fire from a Japanese
25mm gun. The Platoon remained at WAWA during the night. The
2d Battalion 149th Infantry cleaning out isolated enemy
positions on BINICAYAN, received small arms and machine gun
fire from the Northeast corner of the mountain.

Elements of the 1st Battalion 151st Infantry continued
mopping up on Hill Blue 3. One Company and the Battalion
Assault Team worked toward MT HAPONANG BANOY to a position
on the Southwest slope of the mountain against light resistance.
The 3d Battalion met slight resistance on the high ground
800 yards East of Hill Blue 2.

In the 152d Infantry sector the 1st and 3d Battalions moved into defensive positions to hold and secure the MARIQUINA-BOSO BOSO River line. The 2d Battalion was withdrawn and sent to the Division rear area.

During the period 27-28 May elements of the 1st Battalion 149th Infantry supported by medium tanks and 2 flame thrower tanks attacked and captured WAWA Dam. On 27 May our attacking troops were fired on from the dam but on 28 May the attacking forces found the enemy position at the dam abandoned. The 2d Battalion 149th Infantry sent a reinforced Company across the MARIQUINA River with the mission of advancing to MT LAMITA. Other elements of the Battalion cleaned out the last pocket of resistance on the Northeast slope of MT BINICAYAN.

The 151st Infantry continued its advance toward HAPONANG BANOY, the 1st Battalion advancing from the North and the 3d Battalion from the Southwest. Although only light resistance was encountered the advance was slow because of the very difficult terrain.

Company L (Reinforced) of the 3d Battalion 152d Infantry started an advance toward PURRO.

At 1200 27 May the 145th Infantry was detached from the 38th Division.

From 29 to 31 May the 2d Battalion 149th Infantry advanced toward MT. LAMITA against moderate resistance. Movement was slow due to ruggedness of terrain and the problem of resupply. On 31 May the 3d Battalion 149th Infantry came out of Division reserve and went into position on the left (North) of the 2d Battalion with the mission of advanceing to MT LAMITA.

The 1st Battalion 151st Infantry advancing from the North to HAPONANG BANOY, met stiff resistance on 30 May. The enemy was gradually knocked out and the Battalion proceeded to look for a route up to the crest of the mountain. The 3d Battalion 151st Infantry advancing from the South ran into numerous enemy positions in the area East of PAMITINAN which were neutralized as the Battalion advanced.

Elements of the 3d Battalion 152d Infantry in their advance toward the top of MT PURRO met stiff enemy resistance from the high ground 800 yards East of the junction of the BOSO BOSO - MARIQUINA Rivers. Artillery fire was placed on the enemy position after which Company K moved in and secured the high ground.

During the period of 1 June to 4 June the 2d Battalion

149th Infantry in its advance toward MT LAMITA met extremely heavy resistance from the high ground 600 yards Northwest of the junction of the MONTALBAN - BOSO BOSO Rivers. For two days the Battalion was held up by the enemy strong point. Finally a flanking movement by elements of the Battalion proved successful and the high ground was taken. This was a strong, well organized, and dug-in position. Many dead Japanese were found killed by Artillery, mortar, and small arms fire. The 3d Battalion 149th Infantry reached MT LAMITA after numerous contacts with enemy strong points. One by one these were eliminated until the top of MT LAMITA was reached. Here a little sniper fire was encountered but there was no organized resistance.

On 1 June the Intelligence and Reconnaissance Platoon 151st Infantry reached the top of MT ORO making minor contacts enroute. Several enemy defensive positions were located but the Japanese had apparently fled.

In the 151st Infantry sector the 1st Battalion continued its attack Southwest along the East side of HAPONANG BANOY until 3 June when it was relieved by the 1st Battalion 169th Infantry.

From air observers and Prisoners of War reports, it now became apparent that the Japanese were withdrawing to the East. It was decided to make a strong drive from the NEW BOSO BOSO area towards MT MAPATAD and MT CAMPANA. To release the 151st Infantry for this mission XI Corps directed the 43d Infantry Division to take over the sector North of MT PACAWAGAN. In conjunction with this drive, the 112th Cavalry RCT on the South was to advance North to SANTA INEZ.

The 2d Battalion 152d Infantry started an advance up the Southern slopes of MT PURRO against light resistance but advance was extremely slow due to the many bamboo thickets encountered. The 3d Battalion 152d Infantry advancing up the Northwest slope of PURRO met heavy automatic fire from an enemy position on the West slope of the mountain.

On 3 May the 2d Battalion 151st Infantry was relieved of attachment to the 152d Infantry and returned to control of 151st Infantry. Its positions in the NEW BOSO BOSO area were taken over by elements of the 2d Provisional Regiment ECLGA. On 4 May the 3d Battalion 151st Infantry was relieved in place by elements of the 169th Infantry.

The 2d Battalion 149th Infantry continued to run into stubborn enemy resistance on the Southwest slope of MT LAMITA during 5-6 June. During their advance 40 Japanese, apparently

killed by artillery, were found. The 3d Battalion advanced
Northeast and secured the highest ground on MT COMPANANAN
with only minor contact.

On 6 June Company G 152d Infantry reached the highest
peak on MT PURRO after having advanced 2500 yards in 2 days
over thick mountain terrain. Very little opposition was encountered due to the constant well placed artillery fire on
the enemy positions on PURRO. The 3d Battalion 152d Infantry
was relieved by the 1st Battalion 152d Infantry and moved to
Division Rear area. During the period the 151st Infantry was
in Division Reserve preparing for an attack in the NEW BOSO
BOSO area toward MT MAPATAD.

On 7 June the 1st Battalion 149th Infantry made slight
gains in its advance to the junction of the MONTALBAN -
TAYABASAN Rivers. The 2d Battalion 149th Infantry advancing
Northeast toward MT LAMITA destroyed an enemy strong point
which had held up its advance for several days.

At 0925, 7 June a total of 132 planes conducted a very
heavy and effective NaPalm strike in the MT MAPATAD area.
The target area was virtually covered with NaPalm and fragmentation bombs. Observers considered this the finest air
strike in support of ground troops in many months. Immediately
following the air strike the 1st Battalion 151st Infantry
launched its attack toward MT MAPATAD against slight resistance and at the close of the day the Battalion had gained the
high ground 2000 yards directly West of MT MAPATAD. At 1200
the 3d Battalion 151st Infantry started to move East along the
SANTA INEZ Trail with the mission of advancing to MT MAPATAD
from the South. The 2d Battalion 151st Infantry remained in
Regimental Reserve.

Company G 152d Infantry, which on the previous day had
reached the top of MT PURRO, patrolled the sector and met only
minor resistance.

Prior to 7 June the 113th Engineer Combat Battalion built
a dirt trail from MT BAYTANGAN to MT YABANG. Starting 7 June
this trail was improved into a two way gravel road, and an
extension started East toward the SANTA INEZ Trail. This was
graded and graveled to the BOSO BOSO River, and graded and
partially graveled East for nearly five miles. This enabled
the operations in this sector to be conducted rapidly.

On 8 and 9 June the 1st Battalion 149th Infantry continued its advance toward the junction of the MONTALBAN and
TAYABASAN Rivers against moderate resistance, clearing the
draws on both sides of its route. Rugged terrain covered with

bamboo made movement forward difficult in this sector. The 3d Battalion 149th Infantry sent patrols to MT CAYPIPILI and MT COMPANANAN with minor contacts. The 2d Battalion 152d Infantry went into Regimental Reserve.

The 1st Battalion 151st Infantry held its position and sent patrols North to the TAYABASAN River. Movement was slow because supplies were now being dropped from C-47's and some time was needed to consolidate the supplies following the drop. The 3d Battalion 151st Infantry advanced against moderate resistance to the South slope of MT MAPATAD. The 3d Battalion 151st Infantry was also being resupplied by C-47 air drop.

During 10-11 June the 1st Battalion 149th Infantry reached the junction of the MONTALBAN - TAYABASAN and SAPA BUTE BUTE Rivers and Company A seized MT TAYABASAN against slight resistance.

In the 151st Infantry sector Company B moved up the West slope of MT MAPATAD against no opposition. The 3d Battalion 151st Infantry advancing up the South slope of MT MAPATAD ran into considerable enemy machine gun and mortar fire. Numerous Japanese were killed and many found dead, apparently killed by the constant barrages of the Division Artillery.

Throughout the period the 38th Cavalry Reconnaissance Troop patrolled extensively along the SANTA INEZ Trail meeting and killing numerous enemy personnel.

During the period 12-17 June inclusive the 1st Battalion 149th Infantry advanced approximately 5000 yards up the SAPA BUTE BUTE River from the junction of the MONTALBAN, TAYABASAN and SAPA BUTE BUTE Rivers. Many small pockets of enemy resistance were encountered each day during the advance and it became apparent that the enemy was fighting a delaying action. Numerous dead Japanese were found along the river killed by artillery fire. The 3d Battalion 149th Infantry having secured MT COMPANANAN began an advance toward MT CAYPIPILI. Upon reaching the South slope of the mountain the advance of the Battalion was halted by very heavy enemy fire. The enemy's automatic weapons were placed so that they had grazing fire down all the approaches to the top of the mountain. Following several artillery concentrations the Battalion attacked these enemy strong points and wiped them out one by one. On 16 June the Battalion reached the crest of MT CAYPIPILI finding a number of dead Japanese and abandoned enemy strong points.

The 2d Battalion 149th Infantry continued in Regimental Reserve.

The 151st Infantry continued its attack on MT MAPATAD during 12-17 June. The 3d Battalion advancing from the South, met heavy resistance, consisting of machine gun, mortar and small arms fire from well dug-in enemy positions in the side of the mountain. Many well fortified caves were encountered which had to be eliminated by bazooka fire and demolitions. Advance was further impeded by the heavy foliage and sheer cliffs along the side of MT MAPATAD. The objective was taken after a week of hard fighting with Companies K and I attacking up the South slope and Company L hitting the enemy's flank from the East. Upon reaching the top of the mountain a number of enemy dead were found as well as considerable equipment. The 1st Battalion 151st Infantry which initially started to advance on MAPATAD from the West met several pockets of enemy resistance in the KOMEI PLAINS between MT PURRO and MT MAPATAD. Company B advancing on MT MAPATAD from the West, ran into an enemy pocket on the West peak. Assisted by direct fire from 90mm and 40mm AA weapons, this position was destroyed after a days hard fighting. Since the 3d Battalion had secured MT MAPATAD the 1st Battalion patrolled extensively in the KOMEI PLAINS throughout the period. On 12 June the 2d Battalion came out of Regimental Reserve. Initially Company F and Company G assisted the 1st Battalion and 3d Battalion in their attack on MT MAPATAD while Company E advanced East along the SANTA INEZ Trail.

The 152d Infantry during this period ran into an extremely strong enemy position on the Northwest slope of PURRO. During the course of fighting in this sector over 150 Japanese were killed and several enemy weapons were captured.

The 38th Cavalry Reconnaissance Troop patrolled the area South of the SANTA INEZ Trail and found more than 200 dead Japanese. Many small enemy pockets were encountered and were wiped out by the Troop.

All anti-aircraft units aided considerably the infantry troops by their fire on MT PAYACIN, MT DOMIRE, MT CAYPIPILI, and MT MATABA. The front-line troops reported that a number of caves and fortifications had been knocked out and many enemy killed by the fire from these weapons.

Illumination supplied by Battery C 227th Searchlight Battalion was also a valuable aid to troops in their nightly perimeters. A number of Japanese were killed during the hours of darkness because the night infiltration tactics of the enemy were hampered by the illumination of the searchlights. The troops also reported the men were able to obtain more rest at night because they knew the men on guard could detect any attempt at infiltration.

On 18 June Field Order #29 Headquarters 38th Division directed that:

The 149th Infantry secure MT DOMIRE, clean out the MONTALBAN River Valley and destroy all enemy found.

The 151st Infantry secure MT MASOLA, assist the 149th Infantry on MT DOMIRE and destroy all enemy found.

The 152d Infantry upon relief by the 151st Infantry to move to Division Reserve in the vicinity of BAYANBAYANAN.

On 18-19 June the 1st Battalion 149th Infantry continued to advance Northeast along the SAPA BUTE BUTE River against light enemy delaying action. Company A reconnoitered the North slope of MT DOMIRE for a possible approach to the top of the mountain but was unable to find any trails, or any enemy activity. The 3d Battalion 149th Infantry ran into another strong enemy position on the North slope of MT CAYPIPILI. Artillery preparations were fired on the position but the position were not destroyed, and accurate enemy machine gun fire permitted only a minor advance.

The 1st Battalion 151st Infantry continued to advance up the KOMEI PLAINS to a position 400 yards South of the TAYABASAN River against light resistance. In the 2d Battalion 151st Infantry Company G advanced 8000 yards North up the SANTA INEZ Trail to a position 2000 yards Southeast of MT MASOLA against light resistance. Companies E and F ran into considerable enemy resistance 2000 yards South of MT CAMPANA. Approximately 150 Japanese were killed in this area in ravines along the SANTA INEZ Trail. A platoon from Company E patrolled to the top of MT CAMPANA and found no trace of the enemy.

On 18 June Company D 754th Tank Battalion and Company A 82d Chemical Mortar Battalion were relieved from attachment to the 38th Division.

On 18 June the 152d Infantry was relieved by elements of the 151st Infantry and returned to the BAYANBAYANAN area. The anti-tank Company 151st Infantry and elements of the 2d Provisional Regiment took over the defensive positions on MT FURRO formerly occupied by the 152d Infantry.

During the period of 20-22 June the 3d Battalion 149th Infantry reduced the enemy strong point on MT CAYPIPILI which had held up the advance for several days and moved toward MT PAYACIN where again they met an enemy strong point. Following a mortar and artillery preparation Company I attacked and seized the crest of MT PAYACIN after which they were immediately

- 113 -

counterattacked by a large enemy force. After a fierce fire fight the enemy was repulsed suffering 50 casualties and losing several automatic weapons. This was the only enemy counter-attack made after the seizure of WOODPECKER RIDGE. The 1st Battalion 149th Infantry was directed to return to the vicinity of BAYANBAYANAN.

On 20 May the 1st Battalion 151st Infantry, while awaiting a C-47 air drop, was accidentally attacked by 7 P-47's which dropped 10 bombs and made 13 strafing attacks. Casualties numbered about 30 men but fortunately no one was killed. Two litter cases were evacuated by helicopter. On 22 June the 1st Battalion 151st Infantry returned to the Regimental area at BAYANBAYANAN. Company G of the 151st Infantry reached the Battalion objective, MT MASOLA, on 21 June meeting light re-sistance during the advance.

On 20 June the Detachment 13th Armored Group (Flame-thrower tanks) was detached from the 38th Division. On 20 June Battery D 161st AAA Gun Battalion was detached from the 38th Division and on 30 June Battery C 227th Searchlight Battalion was detached from the 38th Division.

On 26 June Company K 149th Infantry advancing North from MT PAYACIN encountered an enemy strong point on the crest of MT MALEMOD. Following an artillery barrage the Company assault-ed and secured the top of the mountain accounting for approx-imately 20 dead Japanese.

From 23 June to 30 June all units of the Division moved to the vicinity of BAYANBAYANAN in preparation for taking over new locations on the Southern section of LUZON.

At 2400 30 June the 38th Division passed from control of the XI Corps and went under control of the XIV Corps, at which time 20547 Japanese had been killed, and 645 prisoners taken since the Division landed on LUZON.

On arrival in LUZON, 29 February 1945, the strength of the 38th Infantry Division was 13,689 officers and men. In four months of continuous action 37 officers and 527 men were killed in action, 109 officers and 1957 men were wounded in action and 1 man missing in action. During this period 3198 replacements were received. On 30 June 1945 the strength of the Division was 12,952 officers and men.

LINGAYEN
GULF

BALER
BAY

SOUTH CHINA SEA

32
38
152

32
XX
43

1 ⊠ 152
• PANIQUI

1 // 3

38 X 43

1 /// 2

2 ⊠ 149

43
XX
38
149

MT ARAYAT

SIBUL
SPRINGS

152 ≡ 149 ⊠ 149

⊠ 152

NORZAGARAY

SAN MARCELINO

SAN FERNANDO

2 // 3 BACOLOR

2 ⊠ 152

1 ⊠ 149

3 ⊠ 152

PULILAN

XX 38
XX 38
/// 151
2 ⊠ 151
3 ⊠ 149

149
151

MT BAYTANGAN

3 ⊠ 151

MARKINA

3 // 2 SUBIC BAY

MANILA
BAY

MANILA

1 ⊠ 151
TANAY

38
XX
I CAV

CORREGIDOR IS.

LAGUNA
DE
BAY

XX

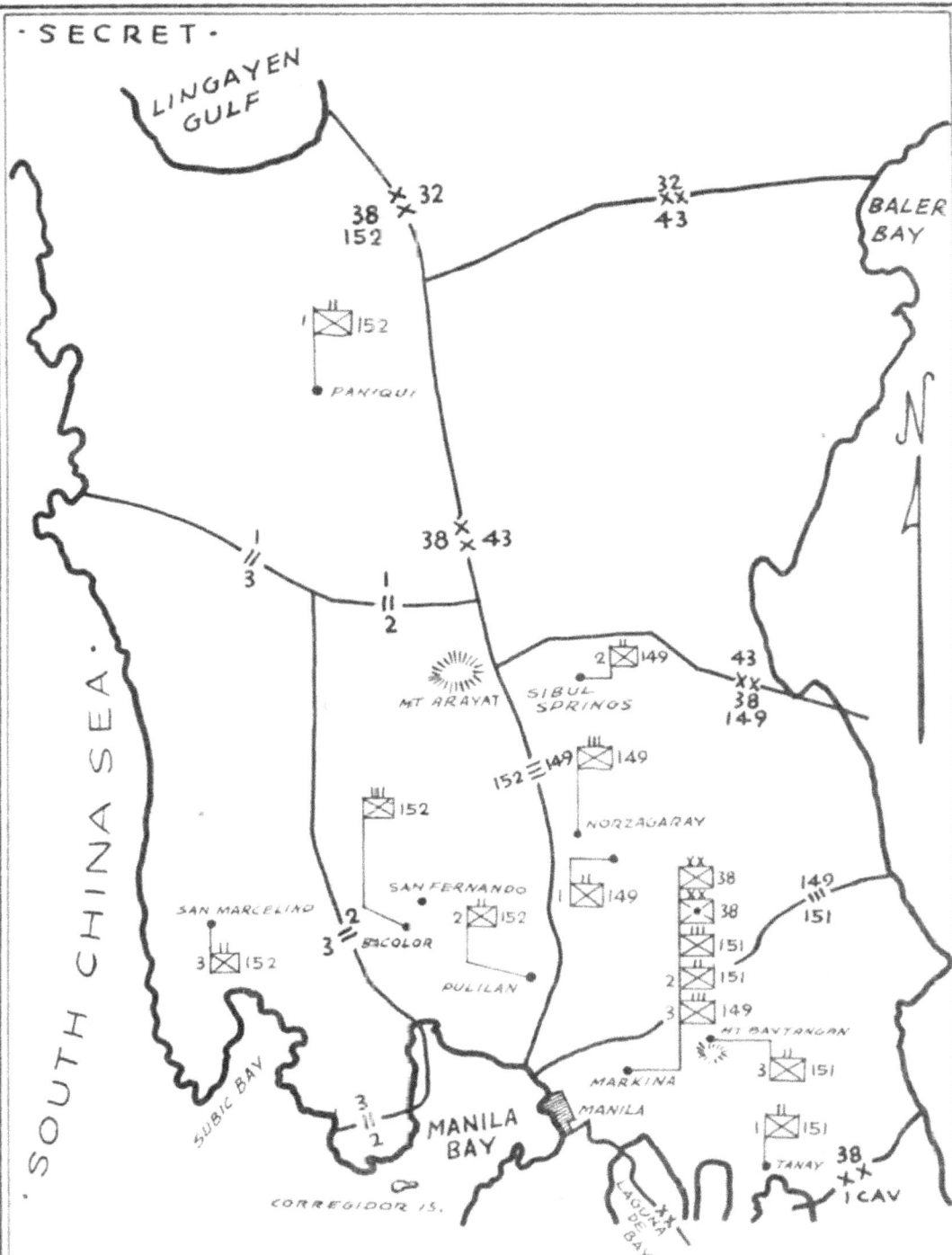

SITUATION AS OF 301800 JUNE 1945

INTELLIGENCE - M-7

INITIAL LANDING -- ZIGZAG

1. Order of Battle

Prior to the campaign, an Order of Battle estimate of enemy strength was included in the G-2 Estimate of the Enemy Situation, dated 16 January 1945, for the M-7 Operation (BATAAN-ZAMBALES).

Since there was a lack of information from captured documents and PsW, two of the most valuable sources of information, the estimate was based almost entirely on guerrilla reports which were furnished by 8th Army. The original estimate for the provinces of BATAAN and ZAMBALES was set at 12,800 and no major combat units were reported in the area. Only one known unit, the 132nd Airfield Bn, had been reported and located at SAN MARCELINO aerodrome early in December. Spot reports on enemy strength were listed as follows:

Place	Province	Strength	Date Reported
SAN ANTONIO	ZAMBALES	300	30 Nov
SAN MARCELINO A/D	ZAMBALES	1200	4 Dec
CASTILEJOS-SUBIC	ZAMBALES	2000	31 Oct
GRANDE ISLAND	BATAAN	1000 (Naval)	4 Dec
PORT OLONGAPO	ZAMBALES	500	19 Nov
DINALUPIHAN	BATAAN	600	22 Dec
ORANI	BATAAN	250	9 Dec
IBA	ZAMBALES	150	1 Dec
LIMAY	BATAAN	800	9 Dec
CABCABEN to MARIVELES	BATAAN	5000	24 Dec
Small Garrisons	BATAAN	1000	
	TOTAL	12,800	

The unopposed landing itself disproved guerrilla reports. No enemy troops had been stationed at SAN ANTONIO and no enemy troops remained at SAN MARCELINO. It was subsequently discovered that the untrained guerrilla ground observers extremely over-estimated in almost every case. However, it is more than likely that assaults by US forces on other islands in the PHILIPPINES and prior landings on LUZON caused the depletion of enemy strength in ZAMBALES and BATAAN prior to our landing.

Further evidence of gross exaggeration came to light when

the 2nd Bn 151st Infantry landed on GRANDE Island, 30 January. As many as 1000 Japanese navy troops had been reported there but none were found on the Island. An undetermined number had previously occupied the Island and had left many guns and ammunition intact.

As our troops pushed towards ZIGZAG PASS they encountered only slight resistance from a screening force at OLONGAPO, ZAMBALES, and did not contact the enemy in force until they reached the entrance of the pass. The first major ground unit to be identified was the 39th Infantry Regiment, 10th Infantry Division. The regiment, commanded by Col NAGAYOSHI, Sanehira, furnished the backbone of the enemy's defense in ZIGZAG PASS and was the core of the "BATAAN Garrison".

The units composing the garrison subsequently were identified as follows:

> 2nd and 3rd Bns, 39th Inf Regt, 10th Div (the 1st
>   Bn was sunk at sea).
> 6th Btry, 10th FA Regt.
> 2nd Co, 10th Engr Regt.
> SAKURA TAI (6th Co, 2nd Prov Inf Bn & 1 MG plat).
> ARAI TAI (2nd Co, 359th II Bn, with part of the
>   105th Div MT unit attached).
> SAISHO TAI (2nd Co, 1st Prov Inf Bn (less 1 plat)
>   and 1 MG Plat).
> MANILA Defense Hq Signal Section.

From information obtained through documents and PsW, the strength of the garrison proper was estimated at 1200. All of it except the 2nd Bn was committed in ZIGZAG PASS. Troops of the 1st and 2nd Provisional Infantry Bns, and of various Airfield Bns, Shipping Engineer and Shipping Artillery units, as well as elements of the OLONGAPO Naval Garrison and a Military Police unit identified in the area, were estimated at 2000, making a total of 3200.

In the battle for ZIGZAG PASS, approximately 2,400 Japs were killed and 25 PsW captured and it was assumed that the remainder of 800 to 1000 was located in BATAAN.

2. Photo Interpretation

Interpretation of the area of our initial landing included the beach at SAN FELIPE and Highway 7 as far as OLONGAPO. The area revealed complete lack of enemy occupied installations although many bunkers were identified in SUBIC and OLONGAPO. Defense positions in OLONGAPO and GRANDE

ISLAND were identified as being those which were built by
the Americans prior to the war. The findings, revealed by
the photos, allowed the conclusion that the enemy left the
area of our initial landing totally unoccupied and unde-
fended. Only after the occupation of OLONGAPO were any
photos of ZIGZAG PASS received, and this was the first time
that Intelligence Officers could acquaint themselves with
the pass. Extremely heavy undergrowth and rugged terrain
concealed the enemy well and it was only after study of
comparative photographs that enemy activity was noted along
the pass. Small arms positions, constructions (believed to be
pillboxes), and trenches were identified.

Later, a ground study of the enemy installations was
made and compared to the photo interpretation report of the
corresponding areas. It was found that the enemy's defenses
were more elaborate than was revealed by photo interpretation. Entrenchments, large caves, foxholes, and pillboxes
were completely concealed from air observation and excellent
camouflage hid them from ground observation as well. However, activity on photographs gave a fair approximation of
the enemy's defense line.

Fifteen strips and about one-hundred and seventy reprints
were received of the areas from SAN FELIPE to DINALUPIHAN.

3. Character of Hostile Opposition

Despite the fact that large numbers of enemy troops were
reported, not more than 100-150 were encountered between the
landing beach area and SANTA RITA, near the Western entrance
to ZIGZAG PASS. The KALAKLAN River bridge, just West of
OLONGAPO, had been carefully prepared for demolition and artfully concealed bunkers constructed to cover all approaches.
For some undetermined reason, the enemy failed to blow the
bridge nor did they choose to occupy the installations in
SUBIC and OLONGAPO that had taken many man-hours to build.
As it was, the guerrillas caused the only delay in our advance by burning several bridges between SUBIC and OLONGAPO.

Enemy resistance began in earnest as our forces
approached the ZIGZAG PASS, East of OLONGAPO, and continued,
in what is believed to be one of the most fierce and determined defenses encountered in the Southwest Pacific up to
that time, until the pass was opened to traffic, 14 February.
Photo interpretation and both air and ground reconnaissance
left no doubt that we were confronted by a strong force
firmly entrenched on extremely rugged and unassailable
terrain. The terrain with its artfully constructed and concealed maze of entrenchments, caves and connecting tunnels,

pillboxes, and emplaced weapons has been discussed earlier in the operations section of this report. These positions were mutually supporting, both to the front and flanks, and organized in depth on each successive terrain feature.

These positions could not be located until our troops were well within the enemy's fields of fire. Maximum use had been made of man-made camouflage consisting mostly of bamboo and, as the positions had been prepared long in advance, natural growth further hid their presence. The most unique examples were mortar pits completely covered with bamboo lattice work in which a small hole had been cut so that a mortar could be raised and fired through the hole. Even air observers in cub planes had difficulty in finding these emplacements.

Our reconnaissance soon established the fact that the defense system was organized along a narrow front, averaging 500 to 2000 yds astride highway #7, and about 6000 yds in depth.

The nature of the terrain and the enemy's defense rendered impracticable a flanking attack and left the commander little choice but to by-pass the entire system and attack from their rear, which ultimately proved highly satisfactory.

From the start of the ZIGZAG engagement until its finish, enemy resistance was stubborn and fanatical in the extreme. Not an inch of ground was given; no withdrawals were made, and it was only by launching furious assaults that advances could be made. The Japanese died in their positions and the few straggler prisoners of war testified that virtually every man in the pass had been annihilated. The Jap commander with a few companions escaped to the South and joined the remainder of the BATAAN garrison (39th Inf Regt), which had not been committed in the ZIGZAG, in the Mt NATIB area of North BATAAN.

BATAAN

1. Order Of Battle

The basis for the strength estimate in the sectors of BATAAN, in the absence of contact identifications, lay in guerrilla reports. Strength in the MARIVELES area was said to be 5,000 and an additional 3,000 troops were reported along the BAGAC-PILAR Road.

Both of these reports were again grossly exaggerated, but it was later learned that a goodly portion of the 1st Provisional Bn on Southern BATAAN had been sent to CORREGIDOR sometime prior to our landing. Opposition after our landing at MARIVELES came not from the BATAAN Garrison proper but from elements of the Japanese 1st Provisional Infantry Bn and such service troops as the "MARIVELES Lumbering Expedition", along with some stragglers from the MANILA Defense Force. A total of about 300 Japs were KIA, found dead, and taken prisoner in the MARIVELES-CABCABEN Sector of South BATAAN and, of course, many of these were stragglers who swam over from CORREGIDOR.

As the original Central Garrison was formed about the 2d Bn, 39th Regt, and a 2d Bn had been identified in ZIGZAG, it was believed that the garrison had been destroyed there.

Later reports from PsW, captured just before relief by the 6th Division, however, established the fact that only the 5th Co had been in ZIGZAG as Regimental Hq guards and that the 2nd Bn referred to there was in fact the 2nd Provisional Infantry Bn. It was revealed that the greater part of the Central Garrison had never been committed and, along with stragglers from the ZIGZAG defeat, was located on Mt NATIB, from whence it intended to forage and engage in guerrilla warfare.

The Central Garrison, located along the BAGAC-PILAR Road, was composed of the following troops:

 Hq, 2nd Bn, 39th Infantry Regt
 5th Company, 2nd Bn
 6th Company, 2nd Bn
 1/3 2nd Engr Company, 10th Engr Regt
 2/3 2nd Bn MG unit
 1/2 Regtl Gun Unit
 Bn Gun Unit
 1/2 AT Gun Unit
 1/3 Pioneer Unit
 2 Wire Sections
 2nd Company, 359th II Bn, with part of the 105th
  Div Transportation Unit attached

It was estimated that his force, along with ZIGZAG and MANILA stragglers, amounted to about 1100 troops of whom 900 were still hiding on Mt NATIB when the 6th Division relieved the 38th Division on 1 May. Our forces accounted for about 200 KIA, found dead and captured along the BAGAC-PILAR Road.

2. Photo Interpretation

Photo Interpretation for the BATAAN operation was started a few days before ZIGZAG PASS was opened. Studies of MARIVELES and Highway #110 as far North as DINALUPIHAN revealed little enemy activity. Coastal guns facing MANILA BAY were left unoccupied and the AA guns and other supporting defenses around the three airstrips in BATAAN were unoccupied. The airstrips at MARIVELES, CABCABEN, and LIMAY were heavily bombed and devoid of any activity. The only place where any enemy activity was noted was along the BAGAC-PILAR Road and along Highway #110 from MARIVELES to CABCABEN. It was quite evident, from the photos, that the enemy did not choose to defend the plains along the East coast of BATAAN. Most of the bridges along Highway #110, running along the East coast of BATAAN, had been destroyed.

A ground survey along the BAGAC-PILAR Road revealed that there were more installations there than were determined from photos, as the enemy's excellent use of camouflage had prevented a too detailed study of the road.

More than ample coverage of BATAAN was obtained. There were over sixty vertical strips and eight hundred reprints received during the operation.

3. Character Of Hostile Opposition

The only active opposition to the landing at MARIVELES was four rounds of coast artillery fire delivered from CORREGIDOR which scored no direct hits on our ships but caused several casualties when a round fell near a loaded landing craft, and when an LCI, in approaching the beach, struck a mine in MARIVELES harbor causing severe damage to the ship and loaded equipment, and inflicting many casualties. There was no resistance encountered on the beaches as our forces landed and fanned out to secure the beachhead. The advance to the East along Highway #110, toward CABCABEN, began immediately and only light sniper fire hindered our progress. As the attack pushed into the hills the route began to rise sharply and the terrain, greatly similar to that in ZIGZAG PASS, although not so impenetrable, became more rugged. About 6,000 yds East of MARIVELES the road entered a series of sharp tortuous loops and turns which was called the

"CORKSCREW" area. Shortly after our advance, reconnaissance elements entered the CORKSCREW where they were subjected to heavy machine gun fire in the vicinity of (25.3-48.3), but tanks soon reduced these nests. That was the only encounter of any strength in the whole of South BATAAN and it netted less than 100 killed. The Japanese had constructed extensive fortifications in the area but intense bombing by friendly aircraft had destroyed many permanent installations and a large number of entrenchments was found to have been abandoned some time prior to our landing. From there on to CABCABEN enemy resistance was negligible and again many well constructed and concealed pillboxes, caves and bunkers were found abandoned along the highway extending from there, North to DINALUPIHAN.

During this time little enemy resistance was encountered by our forces advancing to the South along the East coast of BATAAN. The only opposition of any consequence occurred in the vicinity of ORION when a group of about 100 Japs attacked a 1st Infantry CP at night. A furious fight ensued which resulted in about 85 Japs being killed.

Notwithstanding the negligible enemy resistance encountered by both forces thus far, junction between the two forces was retarded due to the destruction of numerous bridges along the axis of advance both North and South, and it is not known whether they had been destroyed by guerrillas, withdrawing enemy troops, or friendly aircraft.

Guerrillas continued to bring in reports of strong enemy defenses along the BAGAC-PILAR Road where several tanks had been reported sighted recently. The terrain extending West from the coastal plain in the vicinity of PILAR resembled the pattern of the ZIGZAG and CORKSCREW areas. As our troops attacked West through this area it was baffling that the enemy should offer such little opposition from terrain that was so favorable for defense. The route in general was well fortified with the focal point astride the road in the vicinity of MABAHANG PARONG in the (16-70) and (17-70) grid squares. This area had been prepared with a view to repulse enemy landings on the beach at BAGAC and was abandoned when reached by our forces. All bunkers, pillboxes and trenches were facing West and were wholly inadequate in opposing our forces attacking from the East. Many of the positions were wired with double apron barbed wire, and bunkers and pillboxes were constructed to withstand heavy aerial and artillery bombardment. The strongest resistance encountered in the attack from PILAR to BAGAC was met North of Highway #111 and West of BANI where the enemy delivered machine gun and mortar fire on our troops.

However, the enemy forces withdrew during the night and the strength of this group remained unknown. As previously mentioned under "Order of Battle", the entire Central Garrison, due to reverses in ZIGZAG and South BATAAN, had completely withdrawn toward Mt NATIB to the North.

During this time our forces patrolling along the East and South coast of BATAAN made daily contacts with groups of enemy evacuating MANILA and CORREGIDOR.

CABALLO ISLAND

1. Order of Battle

Lt Comdr OGAWA, according to an undated organization chart of "Bay Entrance Defense Force", captured on CORREGIDOR 24 February 1945, and substantiated by a PW, was in command of the CABALLO Island Forces. Supposedly under his command were:

Unit	COMMANDER	Strength
1st Btry (Fort)	WO SAKANSUSHI	38
1st Dual Purpose Btry	Ensign SASAZAWA	80
1st MG Btry	Lt (jg) SAITO	14
2nd MG Btry	WO NIZUSHIMA	17
Land Garrison Unit	1st Lt AMATANI	33
Adm Unit	Ensign SASAZAWA	2
HAMIGUCHI Unit	WO HAMIGUCHI	26
WAKAYAMA Unit	Ensign WAKAYAMA	72
SAKURA Unit	WO SAKURA, Koji	30
331st Const Unit	Tech WO IKUTA	203
Armament Unit (Civilians)	Tech Lt (Navy) GOTO	7
TOTAL		522

With the completion of the occupation of CABALLO approximately 300 Japs were KIA and 3 were taken prisoners. The undated organization chart was apparently out of date since the garrison was considerably smaller. It is likely that many of the so called "Bay Entrance Defense" personnel on CABALLO reinforced CORREGIDOR prior to American landing on the Island, 16 February 1945.

2. Photo Interpretation

Information obtained from a study of vertical and oblique photographs revealed that the enemy had constructed numerous caves and tunnels for the defense of the Island. These were generally located on high ground. Several mortar pits were clearly seen with guns emplaced by Americans prior to the outbreak of the war. Examination of the landing beaches disclosed one portion only that was suitable for an amphibious operation. This beach was not defended by the enemy and the photos did not disclose any underwater obstacles. The photos revealed the land to be barren with precipituous cliffs extending to the water's edge.

3. Character of Enemy Opposition

The Island itself was quite small being some 500 to 600 yds across at the widest part and about 1¼ miles long. The principal terrain features were 3 hills about evenly spaced along the length of the Island.

The landing itself was unopposed and no enemy fire was received until our forces had occupied Hill #1. This resistance consisted of small arms, automatic weapons, and mortar fire delivered from a formidably fortified high plateau adjacent to Hill #2, which towered almost perpendicularly about 300 feet above the sea. There was never any doubt that the enemy's plan was to defend from these positions, which he did to the death, there being only 3 PsW taken. The enemy had no useable heavy mortars or guns larger than 20mm cannon, but they were so emplaced that all-round coverage was permitted and the fortifications so heavily constructed that artillery, aerial bombardment and normal methods of attack were futile. These positions, weapons, and the novel method of attack employed by our forces are further discussed in the G-3 section of this report. It was several days before the fortifications were reduced and the enemy destroyed, and during that time the enemy launched one furious counterattack which failed and cost him almost a third of his total strength.

EL FRAILE (FT DRUM)

1. Order Of Battle

The only enemy information available prior to the landing on EL FRAILE Island (FT DRUM) by elements of the 2nd Bn,
151st Inf, 13 April 1945, was obtained from a document, an
undated **organization** chart of the "Bay Entrance Defense
Force", captured on CORREGIDOR, 24 February 1945. The Japanese garrison strength at that time was found to be 21
men comprising 1 MG Btry (Fort), a Land Party and an administrative unit.

On the 18th of April, after the Fort was blown to bits,
a patrol found a total of 60 dead Japs in the room on the
3rd level. The garrison apparently had been strengthened
prior to our landing, possibly by troops that had evacuated
from CORREGIDOR.

2. Photo Interpretation

Photo interpretation was of little value as complete
plans and drawings were obtained prior to the attack (see
G-3 section of this report), however, photos did indicate
that all exterior guns were inoperative.

The only opposition to the landing were a few scattered small arms shots fired as our troops approached. There
was no fighting on, or within, the "concrete battleship"
itself.

CARABAO ISLAND

1. Order of Battle

Information as to enemy strength, identification and organization of the Japanese forces believed to be on CARABAO
was gathered from two sources, namely, an undated organization chart of "Bay Entrance Defense Force", captured on the
24th of February 1945 on CORREGIDOR, and a PW captured on
the 10th of April 1945.

The organization chart listed the following units, commanders and strength on the island, which was included in
G-2 Estimate of the Enemy Situation, as pertains to CARABAO
and EL FRAILE Islands, dated 9 April 1945:

UNIT	COMMANDER	STRENGTH
11th Btry (Fort)	Ensign WATANABE	76
2nd Btry (Fort)	Ensign SUZUKI	36
1st MG Btry (Fort)	Capt NAKAMURA	213
2nd MG Btry (Fort)	Ensign WATANABE	
Signal Unit	Ensign SUZUKI	
Land Garrison Unit	Ensign SUZUKI	
Armament Unit		8
	Total	333

The PW confirmed the fact that there was a sizeable
force, (approx 500 men), on CARABAO as late as the 24th of
January 1945, but stated that the ICHINOSAWA Independent Bn,
commanded by Capt ICHINOSAWA, was responsible for the defense
of the island.

Inasmuch as ground reconnaissance on the island had not
been conducted since its occupation by the Japs, information
from the above captured document and PW formed the basis
for all estimates.

Though no enemy was contacted, it is significant that
the abandoned defensive positions indicated that a sizeable
force had occupied them as late as 10 days prior to the
attack. The enemy apparently had fled giving up all hopes
of defending CARABAO.

2. Photo Interpretation

Interpretation of photos of CARABAO Island disclosed
enemy defenses very similar to those encountered on CABALLO.
The enemy had constructed numerous caves, tunnels, and
strongpoints for the defense of the island. There was only

one point suitable for an amphibious landing and the photos revealed it to be strongly fortified. No map was available of the Island so one was prepared from the photos, spot elevations were determined and contour lines drawn in.

Prior to landing, ground reconnaissance could not be made, however, patrolling PT boats reported a suspected evacuation of CARABAO but had, on the other hand, recently received ineffective small arms fire from the Island and had observed some lights there.

3. Character of Hostile Opposition

No resistance was encountered during the landing nor was any enemy found on the Island.

1. Order Of Battle

Prior to our troops moving into the West of STOTSENBURG area, 10 March 1945, information concerning the enemy's chain of command, identifications, and estimated strength was gathered from reports of the 43d Infantry Div and 6th Army.

Major General TSUKADA, commanding the RAN GROUP (1st Glider KAKKU) Infantry Group, was responsible for the defense of the area West of STOTSENBURG. Units identified in the area and original strength estimates are as follows:

Units identified:

TAKAYAMA Force -- Lt Col TAKAYAMA, CO

UNITS	UNITS
2nd Bn, 2nd Mobile Regt (plus 9th Co)	3rd Co, 178 IIBn, 103 Div
AT Co, 2nd Combat Unit	4th Co, 178 IIBn, 103 Div
132 A/F Unit (OKAMOTO-9926)	3rd (Naval) Const Unit
137 A/F Unit (18456)	1 Co, 4th Prov Arty Unit (MIYOSHI)
12th Machine Cannon Unit	1 Co, Regt Gun, 2nd Mobile Inf Regt
4th Prov OISHI Labor Unit	
2nd Co (SHIBASAKI Composite Inf Force)	
BAMBAN Naval Force (2 Cos)	1 Maintenance Co
1 Bn, 25th Ind AT Unit (less 1st Co)	6th Co, 2nd Mobile Arty Regt

TAKAYA Force -- Major TAKAYA, CO

UNITS

2nd Glider Inf Regt

OGASAWARA Force -- Lt Col OGASAWARA, CO

UNIT

Composite Signal Unit

OSABUNE Force -- Lt Comdr OSABUNE, CO

- 128 -

UNIT

OSABUNE Naval Unit

NAGA Force -- Lt Col NAGA, CO

UNITS

Working Unit
138 A/F Survey and Construction Unit
1st Raiding Machine Cannon Unit (Capt SUZUKI)
IKDA Guard Unit (Maj KEDA)
1st Sub-depot (MANILA Air Depot)
Remaining Units of 1st Supply Depot, 1st Branch Office
Reserves (Under direct control of Group)
All remaining forces of flying Units

YANAGIMOTO Force -- Capt YANAGIMOTO, CO

UNITS

3rd Bn, 2nd Mobile Inf Regt (less 9th Co)
8th Ind Tank Co

EGUICHI Force -- Lt Col EGUICHI, CO

UNITS

Hq, 10th Air Sector
31st A/F Bn
99th A/F Bn
150th A/F Bn
151st A/F Bn
152nd A/F Bn
8th A/F Co
52nd A/F Co
60th Flying Regt (Remaining Units)
SHIBASAKI Composite Inf Force (2 Cos)
84th Field AA Unit (Bn)
Special Organized AA Unit
13th Machine Cannon Unit
7th Special Organized Machine Cannon Unit
22nd Special Organized Machine Cannon Unit
322nd Ind Truck Co
26th Transport, Regt, Sea Duty Plat (26th Div)
Southern Air Route, MANILA District, CLARK Co
One squad of 56th Construction Duty Co
One squad of 111th Land Duty Co
Other transient forces

Strength Estimates

N Flank -- TAKAYAMA Force	3500
N Central Flank -- TAKAYA Force	750
S Central Flank -- EGUICHI Force	4250
S Flank -- YAMAGIMOTO Force	655
S Central Flank -- OSBUNE Naval Force	1000
Support Units and Reserved	2975
Total Estimated Strength	13,130

In mid March, a captured map, dated 27 February, revealed that the Naval strength in the area was much larger than
was originally estimated. Thus the original estimated **strength**
of 13,130 was increased by 4,000, making a total of 17,130.
From the same map the presence of five combat Sectors was
confirmed in the following approximate areas:

        13th Combat Area----------------Grid Square (17.0-41.0)
        14th Combat Area----------------Hills 1700-1500
        15th Combat Area----------------OBJECT HILL
        16th Combat Area----------------(18.2-36.7)
        17th Combat Area----------------(19.5-38.3)

All these locations were in the area West of FORT STOT-
SENBURG on maps, LUZON Quads, Scale 1/50,000. A Vice Ad-
miral KONDO was in command of all Naval troops in the area.

During the course of two months of fighting in the West
of STOTSENBURG Area, the original enemy organization was
consolidated as the Japs lost men and moved further back
into the hills. Evidence was found that the Army commands
had moved into COMBAT SECTORS which were originally made up
of only Naval personnel.

The enemy intentions at the end of the campaign, when
the area was turned over to the 6th Division, 1 May 45,
seemed to be directed to making a concerted last-ditch stand
at Mt PINATUBO, and, if that effort failed, to withdraw
to IBA, in the hope of evacuating the PHILIPPINES. Already
the division was contacting many stragglers from the RAN
GROUP on the mountain trails and plains between the scene
of action and IBA.

As the reported dead approximated the estimate strength
of 17,130, there were approximately 1000 Japs left in the
area, with the main strength on Mt PINATUBO as of 1 May 1945.

2. Photo Interpretation

Photos of this area revealed a heavily fortified area,

which was SACOBIA Ridge and the adjoining terrain extending
about 4000 yards square, and included SPENCE Ridge, LEWIS
Ridge, and SAWTOOTH Ridge. Gun emplacements, storage areas,
caves, SA defenses, strongpoints, and motor pools were identified in this area. The strongest concentration was found
along the SACOBIA Ridge and SACOBIA River valley. It appeared that the enemy had made excellent use of the terrain for
his defense.

During the course of the operation, due to the lack of
adequate map coverage, wide angle photographs were requested
with a scale of approximately 1:50,000. These were gridded
from LUZON 1:50,000 maps and were used to supplement existing maps of the area. It was found that the Div Arty liaison
pilots could use these wide angle photographs to good advantage in pinpointing enemy gun positions.

The fortified areas located on the photos were confirmed
by both air and ground observation. However, due to the
terrain and heavy vegetation many installations could not be
identified.

400 verticals and 300 reprints of the area were received
along with 4 sets of obliques and 12 reprints from the 43d
Div and XI Corps.

3.   Character Of Opposition

When the 38th Division Task Force began their operations
in the West of STOTSENBURG area, they inherited an area that
had previously been assigned, first, to the 40th Division,
and later, to the 43d Division. Enemy resistance in the general area had initially been encountered in the vicinity of
BAMBAN, and by the time our forces were committed, the Japs
had been driven to the hills West of BAMBAN and FORT STOT-
SENBURG, where the terrain favored defense by the enemy.

After relieving the 43d Division, the attack Southwest
was begun immediately by the 149th Inf in the North and West,
and by the 169th Inf in the East. In the advance Southwest,
little opposition was encountered at first, but as the fingers
of our attack approached the headqaters of the CAUAYAN, MAR-
IMLA, BANGAT and MALAGO Rivers, enemy resistance steadily
increased. The enemy had prepared positions in a vast net-
work of caves on both the forward and rear slopes of SACOBIA,
SPENCE, and SAWTOOTH Ridges from which he could deliver interlocking crossfires. The enemy defensive installations
were generally of one type with certain variations to suit the
type weapons or strength of personnel occupying them. The
works were mostly of earth construction, prepared in and

around caves which were dug straight back into the clay or shale with sufficient perpendicular tunnels to accommodate the occupants, weapons, and supplies. Most of these caves and emplacements were capable of withstanding heavy artillery fire and when they were finally overrun some were found large enough to accommodate as many as 200 men. The Japs had placed riflemen, light and heavy machine guns, knee mortars, and a limited number of 20, 25, and 40mm automatic weapons, which delivered a withering fire on our approaching elements. A few 37mm and 47mm AT guns were also supporting the lighter weapons.

After extremely heavy fighting, the initial positions were overrun and it appeared that the enemy had begun a withdrawal Southwest toward Mt PINATUBO. However, this thought was soon dispelled as he had only fallen back to occupy additional positions. The enemy was determined in his stand and each foot of ground taken by our troops was bitterly contested. The sharp ridges, deep gullies, and heavy undergrowth, characterized the terrain over which our troops must attack, limited flank movement, and dictated, for the most part, frontal assaults. Their dogged resistance never relented until our forces neared the SACOBIA River valley where it became apparent that there was no longer an organized pattern of resistance, and on about 30 March, our forces occupied positions on the ridges North of and overlooking the SACOBIA River generally between the 12 to 15 grid lines. Their action then consisted of mopping up isolated groups of the enemy, patrolling the general area to deny the enemy use of escape routes to the North from the SACOBIA valley, and to protect the right (North) flank of our forces driving toward Mt PINATUBO from the East.

Meanwhile the 169th Infantry had struck a snag in their advance West of STOTSENBURG. They had encountered a formidable fortified area, known as the "MOTOR POOL", in the 20-35 grid square. The enemy defense front was wide and organized from 600 to 1000 yards in depth, with approaches covered by fire from 20mm dual purpose and both light and heavy machine guns, and AT guns. In many cases they were emplaced on the reverse side of slopes which permitted grazing fire on the ridges over which our troops were forced to advance. Innumerable caves were encountered from which interlocking crossfire could be delivered, and they were supported by 37mm AT guns. The advance was hard fought and slow, and on 23 March, when the 169th Infantry was relieved by the 2nd Bn, 152nd Infantry, the area had not yet been taken. The 152nd Infantry was in turn relieved by the 149th Infantry 1 April. Intensified mortar and artillery concentrations laid on the remaining positions and in the numerous draws, finally softened the enemy defenses sufficiently

for the 149th to take them. As the enemy began to give
ground, he displayed excellent judgment, as he has so often
done in the past, in his choice of ground for his delaying
action. His route was generally along the South bank of the
SACOBIA River which flows through a deep gorge. This choice
left commanders no alternative but to follow his trail which
dangerously canalized our advance. However, by this time
the enemy displayed definite signs of weakened physical condition and lack of medical aid, food, and ammunition. Neither
did he possess effective weapons heavier than rifles and a
few machine guns, nor have the advantage of prepared positions.
Earlier, 2 active tanks had been knocked out, and now, as the
advance progressed, 3 additional medium tanks and 1 150mm SPM,
out of gasoline and deserted, were found.

Terrain continued to be the 149th's greatest enemy. The
gorge through which the enemy chose to withdraw was so narrow
that only a squad, and sometimes a platoon in column, could
head the advance. Numerous rock formations lined the only
trail and Japs fighting from these natural barriers placed
our scouts in an unenviable position. Only short advances
could be made following heavy mortar concentrations, and as
the enemy was dislodged, he displayed more ingenuity than was
his usual wont, in preparing numerous booby traps.

Hundreds of badly decomposed enemy dead, blood-stained
bandages, and makeshift crutches littered the way, giving
mute evidence of the effectiveness of our previous air and
artillery preparations. The narrow route, so advantageous to
them now, had been their adversary during the early exodus
from CLARK FIELD and FT STOTSENBURG.

In spite of the obstacles, our push progressed rapidly
and the enemy had no chance to really get set for an effective defense. On 9 April, contact was made with our forces
holding the ridges North of the SACOBIA River, and on 14
April, it was learned from a PW that leading elements of the
2d Bn were within 1000 meters of the RAN Group CP.

The enemy was now in a pitiful plight with no semblance
of organization and our attack advanced quickly to Mt PINATUBO
where junction was made with our forces in ZAMBALES Province
in the West, and other holding elements in the North and South.
The Japanese were no longer capable of conducting an effective
defense and mopping up was in progress when the Division was
relieved by the 6th Division.

<u>EAST OF MANILA</u>

1. <u>Order of Battle</u>

On 1 May 1945, the campaign East of MANILA, in the vicinity of WAWA Dam, officially opened. Prior to our troops
moving in, an Enemy Order of Battle Estimate was furnished
by the 6th Infantry Division which had been in contact with
the enemy for two months. Thus, the situation as of 1 May
was as follows:

The enemy 41st Army (Corps) (Formerly SHIMBU SHUDAN)
commanded by Lt Gen YOKOYAMA, Shizuo, (CG of 8th Div),
according to an Operation Order, dated 29 March 45, was
responsible for the operations in Central and Southern LUZON.
It appeared that Lt Gen YOKOYAMA possibly dissolved his
divisions, and reorganized task forces with area COs as
follows:

```
SHIMBU SHUDAN--Overall Command--Lt Gen YOKOYAMA, Shizuo
BATANGAS Area---------------------Col FUJISHIGE, Masatoshi
ANTIPOLO Area--------------------Maj Gen NOGUCHI, Shizuo
MONTALBAN Area-------------------Maj Gen KOBAYASHI,Takashi
IPO Area--------------------------Maj Gen KAWASHIMA, Osamu
CABANATUAN Area------------------Lt Gen TSUDA, Yoshitake
```

For the purpose of operation, the enemy had divided the
area from Mt MALAGIA, (grid square 04-89) 7500 yds N of WAWA,
to a point 5,000 yds North of ANTIPOLO, into three sectors,
Right, Central and Left, assigning its defense to the
KOBAYASHI HEIDAN, reinforced. The Right Sector Unit occupied
the 9000 yds from Mt MALAGIA to Mt PACAWAGAN (SW of WAWA);
the Central Sector Unit had a front of about 5500 yds from
Mt PACAWAGAN on the North to TILAGAAN (3500 yds SE of SAN
MATEO) on the South; the Left Sector Unit occupied the
remainder of the line, a front of about 5000 yds.

To the North in the IPO area was the KAWASHIMA HEIDAN
with a remaining strength of 5000-6000. South of the
KOBAYASHI HEIDAN, East of ANTIPOLO, was the NOGUCHI HEIDAN
and the KOGURE Detachment with an estimated strength of 2000-
3000. The latest developments indicated that the NOGUCHI
HEIDAN, hard pressed, was being forced into the left flank
of the KOBAYASHI HEIDAN, which might, in time, affect the
strength of that sector.

  . The following were identified:

SECRET

Right Sector Unit	Est. Strength
1st Field Replacement Unit	50
4th Prov Inf Bn	450
7th Prov Inf Bn (3rd Co & 1 MG Platoon)	180
5th Prov MG Co	130
12th Prov MG Co	130
6th Prov AT Co (less 1 Plat)	80
8th FA Regt, 2nd Btry (less 1 Platoon)	100
5th Prov Arty Btry (less 1 Platoon)	100
7th Prov Arty Bn	130
5th Med Inf Mortar Bn (less 2nd Co)	450
2nd Shipping Arty Regt (elms)	100
5th Field Shipping Depot	150
	2050

Left-Central Sector Unit	
10th Prov Inf Bn	450
4th Med Inf Mortar Bn	600
117th Gyoro Bn	100
8th Prov Inf Bn	250
7th Prov MG Co	120
3rd Rocket Gun Bn	730
134th Airfield Bn	500
148th Airfield Bn	500
1 Platoon (6th Prov AT Co)	20
149th Airfield Bn	500
180th Airfield Bn (1 Co)	150
47th Airfield Co	200
22nd Fd Searchlight Co	175
111th Land Duty Co	100
11th Air Sector Hq (later called FUSHIMI Force)	100
77th Fd AA Bn	550
u/i Fd AA Bn	550
5th Prov AT Co	90
6th Prov Arty Btry	130
8th Prov Arty Btry	130
185th II Bn, 105 Div	725
1st and 2nd Prov Engr Co	300
110th Gyoro Bn	450
1 Co, 118th Gyoro Bn	150
1st Prov Auto (truck) Co	150
26th IMR (2nd Bn & Regtl Hq)	650
105th Div Engrs, 8th Co	150
8th Railway Bn	480
106th Gyoro Bn (elms)	100
FUKUI Bn (1st Composite Inf Bn)	750
	9850

Recapitulation of Remaining Strength

	Est Strength	Less KIA	Remaining Strength
Right Sector	2050	400	1650
Left-Central	9850	6700	3150
	11900	7100	4800

Remaining Strength		4800
Add evacuees from MANILA		500
Possible Reserves		3800
		9100

Less Attrition	2000		
Reported KIA by 1st Cav	300		
PsW	55	2355	

Total Est Remaining Strength   6745

Possible Reserves:
OSAKA Unit (118th Gyoro Bn
  less 1 Co) 500 yds NW of
Mt PURRO   300
8th Rcn Regt, 8th Div
  100 yds ESE of Mt PURRO   700
KOBAYASHI Force, vic Mt PURRO 2800
  31 Inf Regt less 3d Bn &
  6th Co (reinforced)
                                              3800

As subsequent information was received and new identifications made (YEBIKO (EBISU) Bn, KAWAUCHI Bn, IMINARI Force,
1st Signal Unit, 63rd L of C Hospital, 22nd Hvy FA Unit,
KATSUME Unit, 182nd II Bn (elms), 186 II Bn (elms), 8th Div
Engr Regt (Hqs, 2nd and 3rd Cos), and the 3rd Bn, 17th Inf
Regt), it became necessary to redistribute strength estimates
of previous identified units and to raise the strength
estimate from the original 15,700 to 16,355.

On 3 June 45, the 43rd Division took over the area of
our right flank North of the MANGO River and an estimated
650 Japs in that area were deducted from the total strength,
and later, after learning that the 22nd Searchlight Co was
the same as the 22nd A/F Construction Co, an additional 175
Japs were deducted. Thus, at the close of the campaign on
30 June 1945, the total estimated strength in the Division
area was 610, based on the following:

```
Total estimated strength                          16,355

Less-
  Estimated transferred to
    43rd Division Area            650
  22nd S/L Co (same as 22nd A/F
    Construction Co)              175
  KIA by 6th Inf Div            7150
  KIA by 38th Inf Div           4350
  KIA by 1st Cav Div             300
  PsW by 6th Inf Div              55
  PsW by 38th Inf Div            240
  Found Dead by 38th Inf Div    2025
  Est fd dead 6th Inf Div        800          15,745

    Total remaining strength 30 June 45          610
```

On 9 May 45, as the division pushed towards WOODPECKER Ridge and the area South and Southeast of NEW BOSOBOSO, an enemy Operation Order, A No. 79, dated 5 May 45, was captured by the 43rd Infantry Division, from which intelligence was gained on an enemy-planned and coordinated counter-offensive, to take place in mid-May, along the whole SHIMBU Line. "X-day", as the enemy called it, was 12 May. Consequently, from the period 14 May to 31 May, fierce fighting prevailed in the Division sector with the enemy attacking in force, using the 3d Bn 17th Inf Regt, reinforced; 5th Medium Mortar Bn; 7th Provisional Inf Bn; elements of the 8th Rcn Regt, 8th Division; 3rd Co, 1st Bn, 31st Inf Regt; and other miscellaneous units, most of which were virtually annihilated.

The next significant contact was made 28 May in the Mt LAMITA area with the FUSHIMI Force (Lt Col FUSHIMI), a provisional unit made up of remnants of Airfield Bns, namely the 148th and 149th, 111th Land Duty Co, 11th Air Sector Hqs and other miscellaneous units. It was estimated that 300 men of FUSHIMI Force and 200 men of the 63rd L of C Hospital were disposed in that vicinity. After taking the area, approximately 270 Japs were killed and the remaining defeated forces fled North and Northeast.

In the Mt PURRC-Mt MAPATAD Area an estimated 1500 Japs were identified prior to our attack on 28 May. The defense was built around the 1st Bn (-3rd Co) and 2d Bn, 31st Inf Regt, and reinforced with the IMINARI Force, 22nd Heavy FA Unit (formed into a provisional mortar unit since they had no artillery pieces), remnants of the 8th Division Rcn Regt, and other miscellaneous units. Approximately 550 Japs were killed at Mt MAPATAD, 500 at Mt PURRO, and the remaining forces were reported to have retreated to the TAKACHIHO Plains West of SANTA INES.

2. Photo Interpretation

A study of the enemy's line of defense, extending from Mt ORO South along the MARIQUINA and BOSOBOSO Rivers as far South as the PAYAGUAN River, revealed a well-entrenched enemy. At Mt ORO, there were many entrenchments extending in depth, with supply points, fortified ridges, and numerous caves making Mt ORO a formidable strongpoint.

The PURAY River was defended with heavy entrenchments, supply points, and caves in the vicinity of (05.5-87.2), LUZON 1:25,000 Mt IRID Northwest. CHALKY Cliff was probably the most heavily defended mountain. Three strongpoints, two guns, and a battery of 6 guns supporting the hill were located at (03.7-83.8).

Mt HAPANONG BANOY held two strongpoints and one gun, and on Mt BINICAYAN and East of the mountain, along the West bank of the MARIQUINA River, one artillery piece, many entrenchments, caves, fortified ridges, and two strongpoints were identified.

Along the East bank of the BOSOBOSO River, three strongpoints, many fortified ridges, OPs, 6 guns, and one light machine gun were identified.

In the vicinity of Mt PURRO, heavy fortifications were again evident and Mt MAPATAD appeared to be well-prepared for defense. Along the PAYAGUAN River, extending West, many caves, strongpoints, and supply points were located. This constituted the enemy's main line of defense. In later photos, activity was noted in the cave area around the SAN YSIDRO River, but there was no indication that it was heavily defended. Furthermore, these photos showed newly-built roads and trails in the vicinity of SANTA INES.

Air and ground observation confirmed photo interpretation reports, although there were additional small arms defenses along the main line of defense which could not be identified due to heavy vegetation.

148 sets of verticals, 16 sets of obliques, and a total of 393 reprints of verticals and 114 reprints of obliques were used.

3. Character of Enemy Opposition

The terrain confronting our forces in the sector East
of MANILA, showed some similarity to that previously
encountered in the ZIGZAG PASS and in the area West of Ft
STOTSENBURG. Rising abruptly from the rice paddies in the
vicinity of MARIQUINA, SAN MATEO, and MONTALBAN; Mt ORO,
Mt PACAWAGAN, Mt MATABA, and Mt YABANG form a mountainous
chain running North and South and favorable to the enemy's
type of defense. East of these mountains, the MARIQUINA,
BOSOBOSO, and PAYAGUAN Rivers become another natural barrier,
overlooked by the higher mountains of LAMITA, PURRO, and
MAPATAD.

On the first series of mountains, vegetation was reasonably scarce except in the draws and along the many small
stream beds. At the river line and Eastward, the mountains
were covered with dense bamboo thickets and thick undergrowth, in which the enemy constructed well-concealed emplacements covering the limited approaches. The mountain
summits were excellent observation posts from which the
entire sector could be viewed and the reverse slopes were
favorable positions for heavy mortars and artillery. Then,
as his positions were neutralized, the MONTALBAN and TAYABASAN
Rivers, flowing generally from the East, were natural routes
for escape.

Enemy defensive installations were constructed mainly
from the available earth and rock, using bamboo and a limited
amount of logs for revetting and camouflage, and were well-
chosen on both forward and reverse slopes.

When the 38th Division assumed responsibility for this
area, the enemy still retained a considerable quantity of
small arms, automatic weapons, mortars, and artillery.
Rifles, knee mortars, and machine guns comprised his main
defensive weapons and 90mm and 150mm mortars, 75mm pack
artillery, and a few 105mm howitzers his main supporting
weapons.

Heavy mortars and artillery, fortunately, were used
sparingly, although large quantities of unexpended ammunition
were later found by our forces. Not many more than 100
rounds were fired in any one day, and those were never in
concentrations of more than 10 to 12 rounds and were scattered
throughout the sector. In several instances, however, the
few rounds fired were very effective, sometimes making a
direct hit with the first round.

Soon after our units began their advance Eastward, extensive enemy positions on WOODPECKER Ridge and TWIN Hills were

engaged. Positions in this area were not elaborate and indicated a hastily constructed earthwork type. Excellent choice of locations for the many caves and emplacements was made in that deadly interlocking cross fires could be delivered from the reverse slopes, thus limiting our approaches along the draws and adjacent ridges. For observation and concealment, the enemy, at all times, controlled commanding ground and possessed an abundance of camouflage material.

The defense of WOODPECKER Ridge was the enemy's heaviest opposition in this sector and was conducted with the same fanaticism displayed in the ZIGZAG PASS. His caves furnished protection from heavy artillery and mortar concentrations, an ample water supply from the MARIQUINA and BOSOBOSO Rivers was available, and it was evident that he was not, at that time, seriously handicapped by a lack of food and ammunition.

About the same time that the 152nd Infantry was attempting to secure WOODPECKER Ridge, the enemy started his mid-May offensive, of which we had been forewarned from captured documents, along the MARIQUINA-BOSOBOSO-PAYAGUAN River line. The type offensive action was not new as it consisted mainly of night infiltration attacks using automatic weapons and knee mortars, and several daylight counterattacks against our units. In some instances, the attacks were supported by artillery and heavy mortars, but these weapons were soon spotted and silenced by our own artillery.

When the enemy lost WOODPECKER Ridge to the 152nd Inf, and Mt BINICAYAN and WAWA Dam to the 149th Inf, his forces withdrew across the MARIQUINA-BOSOBOSO River line and occupied positions on Mt LAMITA, Mt PURRO and Mt MAPATAD. Here, it was quite evident that a delayed defense was his purpose, therefore, the positions were more hastily constructed, narrower in depth, and dispersed to command only the more likely approaches.

The fact that the enemy was withdrawing did not greatly lessen his determination to stem our advances. On the West slopes of Mt LAMITA, the Northwest slopes of Mt PURRO, and a Southern peak of Mt MAPATAD, stubborn resistance was met and the last occupants of the positions were virtually annihilated.

Never again, after losing these defenses, did the enemy offer more than self-preservation opposition. His only thought was to find food and escape East or Northeast.

In retrospect, it was apparent that the heart of the enemy plan was Mt PURRO. It was the center of the zone, it

was an excellent observation post, and the reserves, which
were committed in limited numbers only, were located in the
KOMEI Plains to the East between PURRO and Mt MAPATAD. It
also served as one of the last organized positions to slow
our advance and allow their remaining forces to escape along
the TAYABASAN and MONTALBAN Rivers.

GENERAL

Throughout the entire campaign, standard methods of obtaining combat intelligence, as outlined in current Field Manuals and doctrines, were employed and proved highly satisfactory. The attack elements maintained a continuous flow of information, prisoners of war, and documents through normal intelligence channels, allowing each S-2 the opportunity to function in his proper capacity. Artillery, air, and forward observers were particularly valuable sources of enemy information and their superior radio communication system often facilitated the timely transmission of information obtained by infantry units. Guerrillas were a never ceasing fount of information but due to their tendency to estimate many times the actual strengths, most careful evaluation and verification was necessary.

The most fruitful sources of information were prisoners of war and captured documents. Too much cannot be said about the care and thoroughness with which they should be processed. Prisoners almost always talked freely, were truthful to the best of their knowledge, and in a surprisingly large number of cases they were anxious to point out the locations and assist in the destruction of their fellow countrymen. Documents captured during the campaign were always authentic and sketches were very accurate. Several were captured in the ZIGZAG PASS and the area East of MANILA which revealed enemy positions in great detail even to individual riflemen and knee mortars. The documents captured were not counted individually but would have amounted to several thousands. There was a total of 837 batches processed.

Enemy Casualties

Casualties inflicted on the enemy during the campaign greatly exceeded the average enjoyed by most units. The ratio of enemy casualties to one of ours was particularly gratifying.

29 January to 30 June 1945:

Total enemy KIA and found dead	20,547
Total enemy PsW	645
Percent of PsW to enemy KIA and found dead	3.0%
Number of enemy KIA per 1 of ours	36.6 to 1
Number of enemy casualties per 1 of ours	8.1 to 1

Psychological Warfare

This type of attack was employed throughout the
operation and proved highly satisfactory. Favorable results were observed in the ZIGZAG PASS and the intensity
of its use was increased, reaching the maximum in the area
East of MANILA. The use of propaganda fell into several
categories; leaflets dropped from artillery liaison and
air corps planes, leaflets fired from artillery pieces,
utilization of a public address system, and use of prisoners
of war as intermediaries to influence other Japanese to
surrender. In the latter case, prisoners of war were per-
suaded to reenter the enemy lines to influence other of
their countrymen to surrender, to make broadcasts over the
loud speaker system, to fly over enemy territory, and to enter
forward OPs with intelligence officers to point out enemy
concentrations, CPs, supply dumps, etc.

In employing psychological warfare facilities, the
following leaflet drops and broadcasts were made, and the un-
usually high number of prisoners, some 645, attests to the
effectiveness of this campaign:

AREA	LEAFLETS	BROADCASTS
ZIGZAG PASS	20,000	
BATAAN	998,000	
CORREGIDOR	10,000	1 from PT boat
CABALLO	15,000	1 from PT boat
EL FRAILE		1 from PT boat
CARABAO		1 from PT boat
West of STOTSENBURG	215,000	3
East of MANILA	1,888,000	8
	3,146,000	15

Counterintelligence

There were no instances found where the enemy had gained information of our forces through lack of security, and
the known number of violations within the division were very
few. The enemy's principal source of information appeared
to come from reconnaissance patrols which were very pro-
ficient in sketching our positions and concentrations, as
learned from captured documents.

Little difficulty was experienced in searching enemy
installations for items of counterintelligence value although many were found.

The greatest threat of information falling into the

hands of the enemy was the number of civilians who, of necessity, must have freedom of movement behind our lines. The task of processing these civilians, from whom considerable information of the enemy was gained, and investigation of reported collaborators fell to the CIC detachment. This proved to be quite a burden as little reliance could be placed on the accusations of guerrillas and other civilians, and due to inaccuracies in previously prepared black lists of personalities. The political situation was deplorable. Guerrillas brigands had flourished for three undisturbed years, many local government officials were ruled by guerrilla leaders of questionable character, and honest citizens who had merely failed to allow themselves to be dominated by the self-styled soldier-patriots, were for that reason alone, subjected to provoking charges of collaboration. There were several known pro-Japanese organizations with memberships numbering several thousands, many of whom were victims of circumstances. Thus, the sheep had to be separated from the goats. Of the hundreds interviewed, approximately 200 civilians were thoroughly investigated which resulted in more than 50 interned.

Lessons learned:

Aerial Photographs. Aerial photographs, to be of value to a command, should be received in time for careful interpretation and study by commanders. These photos should have immediate distribution in order that interpretation may be made simultaneous with higher echelon. If this is not done, additional delay results while divisional photo interpretation personnel orient, mount, and conduct further examination before prints are available to commanders.

Intelligence Officers. Regimental and Battalion S-2s have a specific function to perform in evaluation and dissemination of intelligence. These staff officers must spend the bulk of their time at the CP where they can supervise the recording and collating of information, and personally evaluate and disseminate the resulting intelligence. Otherwise, information is forwarded to higher echelon, not intelligence. Their presence at the CP is also essential in order that intelligence may be promptly disseminated to all concerned. Enlisted personnel must not be left to "pinch-hit" for S-2s.

Reconnaissance

Ground: Patrols must be carefully planned and executed. Aerial reconnaissance over densely wooded terrain is inadequate and commanders must therefore rely on ground reconnaissance to supply information of the enemy. Patrols must fix the enemy, determine his flanks and depth of position, locate dumps, vital installations and reserves, and ascertain identity and approximate strength of the opposing force. Patrols must be sent out for extended periods of time with a definite mission in mind, e.g., to capture a PW, locate suspected CPs, observe hostile movement. Too frequently patrols report contact with the enemy and return with nothing more. They must probe the enemy position until flanks are definitely fixed and then seek to determine his depth of position. Their information will enable commanders to move swiftly and decisively to destroy the enemy.

Air: Artillery liaison planes are ideal for detecting enemy movements, especially the shifting of reserves and the arrival of reinforcements. Moreover, they make possible the location of enemy mortar and artillery, and direct immediate neutralization fires thereon. Liaison planes also are valuable in making correction on maps, and in clearing up doubtful targets and installations on aerial photographs. The suspension of enemy fire and movement when the planes are aloft attests their effectiveness.

Reporting information. The worth of information of the enemy is in direct proportion to the speed with which it is disseminated up, down, and laterally. In this, all units were lacking. In the early phase, it was necessary to make frequent calls to subordinate units and inquire: "What is the situation?", "Has contact been made?", "What is the enemy doing?", "How many casualties?", "Prisoners?", "Captured documents?" All information of the enemy - no matter how trivial it appears - must be forwarded immediately, and with personnel specifically delegated to perform this function, it should be spontaneously carried out without prompting. Prompting causes delay which in turn, costs lives and lose battles. Dissemination to lower units often left much to be desired. This was particularly true in distribution of G-2 periodic reports from regiments to battalions. Often, when units were widely separated, receipt by battalions would be as much as 5 or 6 days late and frequently resulted in them having no idea of what was being encountered by sister units in other sectors. It is essential that dissemination of all pertinent information be executed promptly; the lapse of time lessens the worth of intelligence and frequently renders it valueless.

Message Writing

Completeness - Much time was consumed in having to check

incomplete messages with the originating headquarters. The basic requirements of all messages - what, when, why, who, where and evaluation - were, in part, frequently omitted. This resulted in delay in recording, evaluating and disseminating of intelligence as well as imposing a needless burden on communications. Officers and enlisted personnel, alike, must be impressed with the importance of completeness of all messages.

Accuracy - Numerous messages giving wrong coordinates and erroneous information were received. Some messages stated: "We are pinned down by enemy MG fire", "We are surrounded by the enemy", or "The enemy is making a banzai attack". Check all coordinates carefully before forwarding information, and be sure of its accuracy. Surprising though it may seem, coordinates several thousand yards distant from the location of the actual happening were frequently submitted. In extreme, isolated cases, coordinates have been forwarded to division locating ground activity far out to sea. Submit all information to this test: Is the source usually reliable? Is it reasonable and logical? In the light of other information could it have happened?

Searching enemy dead and installations. Much valuable information was lost to the command because enemy dead and enemy installations were not thoroughly searched. In some cases, this failure was prompted by fear of booby traps, and in others, by indifference. A wire hook on the end of a 20' length of cord, or a long pole will enable those who search enemy dead to move the body without danger. Similarly, hand grenades and light demolitions will detonate most booby traps, and, by using a pole and a flashlight (not matches), caves and bunkers can be explored with relative safety. Every dog tag and every scrap of paper may contain information that will contribute to saving the lives of many.

Souvenirs - Too often valuable documents and equipment are destroyed, lost, or overlooked by personnel to whom the collection of information is only incidental in their hunt for souvenirs. Numerous soldiers who were evacuated as casualties, carried notebooks and other printed matter in their pockets. This gives further rise to the assumption that the mania for keepsakes kept valuable information out of intelligence channels.

Prisoners - Although the ratio of PsW to total enemy casualties has been higher than in most divisions in this theater, there were numerous instances where lightly armed

and ineffective Japs were killed. Every PW is a source of
extremely valuable information, which he gives freely to
interrogators. We are the losers when we kill off this
source. It was found that distribution of a copy of PW in-
terrogation or translation of captured documents to the low-
est unit concerned, attested to the great value the division
placed on them and encouraged greater efforts in taking PsW
and documents.

Captured and destroyed equipment - Captured and destroyed enemy equipment was not reported in many cases.
Consequently, evacuation by supply personnel and demolition
by engineers was delayed, aside from the fact that the
division got no credit for capture and destruction of unre-
ported equipment. Location should be noted on maps, and report made promptly of all small supply and ammunition dumps
which do not warrant a guard, and a record of contents be
made and reported when they are destroyed or evacuated. Dis-
regard of these dumps affords enemy stragglers the opportunity of replenishing themselves with food and arms during
the mopping up phase.

All captured equipment, either civilian or military,
used by the enemy, should be accurately reported as encountered, even though it may have been previously destroyed
by air attack, artillery fire, or other means.

Improper Channels - Although the line of demarcation
between S-2 and S-3 information is sometimes obscure, too
frequently G-2 received operational information and G-3
received enemy information. The collection, evaluation
and dissemination of enemy information is a function of
unit intelligence officers, and the proper channel is to
the lower, adjacent or higher S-2 or G-2. Similarly, S-2's
cannot become involved in a maze of information of friendly
troops. Remember: Enemy information to S-2 or G-2; information of friendly troops to S-3 or G-3. In case of doubt
as to where the information should be sent, report to both
staff sections.

Aerial Photographs - Advance planning for the need of
photographs is absolutely essential. This was done by
Division for each change in the situation, redeployment of
our troops, and planning for new attacks. Initial
requisition and distribution of photos was made by G-2 but
needs arose within the Regiments for additional runs which
could not be anticipated by Division. We were fortunate
when 3-day service on new runs was given by the Air Corps,
and frequently it was longer, thus many photos requested by

Regiments on the spur of the moment were worthless when received.

Recommendations

(1) The casualty rate of battalion S-2's in combat was found to be extremely high. Wounds, deaths, battle fatigue, and promotions to battalion S-3 and company commander all took their toll. It is recommended that intensive intelligence training and intelligence schools be conducted for junior officers prior to entering combat. At least one junior officer should be designated as an alternate S-2 for each battalion. This officer should preferably be a 2nd Lieutenant as 1st Lieutenants are naturally looking forward to the time when they may become captains and are not interested in a job which might sidetrack them.

(2) The regimental S-2 has a great need for an assistant and it is recommended that one be allowed. The S-2 cannot avoid being absent from the command post during his necessary visits to the regimental OP and front line units. These absences are often unavoidably long and intelligence functions suffer when a clerk must fill in for him.

(3) Within the G-2 section itself, several changes are highly desirable. The gratifying amount of information received during combat kept the Order of Battle team fully occupied and left them with the urgent need for a driver for their vehicle, which the T/O does not allow.

The necessity of typing their own reports placed a considerable burden on the already overworked language personnel. There was easily enough work to keep two full time clerks busy. It is recommended that two be added to the Language team.

(4) An improvement is highly desirable in the equipment issued to the G-2 section. Duplicating jelly rolls, other than the hard tropical type, were found unsatisfactory in hot climates. It is also recommended that an engineer set of drafting equipment, to include a drawing set, be allowed. It was learned that the present allowance of tools was wholly inadequate for proper accomplishment of the work to be done.

Types of Enemy Installations Encountered

The 38th Division encountered no radically new installations or tactics in this operation. They followed the conventional pattern of construction and employment that American forces have met in the SOLOMONS, NEW GUINEA, the MARIANAS and PHILIPPINES. Those encountered in the M-7 Operation, generally, will fall into these groups.

    (1)   <u>Personnel and air raid shelters</u> (See Figure 1)

        This installation was found both in the ZIGZAG PASS and the area West of STOTSENBURG. It required thousands of man-hours to construct, was used principally for shelter from bombs, artillery and mortars, and would accommodate an entire company. These shelters were capable of withstanding our heaviest artillery.

    (2)   <u>Log and dirt bunkers</u> (See Figure 2)

        Bunkers of this type were found along the ZAMBALES Coast, in towns such as SAN ANTONIO, SUBIC or OLONGAPO, in the ZIGZAG PASS, and along the PILAR-BAGAC Road. Usually of low silhouette, carefully landscaped and camouflaged, and with excellent fields of fire for either AT, MG or small arms, they were the backbone of the Japanese defense.

    (3)   <u>Pillboxes</u> (See Figure 3)

        The conventional pillbox was seldom encountered anywhere except along highways, near road junctions, and around Japanese headquarters. It is more vulnerable to flat trajectory weapons at close range than the bunker shown in Figure 1.

    (4)   <u>Tunnels</u> (See Figure 4)

        The "tunnel area" is another stock-in-trade of the Japs. They are generally more common along roads and trails, where artillery and AT guns may be quickly wheeled out and put into action, although they may be found on higher ground and used for CP's and storage of supplies. They are sometimes mutually supporting, but as a rule, they are <u>without</u> regard to support from adjacent tunnels. These "tunnel areas" are common to every area in which the Division has operated.

    (5)   <u>Foxholes</u> (See Figure 5)

        A - this diagram represents a typical organization of Jap hill-top defense. Foxholes were close enough to be mutually supporting, and so beautifully concealed that they could not be spotted, sometimes, when 10 ft. away. Hand grenades are the best means to neutralize an area thus organized. B - a commonly found fox hole. They permit a degree of comfort and offer considerable protection against grenades or light

mortars since they are partially covered. C - a bowl-shaped
foxhole which allows the occupant to relax while sitting,
and have some protection from air bursts or fires of high
angle weapons. Both B and C may have interconnecting, underground tunnels which enables the enemy to draw fire at one
point, go through the tunnel to another foxhole, and shoot
the attacker from an unsuspected position.

    (6)   Trenches and foxholes (See Figure 6)

        This Jap trench system was frequently used in the
area West of STOTSENBURG, where there was a small amount of
cover and all-around fields of fire were desired. The
connecting trenches, open-type, enabled movement in the
position without being observed, permitted concentration of
fire at desired points, and a considerable latitude for dis-
persal of personnel from any point on the perimeter which
might be under heavy fire.

    (7)   Foxholes (See Figure 7)

        A common installation for covering roads is a
covered foxhole. The lid, made of small saplings and well-
camouflaged, is pulled over the occupant, who had a large
enough opening for his rifle or machine gun to cover the
road or trail. In some cases, mines and demolitions were
placed in the road and detonated by a wire or cord operated
from the foxhole.

20' - 00

7'00"

Bamboo Risers
Bamboo Horizontal
strips

SECTION THRU A   A

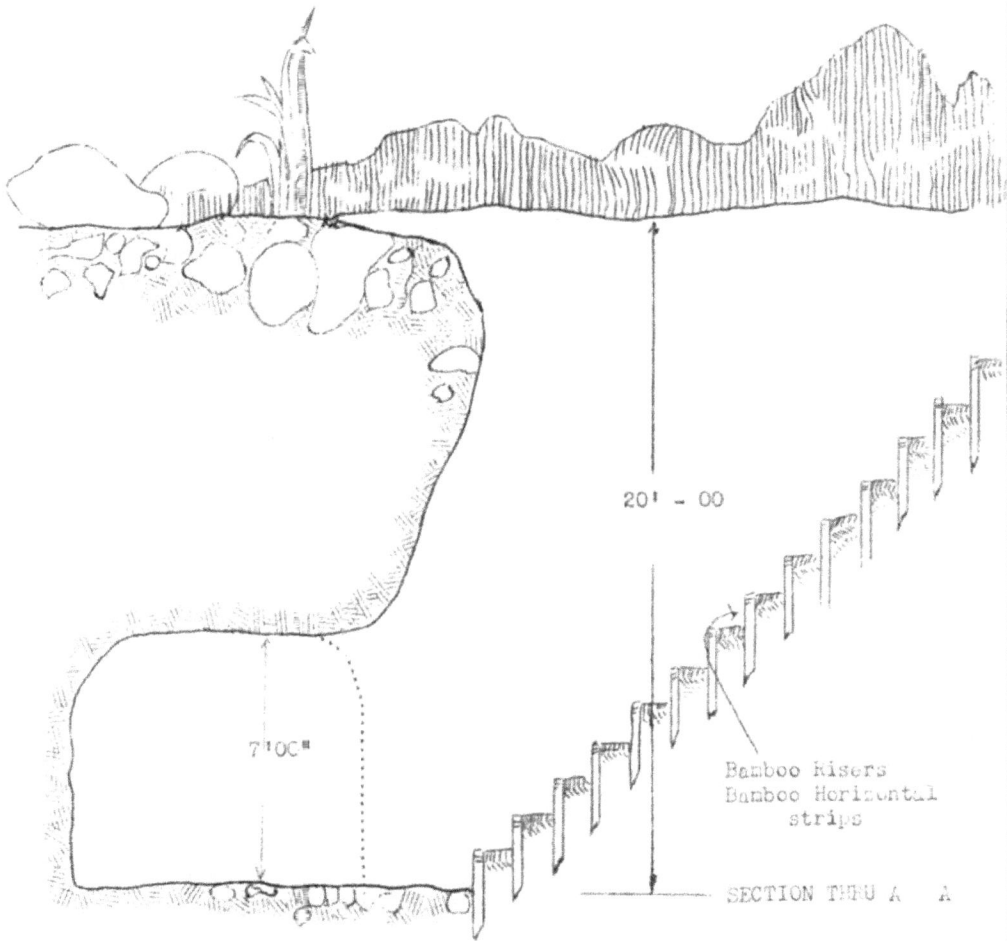

PERSONNEL &
AIR RAID SHELTER

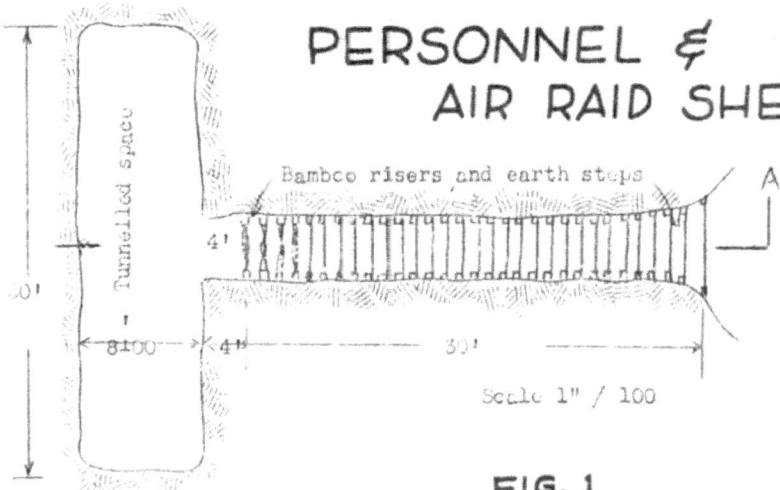

Tunnelled space

Bamboo risers and earth steps

A

4'

.0'

8'00   4'   30'

Scale 1" / 100

FIG. 1

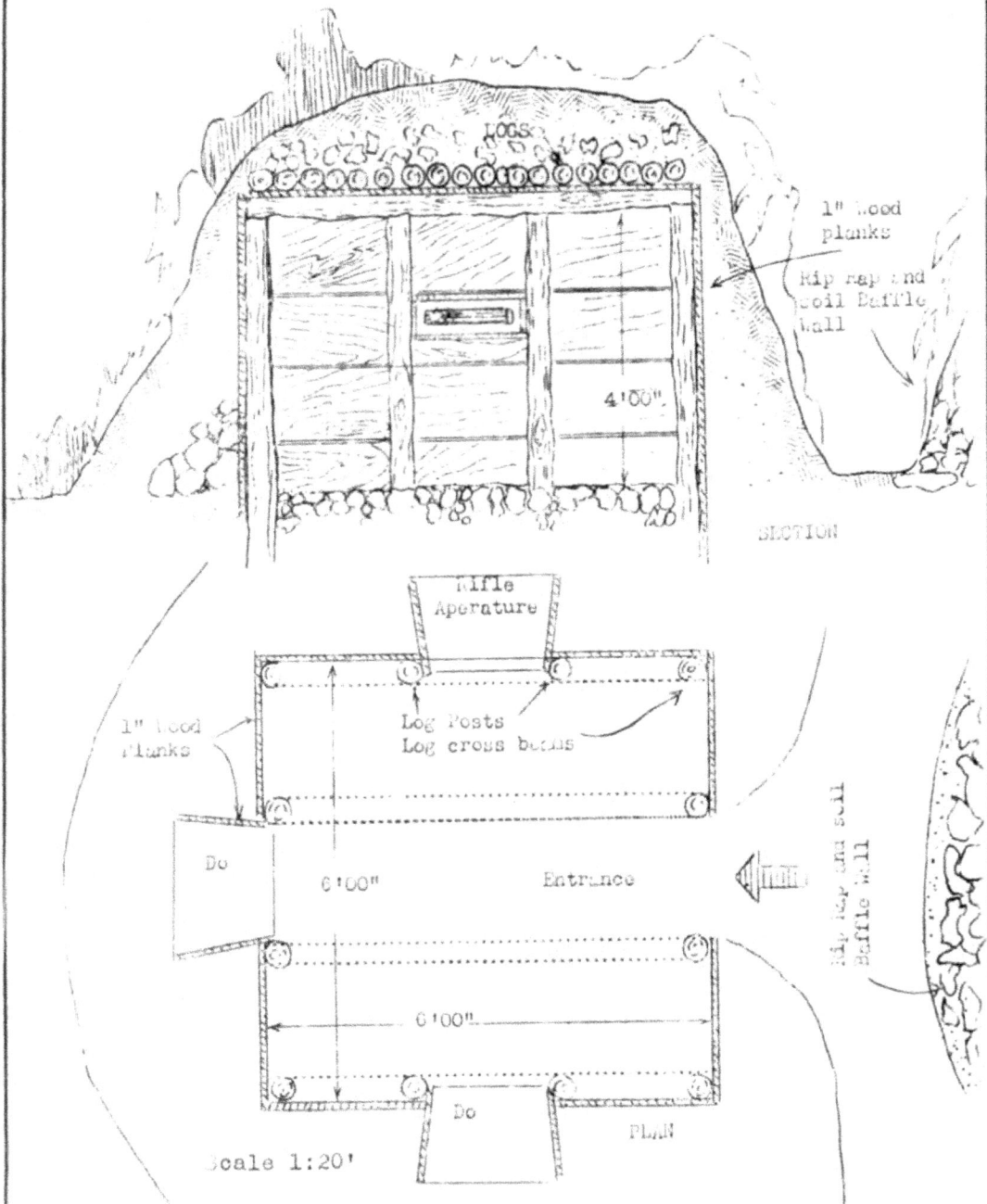

LOGS

1" wood
planks

Rip rap and
soil baffle
wall

4'00"

SECTION

Rifle
Aperature

1" wood
planks

Log Posts
Log cross beams

Do

6'00"

Entrance

Rip rap and soil
baffle wall

6'00"

Do

PLAN

Scale 1:20'

LOG AND DIRT BUNKER
FIG 2

1" Wood Planks

Log Posts
and beams

Stone and dirt
Baffle Mound

4 Ft
Approx

SECTION
Scale 1:20'

Baffle
Mound

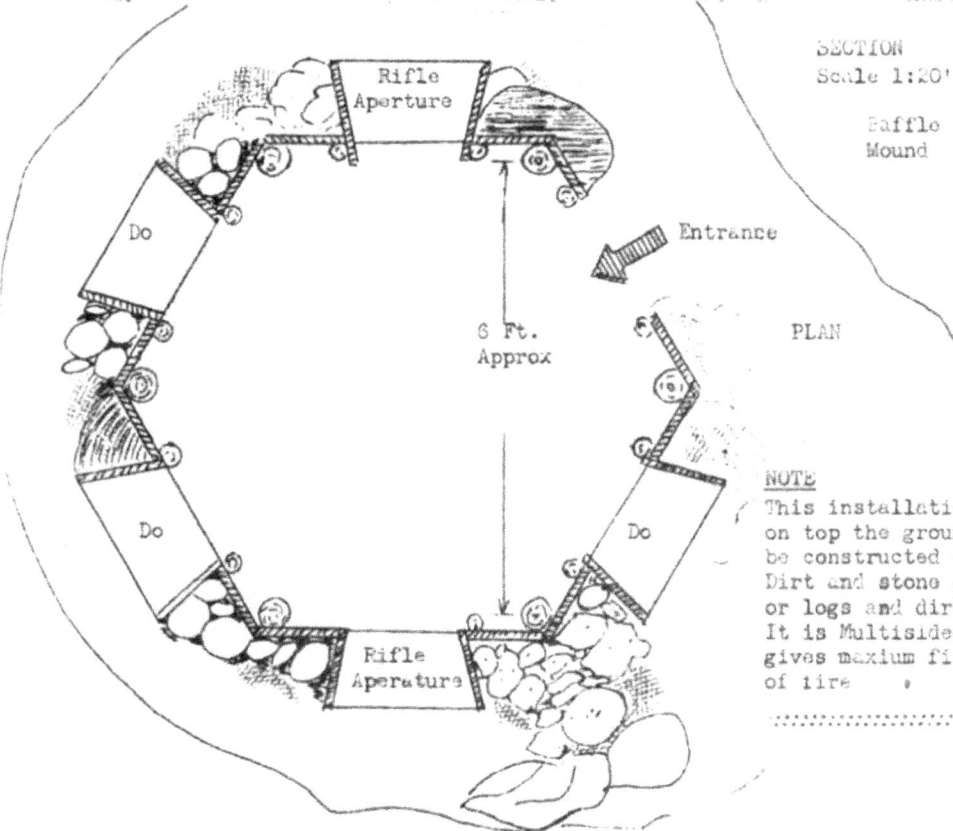

Rifle
Aperture

Do

Do

Do

6 Ft.
Approx

Rifle
Aperature

Rifle
Aperature

Entrance

PLAN

NOTE
This installation is
on top the ground may
be constructed of
Dirt and stone or
or logs and dirt.
It is Multisided and
gives maxium fields
of fire

PILLBOX

FIG 3

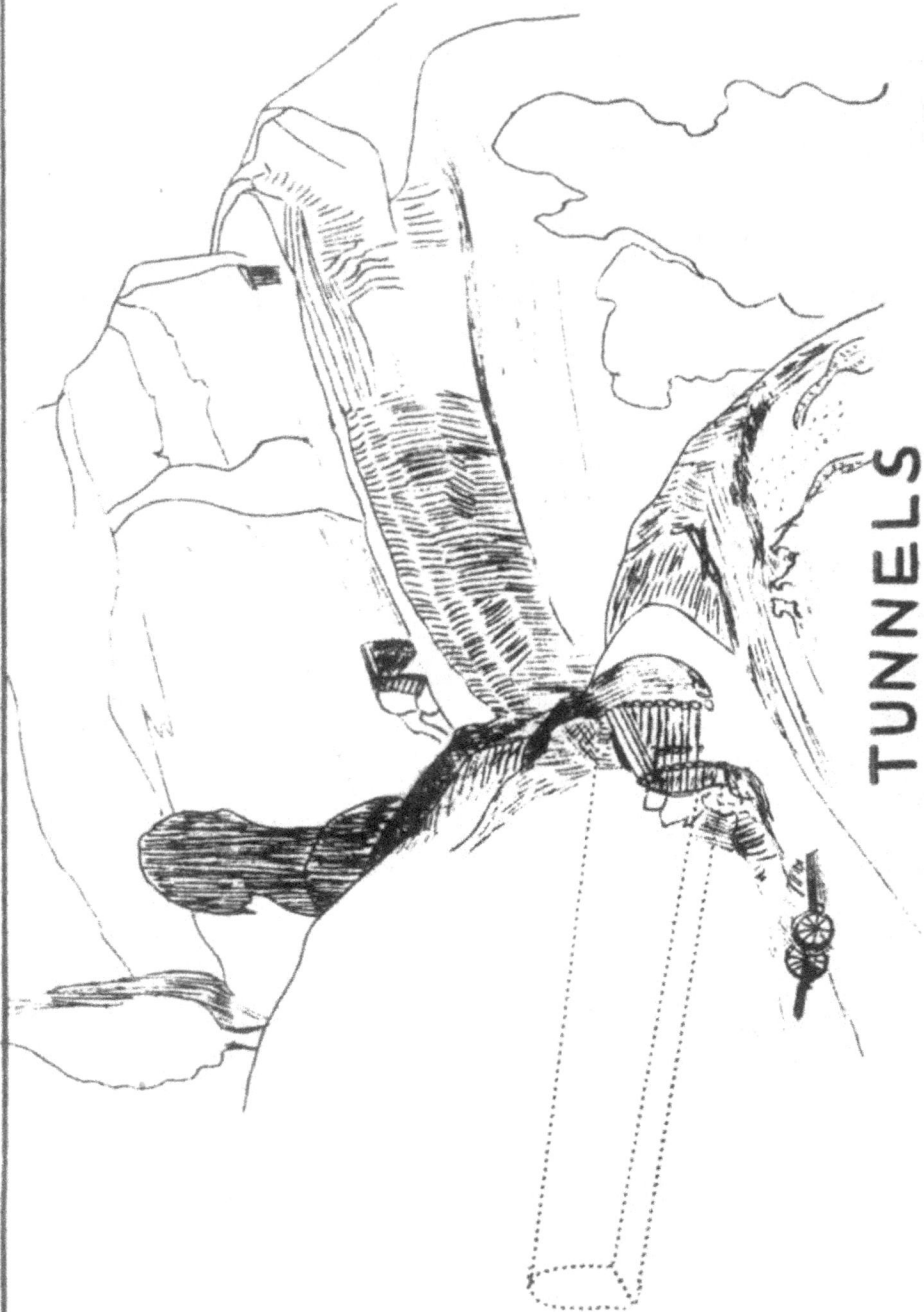

TUNNELS

May be { Guns
used for { Supplies
{ Personnel shelter
{ Shelter for horses (Horse Drawn R.)

FIG 4

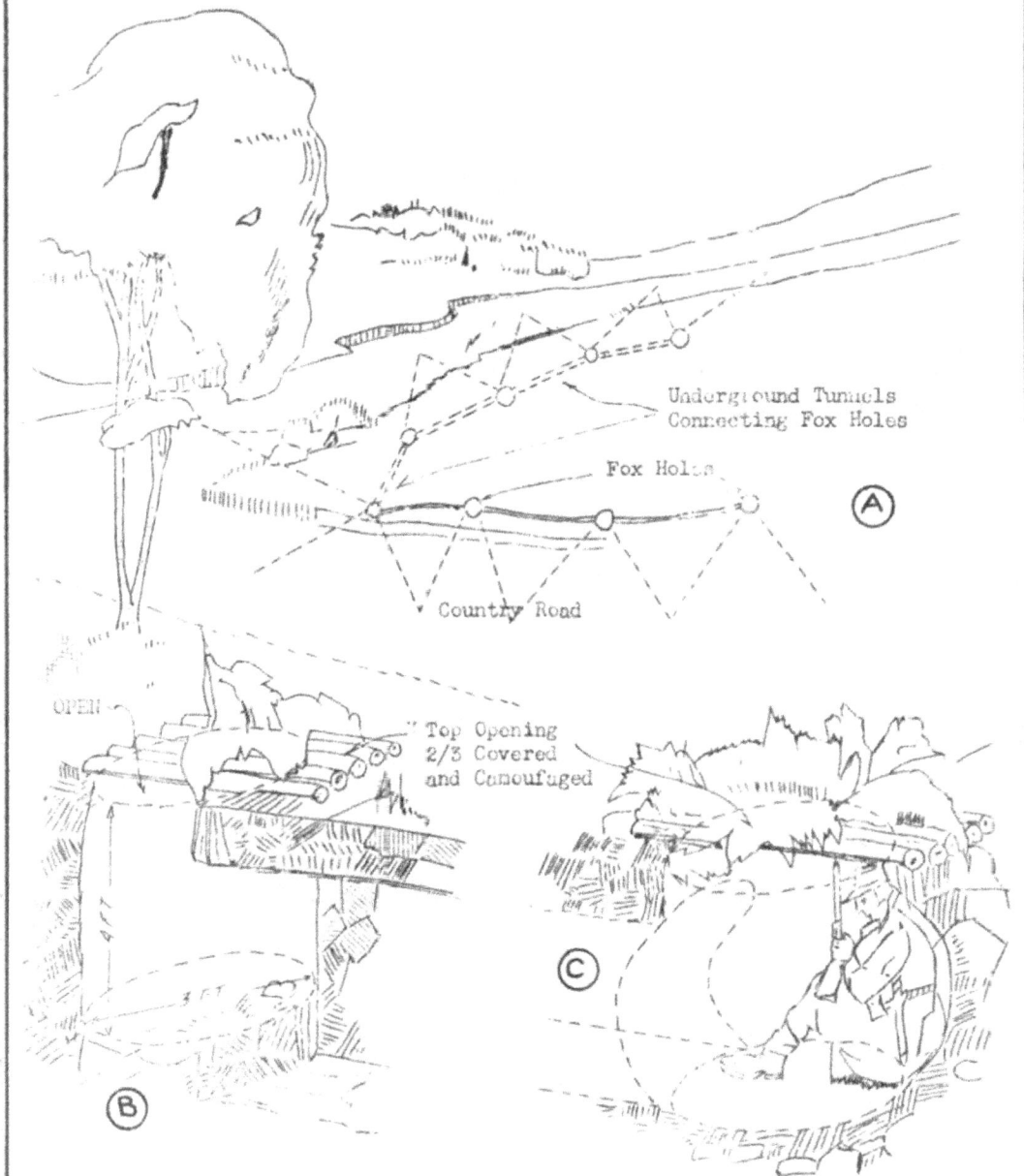

Underground Tunnels
Connecting Fox Holes

Fox Holes

(A)

Country Road

OPEN

Top Opening
2/3 Covered
and Camoufuged

(C)

(B)

CYLINDRICAL TYPE   SPIDER TYPE

FOXHOLES

FIG 5

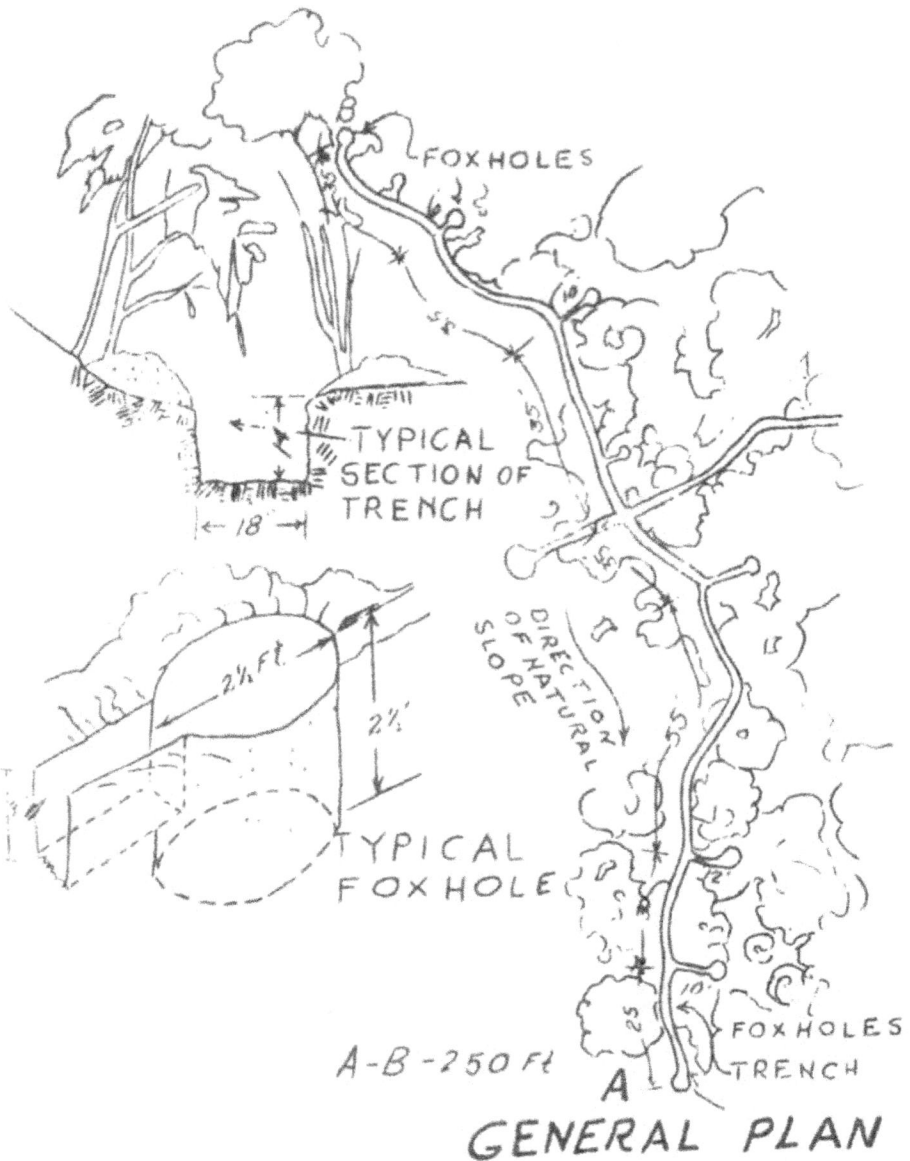

FOXHOLES

TYPICAL SECTION OF TRENCH

← 18 →

2½ Ft.

2½"

TYPICAL FOXHOLE

DIRECTION OF NATURAL SLOPE

FOXHOLES TRENCH

A-B-250 Ft

A

GENERAL PLAN

A SYSTEM OF TRENCHES
AND FOXHOLES

FIG. 6

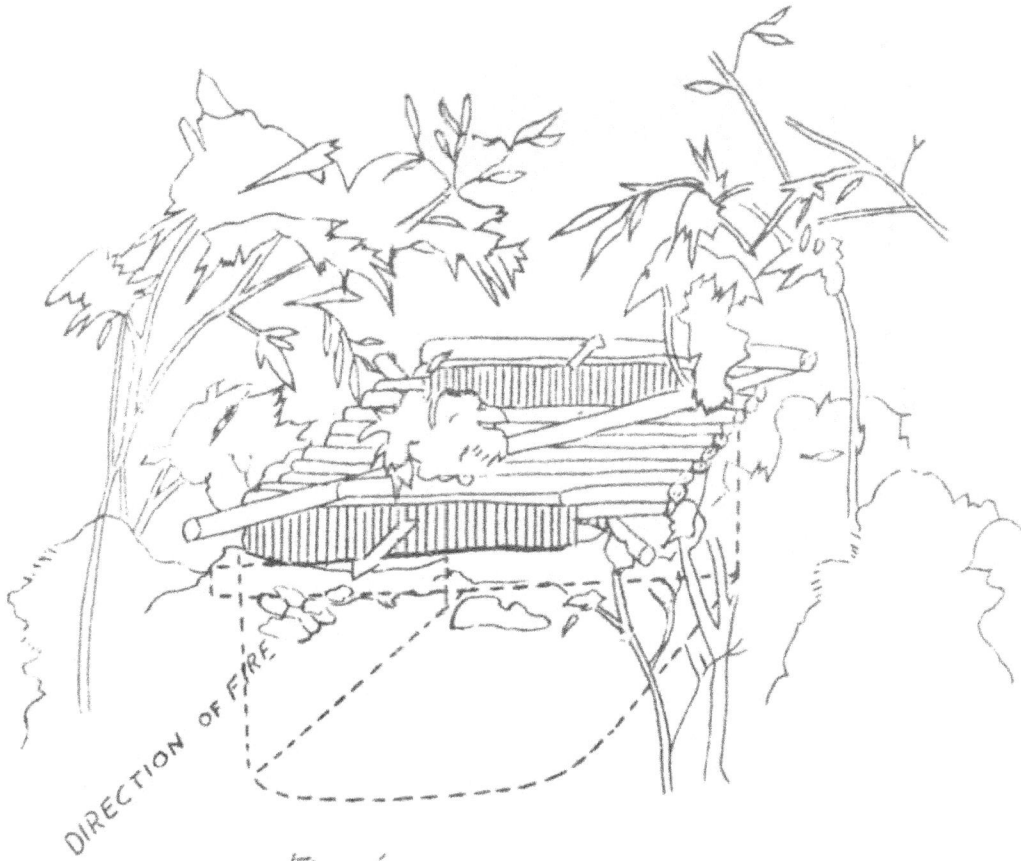

Trees and underbrush

Direction of fire

Trail

PLAN

FOXHOLE

FIG. 7

Pillbox

This installation was found on Bloody Hill in Zigzag Pass. It was 4' high, 6' wide and 18' long. Before its destruction it was well hidden from ground and aerial observation. From its position on a hill it had a wide field of fire. It was used for small arms, machine guns and mortars.

Cave

This photo shows the reinforced and added protection construction around a cave overlooking the beach at
Bagac. The entrance to the cave cannot be seen in the
photo. It is located on the side of a hill, and was probably used as a combination storage and small arms emplacement.

Bunker

This installation is located midway between Pilar and Bagac on the Pilar-Bagac trail. It is 10' off the trail covering a straight stretch of the road. It is constructed of heavy logs covered with dirt and foliage. The opening which is 6' long and 2' high provides a wide field of fire.

It is well concealed from aerial observation.

Slit Trench

This trench is located in the immediate vicinity
of the bunker. There is no pattern of construction and
it appears not to have been used for a considerable
length of time.

Foxhole

This one man foxhole, which is heavily reinforced
with logs and dirt, was located just off the Pilar-Bagac
trail. It commanded a wide field of fire on the road and
was well concealed from both ground and aerial observation.

Personnel Trench

This trench is "Y" shaped and is located immediately behind the bunker covering the bend in the road. It, however, does not connect with this bunker. Excellent concealment is afforded by overhanging trees. Dimensions of each of the three sections of the bunker measure 8' long and 3' deep.

Cave

This installation is dug into the side of a cliff
overlooking the beach at Bagac. The entrance way is about
4' high x 4' wide and extends for a distance of 8' into
the side of the cliff. The cave was probably used for a
personnel shelter and storage.

In front of the cave heavy rocks were emplaced in
a semi-circular pattern. This provided sufficient space
for the location of a coastal defense gun.

Spider Hole

This installation was one of many of similar construction found on Todd's Hill in Zigzag Pass. The hole was 2' wide at the top, widening to 5' in diameter at the base and was 5' deep.

A basket weave of bamboo, camouflaged to blend with the terrain, was used as a lid. The hole was large enough to accommodate two men, one of whom could lift the lid a few inches, while the other fired through the opening.

ARTILLERY SECTION

The employment of the Division Artillery throughout the operation was orthodox in every respect. No technical difficulties were encountered. Movements were of such length that the slow speed tractor was inadequate and shuttling by truck was often necessary. After the initial landing and movement into contact units only moved appreciably between phases.

Though the terrain, opposition, and tactics were very similar throughout the whole operation, for simplicity and clarity it is best to divide the whole into four phases: ZIG-ZAG; BATAAN; FORT STOTSENBURG - ISLANDS - ZAMBALES; MARIQUINA RIVER. Each phase had its own peculiar problems and solutions and should be discussed separately. Phase charts have been made and are appended showing: types of fire delivered and the comparison for each infantry of the amount of artillery ammunition expended in direct support, type resistance encountered, friendly KIA's and enemy killed and found dead.

ZIG-ZAG PHASE:

From positions in the hard rice paddies in the vicinity of Olongapo the Division Artillery and attached units supported the Division thru the rugged, confined, heavily timbered, bamboo choked mountain pass known as the Zig-Zag. Cleared areas were very scarce and then only on hilltops. Ground observation was nearly impossible except for forward observers whose vision was often limited to only a few yards. Therefore, air observation was used to the maximum extent. Air patrols were maintained from before dawn until dark and many times after dark.

The entire action took place in an area about 1500 y ds wide adjacent to the winding road, which was accurately defined on the available maps. Though a target area survey was impossible, all battalions were tied together by position area survey and registration. It was then found possible to mass fires accurately on points, the coordinates and altitude of which were taken from the map.

Though the fortifications encountered were based somewhat on a previous American defense plan, information of these plans did not reach the division until later in the engagement. This hampered the planning of preparations and harassing fires. However a combination of air reconnaissance and the constant study of observers reports and photos gave excellent results. Information from ground troops

about these fortifications, due to the roughness of the
terrain, often came after they had made contact and were
too involved for artillery fire to be safe. Preparations
and fires in direct support of attacks comprised 49% of the
ammunition expended by the Division Artillery and attached
units during this phase.

Although there was very little observation of movement
during daylight, the air observers and pilots quickly developed the ability to locate Japanese installations such
as aid stations, water and food points and supply dumps.
This information coupled with the location of mortar and
light field piece positions enabled interdiction and harassing fires to be particularly effective both during the day
and at night. This type fire made up 10% of the ammunition
expended.

Close defensive fires, requested by the infantry comprised 8% of the total ammunition expended during this phase.
This amount is the highest for this type fire during any
phase. There are two reasons which may be deduced from the
chart of this phase; one: that the troops were inexperienced
and needed the additional assurance that they had adequate
artillery support, two: that the enemy was aggressive and
initially attempted numerous night infiltrations.

Targets of opportunity were located by air observation.
When close to ground troops these targets were fired on in
conjunction with the forward observers. Initially these
targets included many mortar positions. Later as the pressure increased tanks were forced from their caves and pits
and successfully taken under fire. Three of the six encountered were destroyed by indirect artillery fire. During the last part of this period when the organized resistance had been broken, many enemy troops were caught in
the open and destroyed. These targets accounted for 32% of
the ammunition expended.

The remaining charts of this phase show a comparison
of artillery ammunition expended in direct support (exclud-
ing general support), type resistance, enemy KIA and our
own KIA. It will be noted that our artillery fire increased
in proportion to the enemy resistance encountered. In all
three regiments the number of enemy killed and found dead
lagged behind artillery expenditures, indicating that a
great many enemy killed by artillery and mortar fire were
not found until later. Once the enemy resistance was brok-
en and the Jap was forced out of his holes he became an
easy target for both artillery and infantry automatic and
and small arms fire.

- 160 -

During this phase many habits of the Jap were learned
and were put to good advantage in later phases.

BATAAN PHASE:

This phase was a period of scattered resistance where
artillery support was rarely needed. Preparations and
harassing fire produced meager results, defensive fires
were a hang-over from the preceding phase and targets of
opportunity were few and far between. It was a phase of
extended patrol and mopping-up action.

FORT STOTSENBURG-ISLANDS-ZAMBALES PHASE:

This period cannot be treated as a single phase but
rather three - one for each infantry regiment as each
operated in a different sector under different conditions.

The Fort Stotsenburg sector was taken over from another division by a regiment and a battalion of our infantry with three battalions of artillery in support.
Initially one combat team of the relieved division was
attached but its action will not be discussed here.

As the artillery operations in the other areas were
minor the chart showing types of fire for this phase per-
tain to that which took place in the area west of Fort
Stotsenburg. During most of this period artillery ammunition was limited. This limitation was educational in that
it necessitated careful planning on the part of both the
artillery and infantry staffs. It was often necessary to
accumulate artillery ammunition before a particular local
attack could be made. Also as evidenced by the chart,
this shortage limited the expenditure for targets of
opportunity. Defensive fires were virtually eliminated,
due not only to the lack of ammunition but also to the
fact that our troops had become more battle-wise and also
the enemy attempted few infiltrations or counter-attacks.

Early in this phase when ammunition was not restricted, the preponderance of artillery fire was placed
deep in the enemy positions in support of our infantry
encirclement. When forced out of his organized positions,
the Jap again fell easy prey to artillery fire in the open.

As it developed, there were five definite strong
points remaining in the area when the division took over
the sector. These were quite widely separated and not
all interlocking. Three were reduced by concentrated
flank assault, a fourth collapsed as a result of the fall
of the first three and the fifth crumbled under constant

pressure.

The fortification of these strong points was typical and very similar to that encountered in the Zig-Zag Pass.

The reduction of a Jap strong point depends upon several factors: (1) the amount of definite information obtained about the particular fortification to be assaulted, (2) accessibility for placement of automatic and direct fire weapons, (3) the amount of artillery and mortar preparation that can be placed on the target, and (4) the aggressiveness of the foot soldier to close as the supporting fires are lifted.

Jap strong points found in this area were constructed along the precipitious sides of gorges, craters or terminals of ridges, which formed ampitheaters. Some were located in barren lava defiles, while others were in draws, thickly covered with bamboo, undergrowth and large trees. Other fortified areas were constructed on peaks of ridges nearly surrounded by sheer cliffs, canalizing the assault. Many strong points were mutually supporting, while others were self-sufficient with interlocking lanes of automatic weapons fire. Regardless of the type of location there was invariably a complete maze of sub-terrainian passages eminating from large chambers carved out of solid rock. Along these passages were small apertures through which automatic weapons could fire on fixed lanes.

The successful assault of such strong points with proportionately heavy casualties to the enemy was made possible by well coordinated artillery and mortar fires on known installations within a strong point and in the aggressive following of the supporting fires by the infantry. Some lessons learned were (1) that surprise fire at times when the Jap relaxes and comes out of his rat hole for one reason or another, will do much to reduce his fighting efficiency. (This can only be determined by constant study of his actions during the organization period before a well planned attack.) (2) That both artillery and mortar fire are most effective when massed on known targets and accompanied by fire from all available infantry supporting weapons. The foot soldier who finally captures the ground must follow and close with the enemy immediately following the softening up process.

The Island Operations were both spectacular and unusual. The artillery played little part except in the softening up process.

The Zambales Operation was a mopping-up operation where the artillery rendered assistance to strong aggressive infantry patrols or ambushes.

MARIQUINA RIVER PHASE:

At the beginning of this phase the division relieved another division and took over a sector of approximately 40,000 yards. This prevented the massing of more than a few battalions of artillery on any one target, even though the Division Artillery was supplemented by Corps Artillery units.

The enemy was intrenched in his typical spider holes and deep fortifications west of the Mariquina River which he defended tenaciously. His mortar and automatic weapons fires were well coordinated and caused a number of casualties in our forward units. The terrain was very favorable for defense and he made the maximum use of it. Again the heavily covered bamboo draws and hillsides caused much delay and necessitated timbering by the artillery.

Observation from the ground was good but had to be supplemented by air because the Jap emplacements were invariably on reverse slopes. Close coordination of observation from adjacent areas proved very helpful. This was simplified by the common radio channel carried on all 600 series radios. As was the case during the Zig-Zag Phase, radio was the primary means of communication from the front lines and often relay was necessary thru liaison plane radio because of the terrain.

Unlike the Zig-Zag Phase, target area survey was possible and carried out to the fullest extent. When visual survey was impossible due to the mountainous terrain, target area survey was successfully accomplished by using stripped data obtained by firing on the same point with two widely separated batteries. Survey plus the very satisfactory maps made it possible to mass the fires of those units that could be shifted into a particular sector with excellent results.

As indicated by the chart of types of fire, many preparations and close supporting fires were delivered. At times it was difficult to obtain close coordination with the infantry supporting weapons. When the preparations were coordinated the results were more than satisfactory and the strong points reduced as indicated on the charts of the individual infantry regiments. Preparations and close supporting fires comprised 30% of the ammunition expended during this phase.

Targets of opportunity accounted for the largest
expenditure, 46%, while defensive fires were less than
1%. Interdiction and harassing fires amounted to 23%
and again proved very effective. The amount of defensive
fires is an indication again of the aggressiveness of the
enemy and the experience of our troops.

Again constant air patrols proved most useful, both
as an information agency and in adjusting prompt effective fire on targets of opportunity.

SUMMARY:

Throughout the operation a common channel on all
artillery radios proved to be not only useful but necessary. This made possible rapid communications between all
artillery units as well as front line infantry units.

Although not mentioned before, K-20 Cameras were used
extensively for both aerial and ground photos to make
panoramic strips for use by both artillery forward observers and infantry commanders.

For the successful reduction of strong points, the
fire of all weapons must be coordinated both as to target
and as to time. A thorough study of the reactions and
habits of particular Japanese groups encountered must be
made for the proper timing of surprise fire.

Continuous air patrols by the same liaison pilot-
observer teams made it possible for them to accomplish
their missions in a superior manner.

Artillery fire is more effective when massed in surprise time on target.

Target area survey must be accomplished by every
means available.

All troops must develop the ability to determine
their map location accurately so that surprise fire can
be brought close enough to be effective.

TYPES OF FIRE DELIVERED

ZIG ZAG PHASE

149ᵀᴴ INF

PREPARATIONS AND
CLOSE SUPPORT

HARRASSING

DEFENSIVE

TARGETS OF
OPPORTUNITY

ARTY AMMO EXPENDED
IN DIRECT SUPPORT

TYPE RESISTANCE.

FRIENDLY KIA

ENEMY KILLED AND
FOUND DEAD

KIA

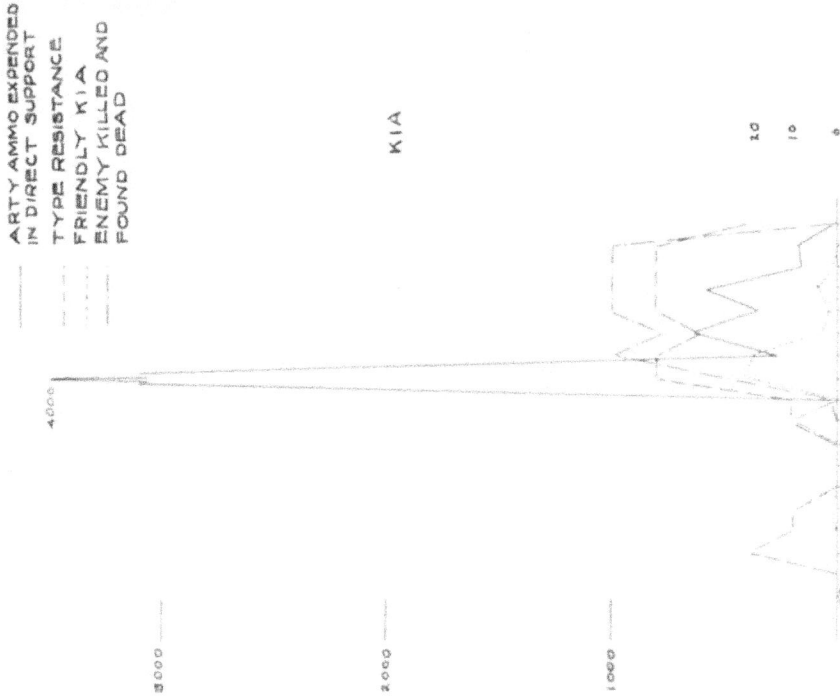

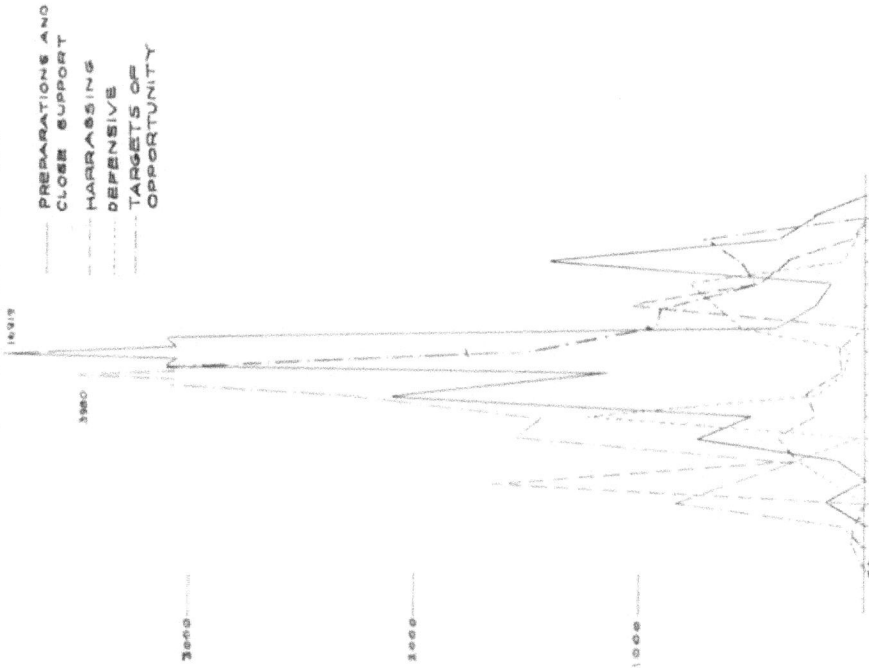

ZIG ZAG PHASE

151ˢᵗ INF

152ᵈ INF

LEGEND:
— ARTY AMMO EXPENDED IN DIRECT SUPPORT
— — TYPE RESISTANCE
— · — FRIENDLY KIA
········ ENEMY KILLED AND FOUND DEAD

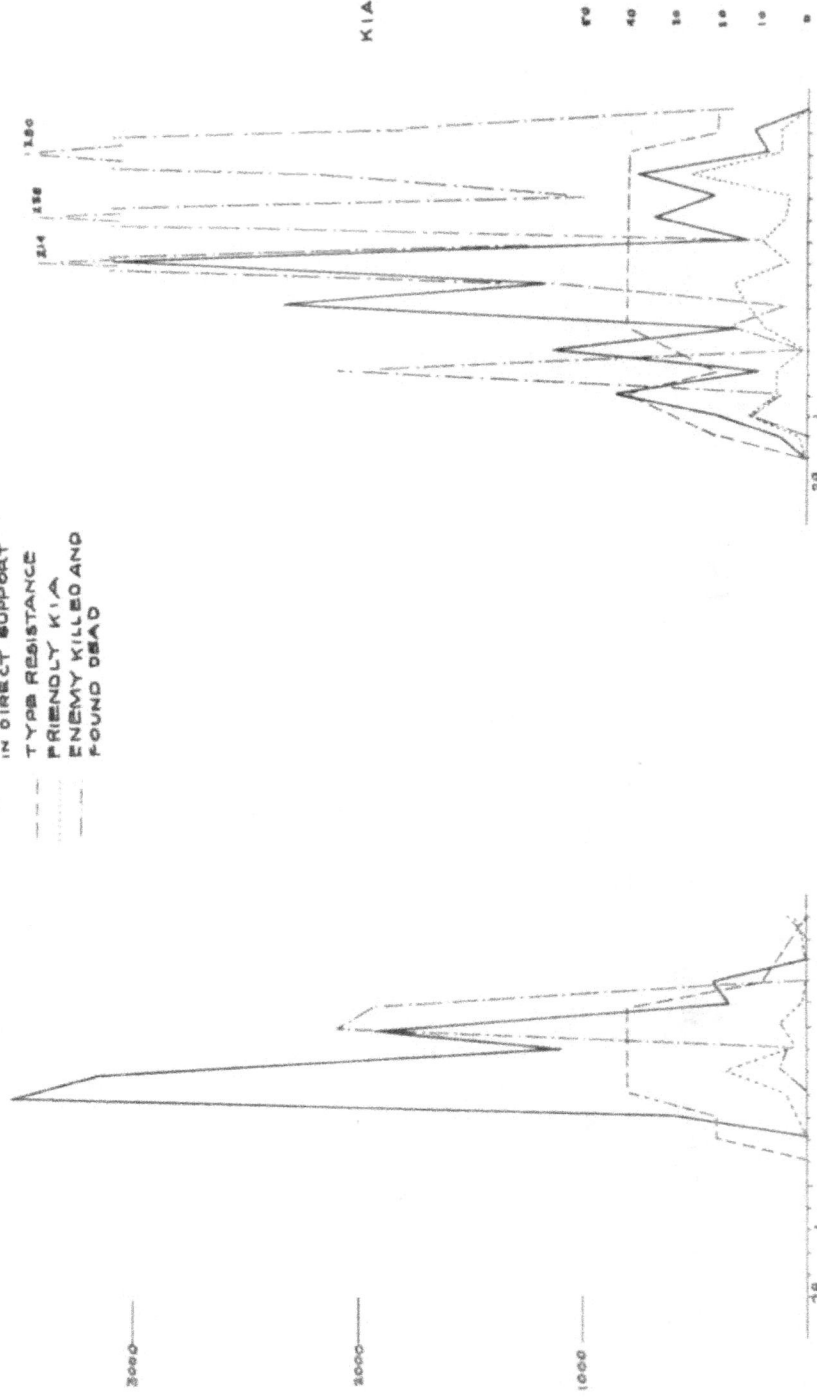

TYPES OF FIRE DELIVERED

BATAAN PHASE

PREPARATIONS AND CLOSE SUPPORT
HARRASSING
DEFENSIVE
TARGETS OF OPPORTUNITY

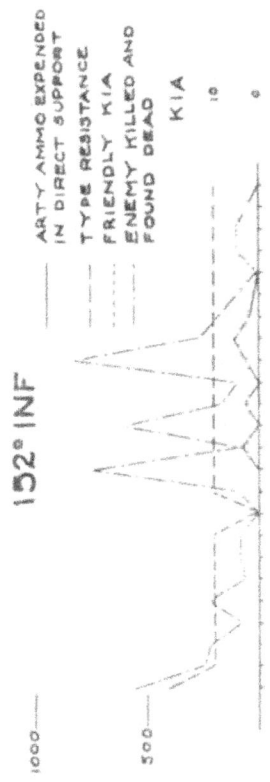

ARTY AMMO EXPENDED IN DIRECT SUPPORT
TYPE RESISTANCE
FRIENDLY KIA
ENEMY KILLED AND FOUND DEAD

152° INF

151ˢᵗ INF

149ᵀᴴ INF

KIA

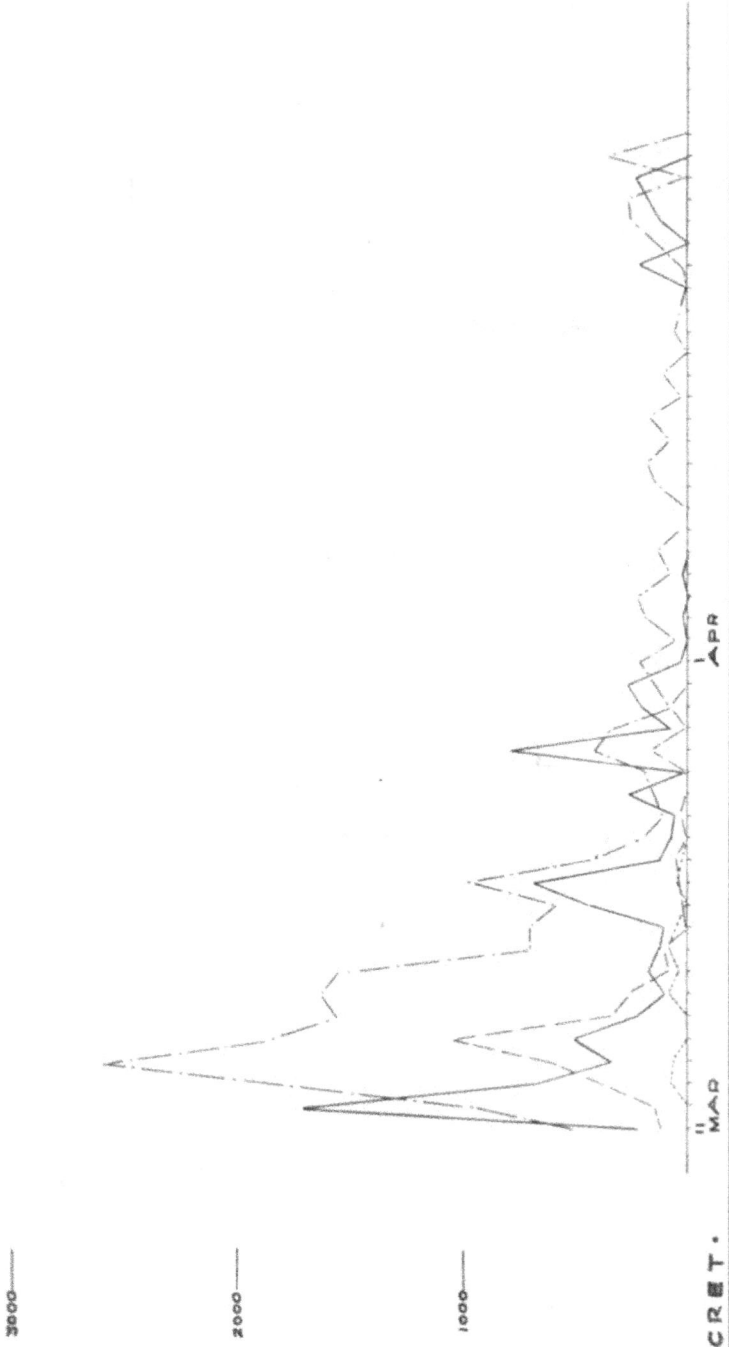

FORT STOTSENBURG—ISLANDS—ZAMBALES—PHASE
TYPES OF FIRE DELIVERED

PREPARATIONS AND
CLOSE SUPPORT

HARRASSING

DEFENSIVE

TARGETS OF
OPPORTUNITY

3000

2000

1000

MAR

APR

4

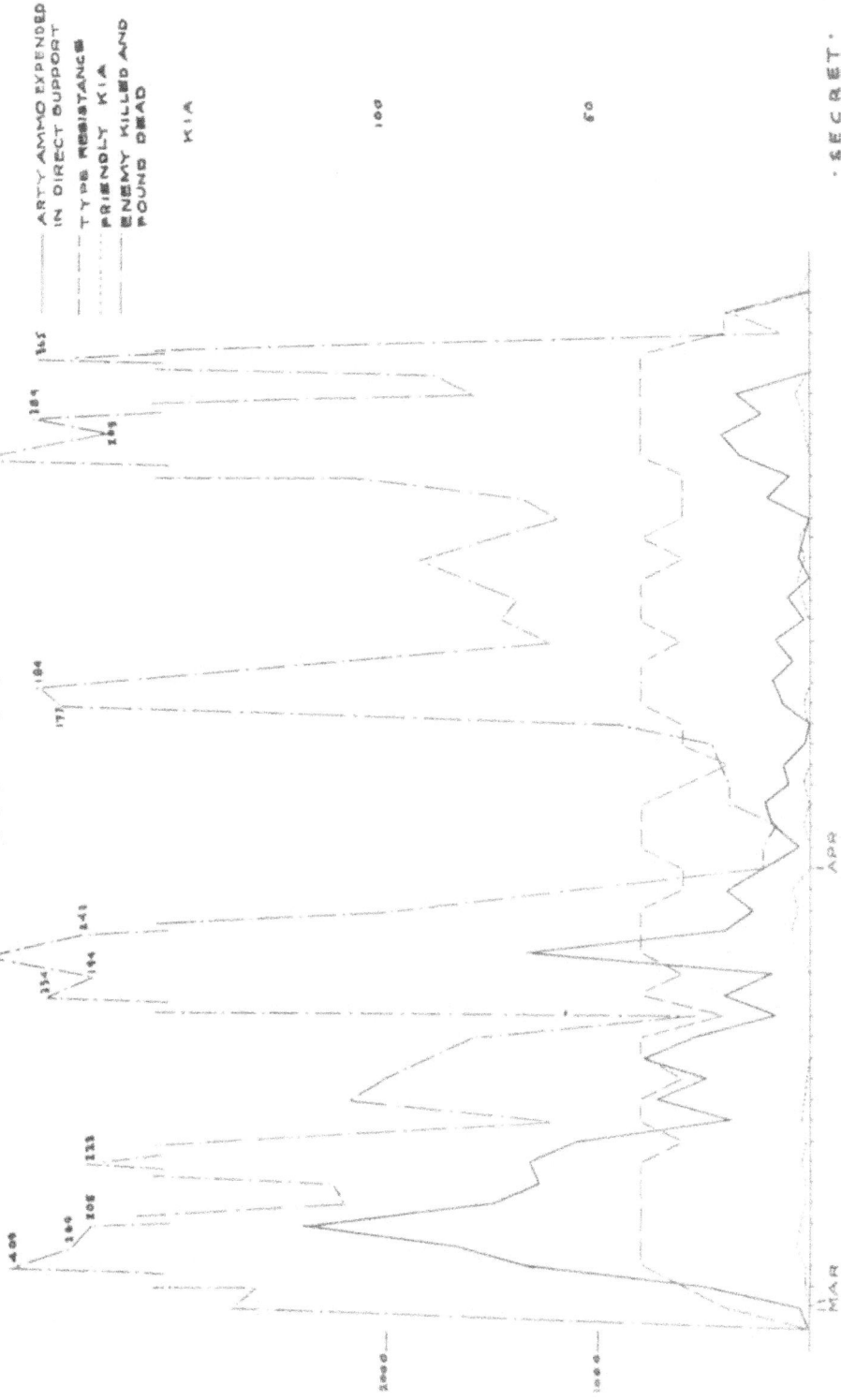

FORT STOTSENBURG PHASE
149TH INF

ARTY AMMO EXPENDED IN DIRECT SUPPORT
TYPE RESISTANCE
FRIENDLY KIA
ENEMY KILLED AND FOUND DEAD

CORREGIDOR — CABALLO — FORT DRUM — CARABAO — PHASE
151ST INF

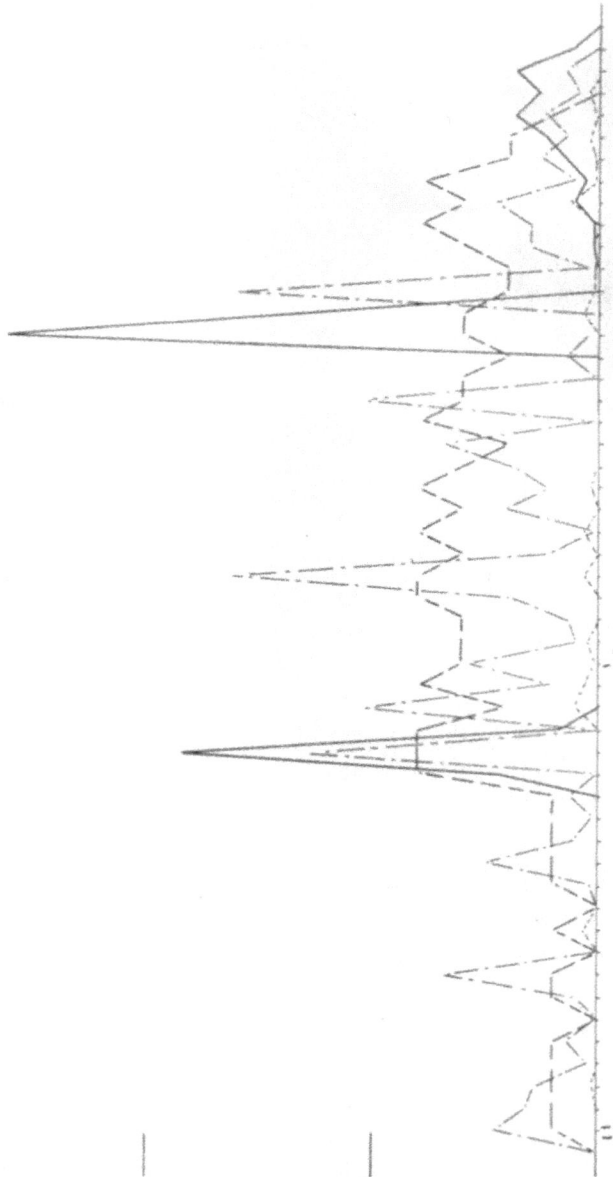

—————— ARTY AMMO EXPENDED
            IN DIRECT SUPPORT

— — — — TYPE RESISTANCE

·············· FRIENDLY KIA

—·—·—·— ENEMY KILLED AND
            FOUND DEAD

KIA

100

50

2000

1000

11
MAR

APR

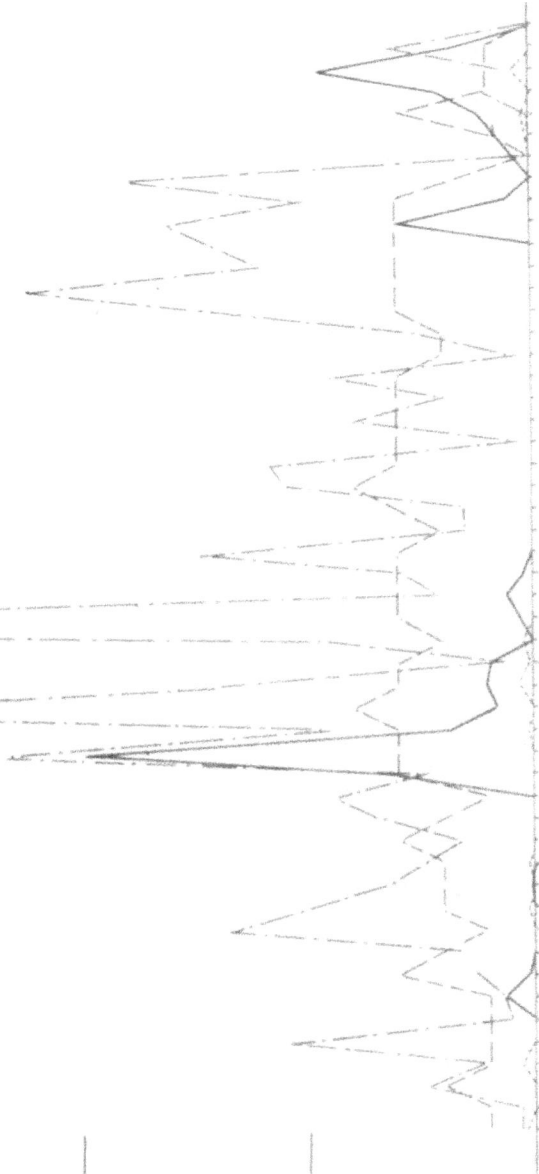

ZAMBALES PHASE
152° INF

ARTY AMMO EXPENDED
IN DIRECT SUPPORT
TYPE RESISTANCE
FRIENDLY KIA
ENEMY KILLED AND
FOUND DEAD

KIA

· SECRET ·

· SECRET · 7

MAR   APR

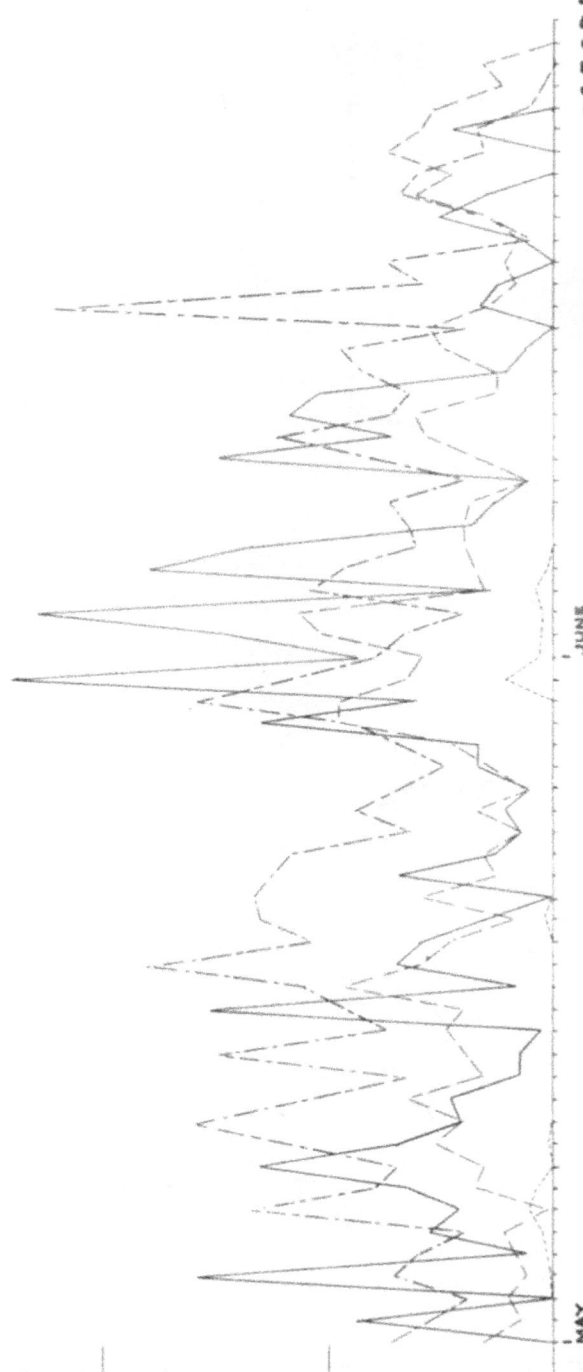

MARIQUINA RIVER PHASE
TYPES OF FIRE DELIVERED

PREPARATIONS AND
CLOSE SUPPORT

HARRASSING

DEFENSIVE

TARGETS OF
OPPORTUNITY

3000

2,000

1000

MAY

JUNE

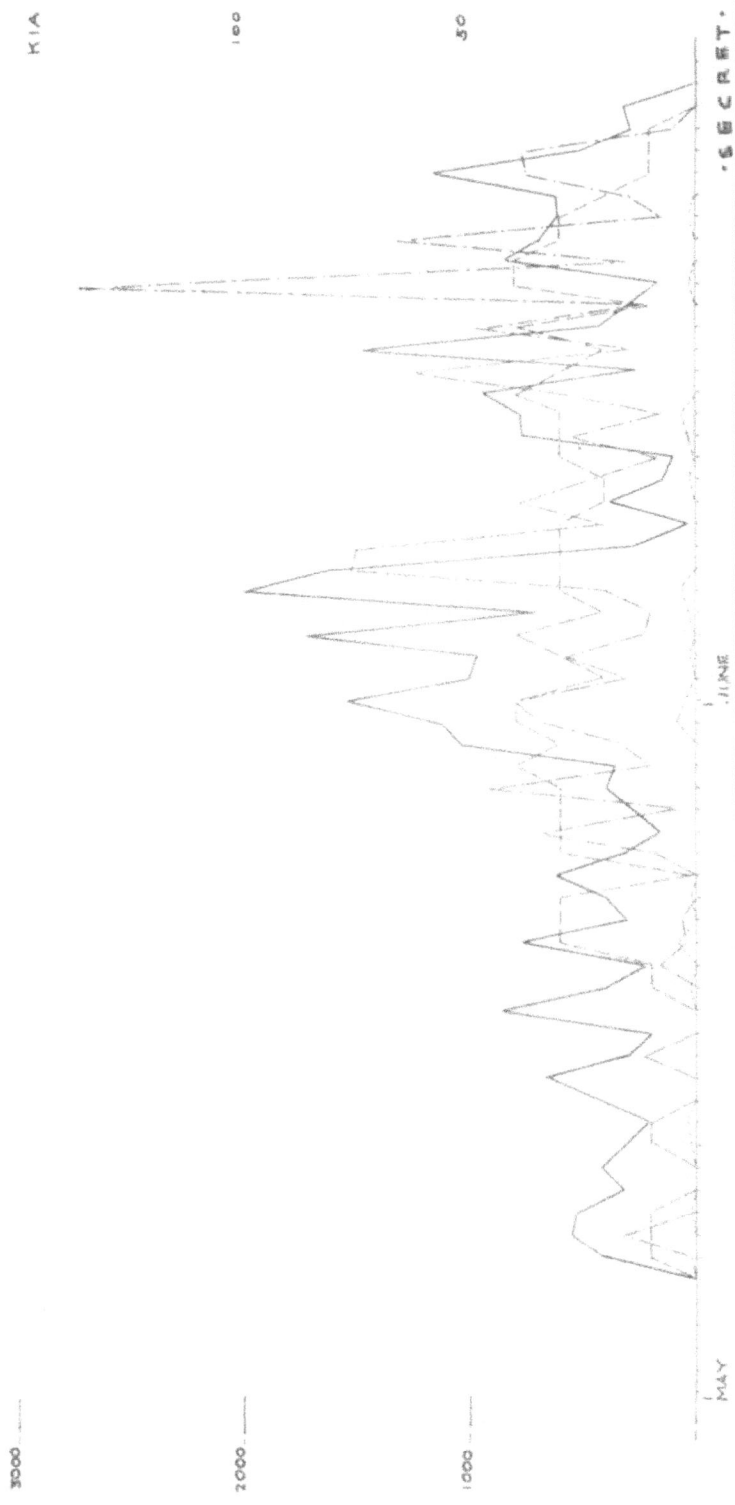

MARIQUINA RIVER PHASE
149ᵀᴴ INF.

ARTY AMMO EXPENDED
IN DIRECT SUPPORT

TYPE RESISTANCE

FRIENDLY KIA

ENEMY KILLED AND
FOUND DEAD

KIA

100

50

3000

2000

1000

MAY

JUNE

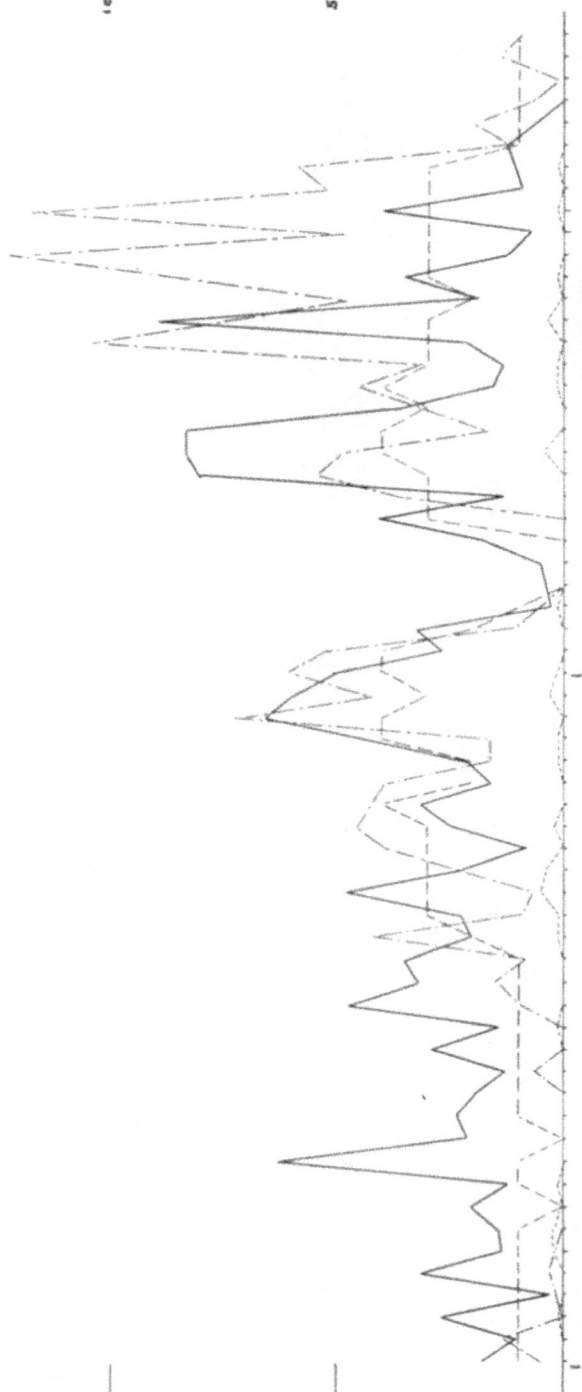

MARIQUINA RIVER PHASE
151st INF

ARTY AMMO EXPENDED
IN DIRECT SUPPORT

TYPE RESISTANCE

FRIENDLY KIA

ENEMY KILLED AND
FOUND DEAD

KIA

100

50

3000

2000

1000

MAY

JUNE

10

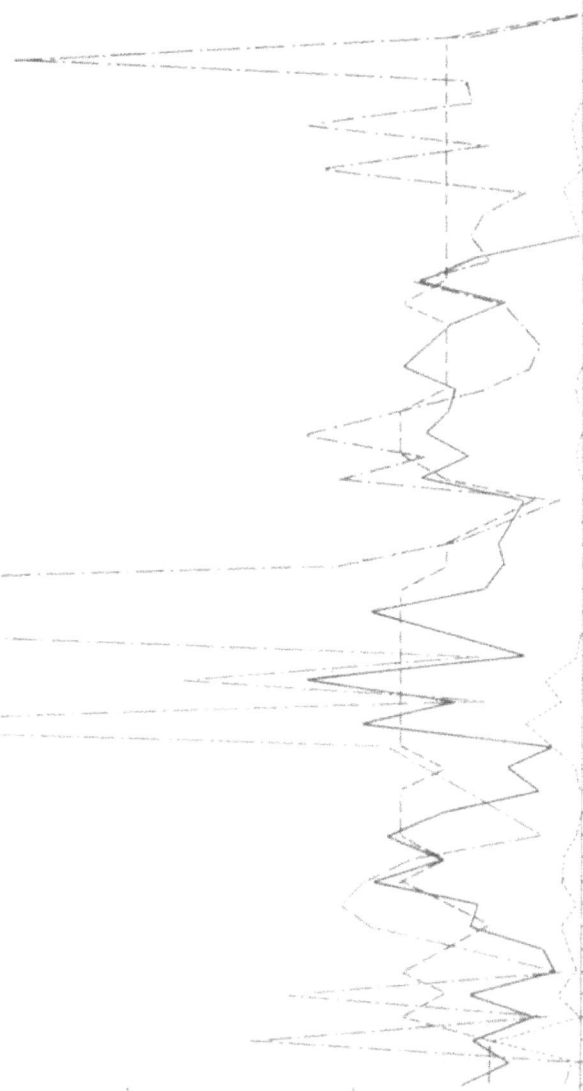

MARIQUINA RIVER PHASE
152ᴰ INF

ARTY AMMO EXPENDED
IN DIRECT SUPPORT

TYPE RESISTANCE

FRIENDLY KIA

ENEMY KILLED AND
FOUND DEAD

KIA

100

50

JUNE

MAY

'2000

1000

261

194

11

CIVIL AFFAIRS AND GRAVES REGISTRATION

In the course of operations on Luzon, this Division was charged with the operation and supervision of civil affairs over an exceedingly extensive area, communication through which was accomplished with considerable difficulty. It was undoubtedly normal and unavoidable that a certain amount of confusion and uncertainty arose initially in the course of operation and administration of the Division's responsibilities in civil affairs. Under the circumstances stated, it was found that the entire time of two officers and two enlisted men was necessary to discharge these functions. Due to the understrength in officer personnel which naturally increased as combat operations continued, the detail of officer personnel for special duty of the character above indicated worked a disadvantage upon such organizations of the Division from which those officers were so detailed. The same conditions were found to be true with respect to the accomplishment of the Graves Registration responsibilities and functions. For example, at one time the Division was charged with the installation and maintenance of military cemeteries at Olongapo, Marivales and Stotsenburg. PCAU and Graves Registration Units attached were, because of the conditions above described, inadequate to meet the problems involved. It is, therefore, recommended if in future operations the Division is to stand charged with the same degree of responsibility over the operation of civil affairs and graves registration that provision be made under Tables of Organization to provide personnel and transportation adequately to accomplish these functions so as not to necessitate the drawing upon divisional organizations, already depleted of officer personnel, to operate such special functions.

G-4 OPERATIONS DURING THE MIKE "7" OPERATION

Planning for the Mike Three operation was instituted on 25 Dec 1944, following an orientation conference with G-4, Eighth Army. In the Mike Three operation, it was contemplated that the 38th Division operate as a task force with the Division Staff operating as a Task Force Staff. The 38th Division was made responsible for bringing all units up to T/E Allowances in serviceable equipment; for the drawing of supply levels authorized; arrangement of the motor transportation to the loading beaches; for planning the shipping of the lift, and for the conducting of the operation.

On 19 Jan 1945, notification was received that the Mike Three operation was cancelled, and that the Division would participate in the Mike Seven operation under the control of XI Corps. The G-4 responsibility remained the same as for the Mike Three operation, with control passing to the XI Corps upon completion of loading. The change from the Mike Three to the Mike Seven operation involved several changes in the plans already prepared, which added to the confusion caused by the lack of sufficient time for a complete planning and organization of the movement. During the period 25 Dec 1944 to 21 Jan 1945, the shipping allotted to the division was changed four (4) times. Each change in shipping allotments necessitated a revision of all loading plans including grouping of units, transportation to be taken by units and revisions in bulk cargo loading arrangements. The final assignment of shipping was made on 21 Jan 1945 leaving only five (5) days for revision of plans and completion of outloading. However, on 26 Jan 1945, loading had been completed and all essential equipment had been included. Changes in shipping allowances made it necessary to leave many desirable items of supplies and equipment and a considerable number of personnel in a rear echelon at DULAG, LEYTE, P. I.

The movement from LEYTE to the landing beaches at LA PAZ, LUZON, P. I., was without incident and landing was accomplished on 29 Jan 1945 without opposition. The XI Corps plan of supply was that the Corps would take over control of the beach dumps initially established by the 592nd Engr Boat and Shore Regiment at both RED and BLUE beaches. The movement of supplies across the beach was very difficult due to the extremely soft and deep sand, however, the units of the division cleared the beach promptly and moved rapidly inward, and the 592nd EB & S Regiment began to stock the beach promptly. The XI Corps having no operating personnel for this phase of the supply operation, attached the entire Division QM Company to XI Corps QM. Since the division did not have access to the 38th QM Truck platoons, it was necessary in the early stages of operation, for unit vehicles to make the long trip from their field train bivouacs to RED BEACH because of lack of advance supply points, which would normally have been established by the Division QM Co. The movement of supplies forward was further complicated by the reduced number of vehicles which shipping facilities had allowed to be shipped for the operation. In spite of these handicaps, division and attached troops were continuously supplied and no undue hardships were observed. The situation progressed rapidly until approximately 3 Feb 1945, when the troops encountered the strong defensive position in ZIG-ZAG PASS.

On 5 Feb 1945, XI Corps began the movement of supply bases from RED BEACH at LA PAZ to OLONGAPO Naval Base. XI Corps supply point for all classes of supply opened at OLONGAPO on 11 Feb 1945. The opening of supply points at OLONGAPO placed all classes of supply in easy access to units of the division, and since QM transportation had been returned to division control, the supply situation approached normal operation. An exception to this was the movement of the 149th Infantry Regiment over a trail paralleling Highway 7, designed to contain the enemy's rear. This movement took place during the period 3 Feb and 14 Feb, and during this time it was necessary to supply the regiment almost entirely by air. This was done successfully with only minor losses in equipment.

The organized resistance in ZIG-ZAG PASS was broken by 14 Feb 1945. This made it possible to supply all units by truck transportation, simplifying the entire supply procedure since distances were comparatively short and main supply routes in most cases adequate.

Following the breakdown of organized resistance in the ZIG-ZAG, the division continued mopping up activities through the ZIG-ZAG PASS area, and down the east coast of BATAAN, which had been secured by a task force composed of 1st RCT from the 6th Infantry Division, commanded by the Commanding General, 38th Division Artillery, and operating directly under XI Corps. At the same time the 38th Division was preparing to land one (1) RCT at MARIVELES, on the southern tip of BATAAN on 15 Feb 1945. Further, the division was given the responsibility of supplying the 503rd Parachute Infantry Regiment and one (1) battalion combat team of the 34th Infantry Regiment which landed on CORREGIDOR on 16 Feb 1945. On 2 March 1945, a battalion of the 151st Infantry Regiment, 38th Division, relieved the 503rd Parachute Infantry and the battalion combat team of the 34th Infantry Regiment on CORREGIDOR, and this unit continued to be supplied by the 38th Division operating LCM's out of SUBIC and MARIVELES Harbors.

On 7 March 1945, 38th Division was given the mission of occupying and mopping up ZAMBALES PROVINCE, BATAAN PROVINCE,

and parts of PAMPANGA, TARLAC and BULACAN PROVINCES, and to
continue mopping up activities on CORREGIDOR. This mission
spread the division over an area of 3139 square miles which
complicated the supply problem. The supply of units was
accomplished by basing some units directly on XI Corps supply
point at OLONGAPO, and others on Army Supply Points at TARLAC
and SAN FERNANDO.

An additional operation to be carried on concurrently
with the mission stated above was assigned on 11 March 1945.
On this date the division was ordered to organize a task force
to conduct operations in the mountains generally west of FT.
STOTSENBURG. This task force was commanded by Commanding
General, 38th Division Artillery, and was composed of the
following troops:

                Det, 38th Div Hq
                  38th Div Arty Hq & Hq Btry
                  139th FA Bn
                  150th FA Bn
                  2d Bn 152d Inf (-Co "E") atchd Co "C" 152d Inf
                  1 Plat 38th QM Co
                  Co "B" 82d Cml Bn (-) (Tactical Control Only)

                149th RCT
                  149th Inf Regt
                  138th FA Bn
                  Co "A", 113th Engr Bn
                  Co "A", 113th Med Bn
                  1st Plat, Co "D", 113th Med Bn
                  38th Rcn Trp
                  Co "E", 152d Inf
                  1 Plat, Co "B", 82d Cml Bn

                169th RCT (From the 43d Inf Div)
                  169th Inf Regt
                  169th FA Bn
                  Col Co, 118th Med Bn
                  3d Plat Clr Co, 118th Med Bn
                  Co "B" 118th Engr Bn
                  Co "B" 640th TD Bn
                  1 Plat Co "B" 82d Cml Bn

The FT. STOTSENBURG task force operating concurrently
with the other operations of the division, necessitated
furnishing the task force commander with a G-4 representative
and certain special staff representatives to supplement his
staff. This deployment of the G-4 section proved to be adequate to supply the task force and the remainder of the division. The supply problem at FT. STOTSENBURG was the most
difficult encountered thus far. The terrain in this area is

extremely rugged and the leading elements of the troops operated along high ridge lines, working through deep draws and
ravines far in advance of any existing roads. The Division
Engineers did commendable work in pushing roads and trails forward to the troops, but the final supply to front line elements
was accomplished by the use of soldier and civilian carriers.
In some cases, carrying parties moved rations, water, ammunition and other supplies for distances up to three (3) miles
over steep mountainous terrain.

Concurrently with the FT. STOTSENBURG operation, other
elements of the division were operating from the IBA-BOTOLAN
area, ZAMBALES PROVINCE, to the east and south toward MT. PINA-
TUBA, which was also the objective of the FT. STOTSENBURG task
force. These units were confronted with essentially the same
problems as were encountered in the STOTSENBURG area. It was
necessary in some instances to supplement the supply of these
units with air-drops, particularly to small forward elements.
In both of these operations, supply to the front line elements
was on the whole, continuous and adequate. Unit supply personnel displayed much initiative and follow-up, and in many
instances, units operating well forward were furnished with two
(2) hot meals daily, in spite of the difficulties occasioned by
the adverse terrain.

The division continued mopping up in the areas already indicated above, and a further mission was assigned. The additional mission was to seize and occupy CABALLO ISLAND off COR-
REGIDOR. The troops participating in this operation were:

    1 Bn of Inf less one Co in reserve on CORREGIDOR
    1 Bn of Light Field Arty supporting the assault
        from positions on CORREGIDOR
    1 Btry of Medium Field Arty in support, from
        positions on the mainland of CABCABEN, BATAAN
    1 Plat of Engrs and necessary small detachments

In preparation of the seizing of CABALLO ISLAND, Infantry
and Artillery ammunition was transported to CORREGIDOR by LCM's
and to CABCABEN by truck. Again on this occasion, a G-4
representative was made available to the Regimental and Battalion commanders, to assist the organic supply personnel, immediately prior to and a few days after the initial assault.
This procedure again proved to be satisfactory and of material
benefit to the local commander. Resistance on CABALLO ISLAND
was reduced and mopping up activities continued in ZAMBALES,
FT. STOTSENBURG, and BATAAN areas.

Up to this time the 38th Division had been operating without the services of the ODQM, and the Service Platoon of the

38th QM Co. On 25 March 1945 the ODQM and the Service Platoon
were returned to division control and the QM immediately re-
gained control of all Quartermaster issues which had, up to
this time, been handled by units operating directly with Corps
and Army Supply Points, except for one or two occasions when
temporary Class I and III supply dumps were established for
parts of the division utilizing special duty personnel.

The division was still operating without the facilities of
approximately 500 special and general purpose vehicles and
other items of equipment which had been left in the rear echelon at LEYTE, due to the last minute change in allotment of
shipping space. All units were further hindered by the fact
that administrative personnel were in the rear echelon and
communication with them was so slow that their value was almost
entirely lost. Repeated requests for shipping necessary to
move the rear echelon to LUZON had been made, but to no avail.
On 13 March 1945, the Commanding General Sixth Army visited the
command post and he stated that he desired that movement of the
rear echelon be consummated at an early date. Following this
visit by the Army Commander, shipping was assigned by GHQ but
it was necessary to turn in 411 of the division's vehicles left
on LEYTE, and only 91 were shipped to LUZON, which did not begin to alleviate the transportation difficulties of the division. The majority of the bulk cargo of the rear echelon together with rear echelon personnel arrived at SUBIC BAY, LUZON,
on 31 March 1945, aboard two (2) LST's.

On 3 April 1945, the division was ordered to capture,
occupy and reduce FT. DRUM, on EL FRAILLE ISLAND, commonly
known as the "CONCRETE BATTLESHIP". This mission required the
development of an ingenious device consisting of a scaffold
and ladder arrangement for boarding the battleship, and a pump
arrangement mounted on an LCM, fitted with Navy Ponton Cubes,
to pump oil into the ship. The device was used successfully
and when the oil was ignited, a tremendous explosion occurred
which blasted a large hole through the reinforced concrete and
armor plate of the deck, and killed all enemy below decks.

Concurrently with the FT. DRUM operation, the division was
to attack, seize and secure CARABAO ISLAND. The scheme of maneuver for this operation was that a small landing force would
land on CARABAO ISLAND, supported by a battalion of light field
artillery, two (2) platoons of M-7 SPM's, and one (1) platoon
of 4.2 Chemical Mortars, firing from positions on the west
coast of MANILA BAY, in the vicinity of TERNATI and LIMBONES
coves. The Navy furnished six (6) LCT's for the movement of
the fire support group which was embarked from SUBIC BAY on
15 April 1945. LCM's were obtained to mount the Infantry Battalion making the assault, and to handle the re-supply of all
elements. On 19 April 1945, this mission was completed and

Infantry elements were evacuated from CARABAO ISLAND by LCM, without incident. The fire support group was returned to the division by LCT, on 26 April 1945.

On 20 April 1945, orders were received from XI Corps, for the 38th Division to relieve the 6th Infantry Division which was engaged with the enemy in the foothills of the SIERRA MADRE mountains, east of MARIKINA. The relief was accomplished by 1 May 1945, and the division continued on its mission. The operation in the SIERRA MADRE's was again characterized by terrain difficulties somewhat similar to those encountered in the FT. STOTSENBURG area. Road building was given first priority, but it was still necessary to supply many front line units by carrier and air-drop. The operation progressed satisfactorily in spite of the terrain and supply difficulties.

With the approach of the rainy season in this area, it became necessary to divert a portion of the division engineers for the construction of a wet weather camp for the division. This diversion of engineer equipment and personnel reduced the progress of road building, and made supply more and more dependent on carrying parties and air supply to units which were far beyond roads and trails.

As operations continued in the MARIKINA area, the division secured WOODPECKER RIDGE and captured WAWA DAM intact. The SHIMBU line had been broken and operations now consisted of pushing the enemy farther and farther into the hills, reducing successive strong points and defensive positions. The supply problem continued to be to supply units of regimental and battalion size far in advance of roads or trails. This was accomplished only by extending roads as fast as possible and supplying from the end of these roads employing native civilian, guerrilla and soldier carriers, supplemented with air supply.

On 20 June 1945, the 38th Division first used Heliocopters for evacuation of seriously wounded soldiers from isolated mountain positions which would have necessitated a two (2) day litter carry if evacuation had been made by native carriers.

This phase of the LUZON operation was rapidly nearing completion and on 21 June 1945, part of the division was withdrawn from the SIERRA MADRE mountains for a short period of rehabilitation in preparation for further operations in other sectors on LUZON. The LUZON campaign ended on 30 June 1945 with the division deployed over a large area and still mopping up.

LESSONS LEARNED

PLANNING AND LOADING PHASE

For an operation similar to the Mike Seven operation, the Division Staff should have a minimum period of thirty days after the assignment of shipping for planning, coordination and inspection of attachments, equipping of units, formulation of loading plans and the accumulation of the required levels of supply of all classes.

Ships characteristics should be made available to G-4 as soon as shipping is assigned and some provisions should be made for a preliminary conference between Naval and Army TQM's, so that all planning can be done using the up-to-date character- istics for each ship. This will make for better overall plan- ning and eliminate many of the disrupting changes which occur when planning is done without full information and a complete understanding with the Navy.

Outloading of an operation can be expedited by an early assignment of loading slots, provisions for advance stocking of these slots and the assignment of sufficient transportation and labor to support the outloading.

Palletization of bulk cargo would have expedited unload- ing and beach stockage on LA PAZ landing beaches. Pallet- ization should be given serious consideration for future oper- ations.

OPERATIONS PHASE

When an Infantry Division is to operate as a task force the attachment of certain support groups is an absolute necessity. In this operation the services of an Ordnance Ammunition Company and a Quartermaster Truck Company were necessities. The Ordnance Ammunition Company was necessary to establish, advance and maintain Ammunition Supply Points. At least one QM Truck Company in addition to the full organic transportation of a division is required to advance supply points where they are accessible to the troops. This was particularly true in the Mike Seven operation in which supply lines were extended very rapidly, straining the unit supply transportation almost to the breakdown point.

In all operations the force rear echelon should be landed by not later than D plus 10 days if the tactical situation will permit.

During the entire LUZON operation the need for organic

liaison type aircraft, both L-5 planes and Heliocopter, was proved beyond question. Aircraft of this nature should be provided in addition to the organic L-4 planes of the Division Artillery. Three L-5 airplanes should be assigned to a division headquarters for air evacuation, reconnaisance, and courier service. When available, Heliocopters could be used advantageously for medical evacuation from localities not accessable by road or to L-5 landing strips.

The Infantry Division Engineer Battalion should be enlarged to an Engineer Regiment. The present Engineer Battalion has neither the men nor equipment to adequately support an operation similar to the operation on LUZON. It is believed that a construction battalion should be added and the size and equipment of the Engineer Headquarters and Service Company should be increased. The Engineer supply of a division suffers for lack of sufficient supply personnel and maintenance facilities, and the supply of front line troops is seriously handicapped by lack of adequate engineer support.

MEDICAL ACTIVITIES, M-7 OPERATION

1. Planning phase:

    a. The planning phase was characterized by diffi-
culty in making contact with the medical units which were to
accompany the force, due to the fact that although all units
were staged in Leyte, many of them arrived from other bases at
a late date. Due to the paucity of bivouac areas the various
components of the task force were widely separated, and since
transportation and communication facilities were limited, planning conferences and the assembling of logistical data were
very time consuming.

    b. Several of the medical units were partially moved
to the staging area by transporting personnel and a small
amount of impedimenta on hospital ships. Because of a shortage
of heavy shipping at the southern bases, it was impossible to
move the remainder of equipment and except for a few of the
shortages which could be supplied at the staging base, the
units were forced to proceed to the operation partially supplied. It is thought that the use of hospital ships for this
purpose is not of advantage, since heavy shipping sufficient
to transport the materiel of a unit, will in almost all cases,
also accomodate the personnel.

2. Supply phase:

    a. Shortages of expendable medical supplies and the
absence of non-expendable items on the island of Leyte inter-
fered with the completion of the supply phase. Two of the
infantry regiments were short one-half a battalion aid station
equipment each, due in one instance to the loss of one loaded
vehicle in Leyte bay, and in the other case to the burning of
two holds of a transport prior to disembarking at Leyte. The
battalion shortages were minimized by reallocation of equipment in each regiment.

    b. Shortages in the T/E allowances of expendable
supplies were filled from the 30-day maintenance reserve which
the division moved to Leyte.

    c. The reconstitution of the 30-day maintenance
stock and it's conversion to a combat reserve was difficult
due to shortages of expendable items in the base depots.

3. Loading phase:

    a. Shortage of shipping space did not limit the
amount of bulk cargo which was carried, due to the relatively
small proportion of space which is occupied by medical items.

    b. Collecting Stations, Clearing Stations, and the
Portable Surgical Hospital were limited in the amount of T/E

equipment which accompanied the original movement due chiefly
to limitation of number of vehicles which could be transported
in the shipping available. In each case careful consideration
was given to the problem and the vehicles and equipment which
could be most easily spared during combat were reserved for
later shipment.

     c. Each Collecting Company was moved without the
following motor equipment:

         Co. A - 1 - 3/4 ton W/C   1 - $\frac{1}{4}$ ton trailer
         Co. B - 1 - 3/4 ton W/C   1 - $\frac{1}{4}$ ton trailer
         Co. C - 1 - 3/4 ton W/C   1 - $\frac{1}{4}$ ton trailer

     d. The Clearing Company and Headquarters & Head-
quarters Detachment of the Medical Battalion moved without the
following motor equipment:

         1 - 3/4 ton C & R
         1 - 2$\frac{1}{2}$ ton 6 x 6
         3 - 1 ton trailers

   4. Debarkation phase:

     a. Unloading and landing of the tactical medical
units was accomplished without incident.

     b. Aid men accompanied their platoons. Battalion
and regimental aid stations were landed with their respective
organizations. Aid Stations were divided equally and dispatched in separate waves.

     c. Collecting Stations were divided and landed in
separate waves, litter bearers being placed in the late organized waves of the assault battalions. The Collecting Station
Sections and motor transport was given a landing priority which
placed them on shore after the assault battalions and for the
most part ahead of the reserve battalions.

     d. Clearing Stations were likewise landed in several
waves and were timed to arrive after the infantry battalions
and during the time the regimental special units were landing.

     e. The Portable Surgical Hospital was attached to
the Clearing Company and came ashore immediately after it.

     f. The 30-day maintenance supplies were mobile loaded
to the maximum extent possible with use of medical unit vehicles. The half of the ambulances which were unloaded last were
loaded with expendable supply to a limit of 500 pounds per
vehicle.

     g. The remainder of the 30-day maintenance supplies

to the extent of 17 tons was bulk loaded. They were successfully unloaded and placed on the landing beaches. However
safeguarding and control of these items during the first three
days was extremely difficult due to absence of personnel which
could be utilized for this purpose. The containers, having
been marked with unit designation were later located in the
miscellaneous beach dumps and brought under control.

5. Supply during combat:
a. The Division Medical Supply Point was maintained
in the vicinity of the Clearing Station. Movement and distribution of replacement supplies was accomplished by use of
normal medical channels. Each medical unit was instructed to
fill informal requisitions made by the next unit forward, to
the extent possible, from their own stocks and to request replacement from the medical unit to their rear. By this method
it was possible to maintain an adequate stock of expendable
items with aid men and in aid stations at all times. Collecting Stations carried more than the usual stockage of those
articles which are consumed rapidly in combat in ambulances,
in order to quickly restore the normal balance in infantry
battalions.

b. The shortages referred to on paragraph 2c above
did not develope into a critical situation in combat, since
those items which are absolutely necessary in combat were resupplied by the first resupply convoy, unloading of which was
completed on D plus 15.

c. As a result of participation in three months of
combat, the amounts of various items in the 30-day maintenance
stock were revised for future stockage. This was accomplished
by maintaining a stock supply record during combat, and deter-
mining from this the rate of consumption for the individual
items.

6. Evacuation during combat - Zig Zag Pass, Olongapoa.

a. Casualties were evacuated to the Division Clearing
Station by normal methods. The infantry regiments prescribed
the forward limit for movement of ambulances, and there was no
loss of vehicles due to direct enemy action. A few small arms
projectiles struck ambulances, but without significant damage.
During combat through Zig-Zag Pass, the only access road was
subject to mortar fire and attacks by infiltration throughout
hours of darkness, and it was customary to withdraw all vehicles from the immediate combat area prior to dark. Casualties
occurring during the night were retained and treated in perimeters. In no case did the casualties suffer from the evacuation delay to a degree sufficient to justify the operations

of vehicles after dark.

b.   During combat on Corregidor two ambulances were damaged, one beyond repair, by the occurrance of a huge subterranean explosion. This occurred during evacuation of casualties and could not have been prevented.

c.   During the five-week period ending 2 March 1945, a total of 1011 battle casualties were evacuated. 8.2 of these were handled during the 14-day period in which the Battle of Zig-Zag Pass was fought. The Clearing Station was set up well forward at all times, and at no time was the evacuation system under strain.

d.   Nontransportable surgical cases were cared for in a most adequate fashion by 3 Portable Surgical Hospitals, one of which was attached to the division, and 2 of which were under Corps control in support of division. They were all operated within one to two miles of the front lines, and enabled the division to evacuate seriously wounded after definitive treatment had been accomplished near the front.

7.   During the battle of Zig-Zag Pass, one infantry regiment outflanked the enemy organized position by a foot march over mountain trails. This phase of the operation occupied 11 days. The original supply was hand carried by the troops and a limited number of native bearers, and resupply was affected from the air by parachute and non-parachute droppings, and after construction of an air strip by landing fragile supplies such as whole blood in liaison planes. The regiment was supported by a collecting company less motor elements, and by a Portable Surgical Hospital. Evacuation of casualties from the hospital was established on the 7th day by the use of L-5 planes operating from an air strip built by the medical personnel of the regiment aided by native labor. Evacuation to the portable hospital was by litter and carabao carts. A total of 123 casualties were evacuated from the area, and 67 casualties were treated in the operational area and returned to duty. The medical supply was excellent during this phase.

8.   In Zig-Zag Pass, infantry aid men were able to evacuate two casualties from a burning tank, having received training in this maneuver previously, in accordance with Training Memorandum published by Headquarters, Armored Force.

9.   The 151st RCT was supported medically in its Marivelles landing by one Clearing Station which was established on the beach, and by a Surgical LST which received patients at anchor in Marivelles Bay. Patients requiring immediate operation and all seriously wounded were evacuated to the LST, minor

wounds were cared for by the Clearing Station. The LST remained in the area for three days, after which time the Clearing Station, reinforced by a surgical team cared for all sick and wounded, and was evacuated by L-5 planes from the Marivelles strip. The medical service for this operation was more than adequate and functioned in an excellent manner. Air evacuation was extremely valuable, since the route of ambulance evacuation would have been over a rough road along the east shore of Bataan, at a time when the route was subject to enemy infiltration, and water evacuation was limited to use of LCM's.

10. One infantry battalion relieved a battalion of the 34th RCT after the main action was completed on Corregidor. This battalion was supported by a Portable Surgical Hospital which had been established on Corregidor for the troops making the initial assault. The Clearing Station at Marivelles received sick and slightly wounded from Corregidor by LCM's, and was evacuated during this phase by L-5 planes.

11. The assault of Caballo Island was supported by a Clearing Station on Corregidor which received patients with minor wounds by LCM's. A surgical LST was able to beach on Caballo and received all seriously wounded during the first two days. Collecting Company litter bearers were landed on Caballo to evacuate the battalion aid station and a sorting station was maintained on the Caballo landing beach by the Collecting Company. Ambulances were utilized on Corregidor and the Collecting Company established a station at the debarkation beach for care and sorting of casualties destined for the Clearing Station. After the LST departed the area, evacuation was by air from Marivelles.

12. Infantry action in the area west of Fort Stotsenburg was characterized by assault of well organized positions dug in the sides of a series of precipitous ridges. The terrain was such that control of the high ground was essential, and supply and evacuation operations were necessarily confined to the crests of ridges, draws and ravines being under enemy fire. The high ground varied from a height of 1500 to 2500 feet above the plains, with steep rises amounting to cliffs in some situations. The engineers were able to construct ridge roads for access, but because of the ruggedness of the terrain, vehicles could never operate closer than 2000 yards from the front lines.

13. Litter carries were long and hazardous. As many as 25 litter bearers were used as a team in transporting casualties over the most difficult portions. Natives were employed to reinforce the personnel of the Collecting Company. The time required to carry a loaded litter from aid stations to the for-

ward ambulance positions varied from six to twelve hours. At times litter patients were lowered down declevities. In order to combat shock in the seriously wounded during such a long evacuation process, the Collecting Company established way stations for the administration of plasma, morphine, and dressings. In one instance the terrain required one more plasma station than was possible to maintain with the personnel available. At this point radio communication was used to announce the departure of a seriously wounded patient from the aid station, and a litter team went forward with plasma for administration at a half way point. Under this system even desperate cases were evacuated to the Clearing Station in a satisfactory condition. Several of the wounded received as much as 6,000 to 8,000 cc of plasma on the route. At the end of the period the Fifth Air Force was obtaining helicopter planes with a view to evacuating the ridges by air.

14.   During three weeks in April the division area approximated 3139 square miles. Active combat operations were being carried on at the two extremities of the area, and the remainder was covered by patrols and bridge guards. To support this greatly dispersed force the division clearing stations were established close to the two areas of active combat. In each regimental sector the collecting company operated a provisional clearing station, with a capacity of 50 patients. Due to the large number of liaison air strips it was possible to evacuate patients from distant points by L-5 planes. The infantry battalions held a roving sick call for bridge guards and isolated detachments.

15.   The division was engaged in combat in the Sierra Madres Mountains, east and slightly north of Manila, from 28 April 1945 to 1 July 1945. Engineer constructed roads gave access to the division zone in two places, each road being located close to the center of the two zones of greatest tactical importance. The road leading up Mt. Pakawagan, was so steep that heavy vehicles could not negotiate the climb except with the aid of tractors. Accordingly $\frac{1}{4}$ ton Trucks were utilized to transport casualties to the base of the mountain, where they were transferred to field ambulances. At the onset of the rainy season, a provisional portable surgical hospital was formed from one platoon of the Clearing Company. This hospital was moved close to the front line in the South Sector and was established high in the mountains, in order to provide surgery for non-transportables, and also for all casualties in case the mountain road became impassable, because of rain. The 38th Portable Surgical Hospital, was attached to the division during this operation, and was established for two weeks close to the base of the mountain at the north flank.

16.   On 28 May, the 19th Portable Surgical Hospital was
made available to the division, and replaced the provisional unit
in the front lines. As the advance proceeded over the New Bogo
Boso River, its station was moved down a steep section of the
road (impassable in wet weather) and established to care for
seriously wounded, and all casualties who could not be evacuated
at times when the road to the rear was impassable. At about this
same time the 38th Portable was moved from Wawa Dam area and took
an advanced position near the Mariquina River, in front of as
much of the critical roadnet as possible. In this area each
hospital supported a regiment.

17.   On 20 June one regiment advanced into hilly terrain in
which a road could not be constructed. The 38th Portable was
transported with the troops on a 48-hour hand carry. It was resupplied by air drop.

18.   In the Sierra Madres Mountains helicopter evacuation
was used by the division for the first time. Suitable landing
sites were scarce because of the steepness of the hills and the
narrowness of the valleys. A few landing areas were found on the
plateau and six casualties were successfully removed by the planes.

19.   Medical Administrative Corps officers occupy the position of assistant infantry battalion surgeons in the 38th Division.
They had been assigned to the division for a period of 7 months
prior to the operation and had received a course of instruction
in surgical first aid, and in infantry tactics subsequent to assignment. Eight of these officers rendered excellent to superior
service in combat. One officer was relieved and recommended for
reclassification on the basis of unsuitability for combat service.
There is no doubt on the part of line and medical officers that
these officers performed the tasks previously allotted to medical officers, and did so in a superior manner.

20.   Separation of tactical units and active combat interfer-
ed considerably with the division dental service. During operations the dental officers served as assistant surgeons, and as
Graves Registration Officers, and accomplished these missions in
a superior manner. When ever possible the troops were served by
transporting the dental dispensary to company and platoon bivouacs. The two dental officers of the medical battalion were engaged full time in caring for personnel of other division units
when they were in the vicinity of the clearing stations.

21.   The report of the Division Neuropsychiatrist to the
Surgeon, Sixth Army, concerning the psychiatric experiences of
the division during the four month period February to May, 1945,
is appended an Annex No. 1.

22.   During the operation, both Clearing Stations were at station, except for short periods required for moving.   A total of 10680 patients were admitted.   The Collecting Companies evacuated a total of 8222 patients during the same period.   The average number of Clearing Station beds occupied during the operation was 139.

COMBAT PSYCHIATRIC PROBLEMS IN AN INFANTRY DIVISION

1. This is a report of psychiatric experiences in the 38th
Infantry Division during four months of combat from February
through May 1945 inclusive. It covers the greater part of the
Luzon campaign of the Division, the first campaign in which the
Division as a whole participated. The initial landing was made
29 January 1945 without enemy opposition in the southwest corner
of Zambales Province on the west coast of Luzon. A break-through
into Bataan was achieved after bitter fighting for Zig-Zag Pass.
A South Force, which was then dispatched to seize Mariveles at
the tip of Bataan, participated in the battle for Corregidor, and
stormed the nearby islands of Caballo, Carabao, and Fort Drum, to
clear Manila Bay. A North Force engaged in extensive mopping-up
operations west of Fort Stotsenberg, while elements of the Division took control of the large area from Tarlac to Mariveles.
Around the beginning of May 1945, the Division was transferred to
the Marikina Watershed Area, northeast of Manila, to root the
enemy out of strongly entrenched mountain positions cutting off
the Manila water supply. Final mopping up operations are now in
progress in this area.

2.   There were 779 neuropsychiatric patients admitted to the
Division Clearing Station during the period covered by the report.
This includes every type of psychiatric problem, from psychoses to
mild fatigue states which could as well have been cared for in a
rest camp. There were two important factors in the relatively
high number of combat reactions: the lack of previous combat
experience and the rough fighting into which the men were thrown
for their first baptism of fire. Of these 779 cases, 558 or 71.6%
were returned to duty directly from the Clearing Station; 221 or
28.4% were evacuated further. Of these, 76 or 9.7% are back with
the Division, making a total of 81.4% returned to duty, as of 15
June 1945. There were 71 repeaters, of whom 47 are still on duty,
and 24 have been evacuated. There were 27 psychotics.

Table 1

Total N.P Cases	779	
To duty from Clearing Station	558	(71.6%)
Evacuated to hospitals	221	(28.4%)
To duty from hospitals	76	(9.7%)
Total to duty	634	(81.3%)
Remaining - disposition unknown	145	(18.7%)

3.   The neuropsychiatric cases represented 9.6% of total
casualties, and 36% of battle casualties. The regiments had the
bulk of cases, 734, as compared with 45 for all other units of the
Division. The heaviest fighting occured in February and May, and
88% of the psychiatric cases were admitted during those two

months. If all cases which could be diagnosed as "Exhaustion, overexertion" were excluded, the total number of psychiatric cases would be very much lower. However, these cases were all treated in the psychiatric section; they were given the same routine of treatment; and psychiatric factors were undoubtedly essential contributing elements to the development of the exhaustion state.

4.   The chief problem in combat is that of handling large numbers of patients within the limited medical facilities of the Division, which include the Clearing Station, the Regimental Aid Stations, the Collecting Stations, and the Regimental Train Areas. Battalion Aid Stations are usually too far forward to hold patients for treatment, but a good many men receive comfort, reassurance and support even from a brief contact with the Battalion Surgeon who knows them and can take advantage of a rapport which has already been established. Psychiatric treatment forward of the Clearing Station is a continuous process, and takes care of many soldiers who are in need of rest and relaxation. Almost all men in the front lines develop tensions and anxieties which they may temporarily find hard to handle; and judicious use of forward facilities may go far to sustain combat effectiveness.

5.   If 70% of psychiatric combat reactions can be returned to duty from the Clearing Station, it would seem advisable to hold all but psychotics within the Division to watch their progress and evaluate their capacity to regain control of their anxiety. During the first few days of combat, many patients were evacuated for other than psychiatric reasons: because of rapid change in the location of the Clearing Station (4 moves in 5 days); and because of inexperience of ward personnel. To provide for a rapid influx of patients, a Reconditioning Section had been planned, and was set up several days after the landing. It was a section of the Clearing Station, actually nothing more than a fly, under which patients slept on the ground, after a night or two of ward care, to make room for new admissions. We had run out of cots and litters. In this way, 102 patients were given the additional time they needed for complete recovery before return to duty.

6.   Ward personnel learned the routine of treatment in a surprisingly short time. They soon adapted themselves to the needs of the patients, giving them the necessary care, comfort, and companionship. Sedation was used only at night, and never in the daytime, when patients were encouraged to be active, to get themselves washed and shaved, and to be up for chow. Most of the men were assigned to duties in and around the Station: helping on the wards, in the kitchens, policing and improving the area. Hot drinks were served at night; showers, barbers, and laundry facilities were available for all patients. The Red Cross worker provided the drinks, and distributed comfort articles, reading material, and writing paper, and supplemented the cigarette

ration. The Division newspaper was circulated daily, and a map board was prominently displayed.

7. During the month of April, the North Force operated a Rest Camp, which was located in the recreational buildings of a sugar plantation. There were two large buildings, one used as a dormitory for 125 soldiers; the other used as a Red Cross Center. Adjoining were a swimming pool and a ball park. Admission was on a quota basis. No recognized psychiatric patients were sent to the Rest Camp, but it served a valuable preventive function. Soldiers were at first kept for 2 days and later for 4 days. The T/O & E for such a project is outlined in the following table:

Table 2
T/O & E for Rest Camp

Personnel

5 Officers, including 2 in charge of administration and details; 1 Sanitary Officer; 1 I & E and Special Service Officer; 1 PX Officer.

23 Enlisted men, including:
    1 Mess Sgt with 6 EM and 1 Baker.
    1 Tech Sgt in charge of details with 1 Tec 5 and 8 EM.
    1 Sgt and 1 Tec 5, Medical Department.
    3 EM to assist the Red Cross.

(2 Female and 1 Male Red Cross workers ran the Recreational Center. Medical Officers and Chaplains provided part-time service. There was an ample supply of native labor).

Equipment

1 Field range per 50 men plus 1 for baking.
Kitchen equipment.
Box latrines.
Cots and mosquito bars.
1 Water trailer (navy cube) per 125 men.
1 Shower head per 25 men.
1 Generator and electrical equipment.
1 Movie projector.
1 Barber per 50 men.
Laundry service (by natives)
Athletic equipment.
Clothing and mess equipment.
Radio-phonograph.
Reading and writing material.
Money.
Comfort articles.
(Pro Station)

The Rest Camp is valuable not only for what it offers in relaxation and rest but because it demonstrates to the soldier command's interest in his welfare, and may be used as to set up for each soldier a series of time limits during long periods of combat. If a soldier knows that he will be sent to a rest camp after a definite period of front-line duty, it will help to relieve the feelings he tends to develop of endlessness, and hopelessness of survival.

8. A large number of replacements were received during the four month period. They were all assigned by the Division Classification Officer, and men with special skills were given proper assignments whenever possible. As each group of replacements arrived, they were welcomed by the Commanding General, given some information on the history and tradition of the Division, and told of the General's personal interest in their welfare. After arrival at their units they were whenever possible given minor assignments such as patrolling or littering, to give them time to get to know their future companions and to adjust themselves gradually to flying bullets. This policy of handling replacements proved very successful, and only a handful turned up as psychiatric patients in the Clearing Station.

9. Reassignment is of course necessary for a number of men who show a lack of tolerance for their anxiety. Although they are unable to serve as front-line soldiers, they often have intense loyalty to the Division, and are eager to do a job to help their buddies up front. Very often they are of more value in a Division rear echelon job than any new replacement could be. Moreover they present no psychiatric problem as long as they are not in the front lines. They can tolerate short periods of anxiety, but not the sustained tension of front-line duty. Thus far about 50 men have been recommended for reassignment. It has been recommended that a Board of Officers be appointed, consisting of the Personnel Officers of Division Artillery, the Engineers, the Medical Battalion, and Special Troops; the Division Classification Officer; and the Division Neuropsychiatrist; to review all cases referred for reassignment, and to suggest suitable disposition. There is, of course, a saturation point beyond which reassigned personnel cannot be absorbed by the Division.

10. It is planned to follow up all psychiatric patients who have been returned to duty, and to institute a screening procedure on the basis of combat performance. It is the experience of the writer that combat performance is the only reliable criterion for screening. Of several hundred soldiers who were referred for psychiatric examination during a period of a year prior to combat, only a few (not more than 10) turned up as psychiatric combat reactions.

A follow-up program will also serve the purpose of bringing psychiatric combat problems to the attention of line officers and senior non-coms.

Conclusions and Recommendations

11. The prevention of manpower losses due to psychiatric disability is primarily a command function, depending on multiple morale factors of which confidence in leadership is the most important. This can be most strikingly illustrated by comparing the incidence of psychiatric cases in the various companies, battalions, and regiments. The regiment which accounted for the most enemy dead had 143 cases, while the one which accounted for the fewest had 297 cases. One battalion in the former regiment had only 12 cases, whereas one battalion of the latter had 154 cases. Since the first regiment had by far the more difficult combat assignments, it is apparent that the difference in incidence of psychiatric cases was based on a difference in leadership effectiveness.

12. The supporting role of the medical detachments is also an important factor in maintaining the combat effectiveness of a unit. The aid stations should be kept as far forward as possible, so that the personal influence of the battalion surgeon can make itself felt where it is needed most; there should be a policy of not evacuating further any cases which can be treated in a more forward installation; and the medical criteria for evacuation should be strictly maintained. Without the active co-operation of forward medical personnel, it is almost impossible to do an effective job of minimizing loss due to psychiatric disability.

13. In periods of intensive combat, the facilities of the Clearing Station are taxed by large numbers of psychiatric patients. Provision should be made for expansion of these facilities, in terms of personnel and equipment. The basic factor in treatment is the provision of adequate personnel to insure that every patient receives personal attention.

14. The establishment of continuous rest camp facilities, because of its morale value, can be an important aid in psychiatric prevention.

15. The need for reassignment of men during combat has been most apparent, and a flexible method of providing for such reassignment should be ready for use. The simplest method during combat is to give the Division Classification Officer the authority to make reassignments on the recommendation of the psychiatrist. In post-combat periods, screening and reassignment can be carried out by a Board of Officers, as outlined above.

SIGNAL COMMUNICATIONS, M-7 OPERATION

1. **GENERAL**: Signal communications were established at H hour, 29 Jan 1945, and were continuous throughout the M-7 operation. At no time did the Division communications system bog down. Service interruptions were held to a minimum, with alternate means habitually available.

2. **WIRE**: A complete Division wire system was established by 2100, D-Day, and maintained continuously. In the early phases, existing commercial wire was rehabilitated and used effectively. During operations over extended distances, many long circuits of 20 to 40 miles were installed, requiring continual use of all repeaters available. Division wire circuits were habitually put in the air on existing poles, or on bamboo or lance poles installed by Division teams. Field wire maintenance during the first two months operation was a serious problem, due to the extremely poor condition of field wire available.

3. **RADIO**: Maximum use of voice and CW radio was made to supplement wire communications. During amphibious phases, alternate voice nets utilizing radio sets SCR-193, 694, 610 and 300 provided unfailing communications. During operation over extended distances, CW and voice nets performed satisfactorily over ranges up to 70 miles. Radio relay stations in L-4 planes were used successfully with long-range patrols. When it was demonstrated the enemy could take no counter measures, low powered voice radios were used extensively in the clear.

4. **MESSAGE CENTER**: Normal message center service was unceasing. During assault phases, the Combined Assault Code was used for two hours, but discontinued in favor of M-209 systems because its use was delaying traffic. There being no initial opposition, SIGABA'S were taken ashore the first day.

5. **MESSENGER**: Scheduled and special messenger service was provided throughout the operation. Safehand Courier service was handled by the Division the first two months. Frequent use of L-4 planes facilitated courier and messenger service over the long distances involved.

6. **PIGEON**: A pigeon loft was attached to the Division for the period 15 March - 30 April. Pigeons were used on two long-range patrols, and in training flights. Good recovery of birds over distances up to 40 miles was experienced.

7. ENEMY COMMUNICATIONS: a. No appreciable Japanese wire installations were discovered. The enemy cut our wire lines on only a few occassions. One incident of Japanese wire tapping was reported. None of the enemy switchboard and telephone equipment captured was installed when siezed.

b. Intermittent enemy radio jamming was experienced throughout the campaign, in the form of jabbering in Japanese and broken English. Two spurious CW and several voice transmissions were attempted by the enemy, but were promptly detected. These incidents of enemy interference were of nuisance value only.

LESSONS LEARNED AND RECOMMENDATIONS

There is no substitute for training in mountainous and hilly country without roads. Since operations in every theater inevitably require fighting in mountainous terrain, all units should be given this training.

Units must follow supporting fires very closely. It is better to start the infantry moving forward and lift fires on signal from the troops than to lift the artillery or mortars at H hour. This procedure was followed in several successful attacks by battalions of the Division.

It is essential to hold ground gained, and not pull back. The Japanese will follow up quickly and effectually. Casualties suffered in holding normally will not exceed those suffered in regaining the ground again. The morale factor in this respect is of the greatest importance in succeeding actions of the unit. All troops should be taught to hold their positions.

Men do not fire their rifles and small arms enough. The long training not to fire unless you see the target does not fit troops for combat in this theater. You seldom if ever see the Japanese, even when they fire at you. Men should be trained to sweep the roots of the trees and bushes with distributed small arms fire, whenever fired upon. In the final assault all ranks must move in with all weapons firing.

The greatest advantage to the enemy of his night infiltration is the mental strain placed on our troops, rather than the physical injuries suffered. The use of searchlights to enable the guards on the perimeter to see around them, permits the remainder of the unit to obtain more rest. It is recommended that searchlights be available for this purpose.

Separately organized assault detachments, although undoubtedly a fine medium for the accomplishment of specific tasks, can not be maintained intact after a few days of hard combat. When the strength of units becomes depleted the need for personnel is such that the employment of these detachments in some manner is inevitable; consequently, the missions for which they were organized ordinarily fall to an infantry squad or platoon closest to the situation. Certain personnel in each infantry squad should be trained in the use of the flame-thrower, and the squad, as a whole, instructed in the principles of the establishment of a base of fire and employment of supporting weapons in connection with flamethrower operations. This will greatly facilitate the performance of a mission by any rifle squad or platoon with whatever supporting weapons are available.

Thorough, systematic, daily patrolling and mopping up by all units, including service and rear area units, is necessary. This will prevent sniping, give a sense of security to the units, and train the men.

Air support, particularly fighter-bomber, can be pulled in to within 200 yards of the front line troops by experienced SAP's and bomber squadrons with telling effect on the enemy. This was successfully done on WOODPECKER Ridge. It is recommended that combined training in this be given combat troops prior to commitment in battle.

NaPalm strikes have a definite effect on the morale of the enemy, but to be destructive, must be concentrated. In green jungle the first strike kills the vegetation, and if followed by a second four or five days later intense hot fires that denude the ground will result. Strikes are most effective if the troops can occupy the ground the same day, otherwise the Japanese will reoccupy it.

Marking for air drops should be practiced by company and battalion units. The unit commander should be flown over the dropping ground to see the markings from the pilot's point of view.

For efficient operations on large land masses, no reduction should be made on the vehicles to be taken with the Division. If a reduction is made for the initial assault, the balance of the vehicles should be landed by D ≠ 5 or D ≠ 10.

For operations over large areas each liaison officer in the Division Headquarters should be given an individual vehicle and driver if he is to function properly. This should be an addition to the present T/O & E.